Reading from the Underside of Selfhood

Bonhoeffer and Spiritual Formation

LISA E. DAHILL

With a Foreword by H. Martin Rumscheidt

PICKWICK *Publications* · Eugene, Oregon

READING FROM THE UNDERSIDE OF SELFHOOD
Bonhoeffer and Spiritual Formation

Princeton Theological Monograph Series 95

Pickwick Publications
A Division of Wipf and Stock Publishers
199 W. 8th Ave., Suite 3
Eugene, Oregon 97401

www.wipfandstock.com

ISBN 13: 978-1-55635-425-0

Cataloging-in-Publication data:

Dahill, Lisa E.

    Reading from the underside of selfhood : Bonhoeffer and spiritual formation / Lisa E. Dahill. Foreword by H. Martin Rumscheidt.

    xvi + 268 p.; 23 cm. — Includes bibliographical references and index.

    Princeton Theological Monograph Series 95

    ISBN 13: 978-1-55635-425-0

    1. Bonhoeffer, Dietrich, 1906–1945. 2. Spiritual Formation. 3. Spirituality—Christianity. I. Rumscheidt, Martin. II. Title. III. Series.

BV4011.6 D33 2009

Manufactured in the U.S.A.

Princeton Theological Monograph Series

K. C. Hanson, Charles M. Collier, and
D. Christopher Spinks, Series Editors

Recent volumes in the series

Linda Hogan and Dylan Lee Lehrke, editors
Religion and the Politics of Peace and Conflict

Jeanne M. Hoeft
*Agency, Culture, and Human Personhood: Pastoral Thelogy
and Intimate Partner Violence*

Philip Ruge-Jones
*Cross in Tensions: Luther's Theology of the Cross
as Theolgico-social Critique*

Jerry Root
*C. S. Lewis and a Problem of Evil: An Investigation
of a Pervasive Theme*

Christian T. Collins Winn
*"Jesus is Victor!": The Significance of the Blumhardts
for the Theology of Karl Barth*

Charles K. Bellinger
The Trinitarian Self: The Key to the Puzzle of Violence

Michael S. Hogue
*The Tangled Bank: Toward an Ecotheological Ethics
of Responsible Participation*

Mary Clark Moschella
*Living Devotions: Reflections on Immigration, Identity,
and Religious Imagination*

Kevin Twain Lowery
*Salvaging Wesley's Agenda: A New Paradigm
for Wesleyan Virtue Ethics*

Reading from the Underside of Selfhood

Contents

Foreword

IT IS ALMOST IMPOSSIBLE TO RENDER IN WORDS THE EXPERIENCE OF looking down from Pacific Lutheran Theological Seminary over the city of Berkeley, California, and out onto the Golden Gate Bridge on a perfect summer evening. In that setting, Lisa Dahill and I had a lengthy conversation about the spirituality she had discovered in Bonhoeffer's work and which she believed to be evocative of a liberating "spiritual formation" for people whose journey is marked by the "underside of selfhood."

Her phrase "from the underside of selfhood" is an allusion to and adaptation of those evocative sentences Bonhoeffer had written shortly before he was arrested by the Nazis in early 1943. It is useful to repeat the relatively brief but crucial passage from the essay "After Ten Years," for the spiritual formation Lisa Dahill develops in her study is meant for those who, as a result of suffering abuse, oppression, and repeated violation of basic human rights, have lost or never found the way to what the catechism declares to be the chief end of the human being: to praise and enjoy God. Bonhoeffer had composed that essay at the height of his and his fellow conspirators' resistance against the tyranny of Hitler, against Germany's terrifying crime against humanity, which, as we now know, opened the floodgates for so much that made the twentieth century "the genocidal century."

> It remains an experience of incomparable value that we have for once learned to see the great events of world history from below, from the perspective of the outcasts, the suspects, the maltreated, the powerless, the oppressed and reviled, in short from the perspective of the suffering. If only bitterness and envy have during this time not corroded the heart; that we may come to see matters great and small, happiness and misfortune, strength and weakness with new eyes; that our sense for greatness, humanness, justice and mercy may have grown clearer, freer, more incorruptible. . . . But it is important that this perspective from below must not lead into taking sides with the perpetually dis-

satisfied. From a higher satisfaction the foundation of which really lies beyond below and above, we do justice to life in all its dimensions and thus affirm it.[1]

The sheer incongruence of the perfection of that Californian evening surrounding us, on the one hand, and the evil Lisa told me she was addressing in her work, on the other, was startling. Escaping into the transfiguring beauty of the vista was easy and I chose to let it hold me instead of looking with and through Lisa's eyes into the abyss.

Professor Dahill and I work with several colleagues on the translation of the new German critical *Gesamtausgabe* of Bonhoeffer's work; that is how we met. Not long after that evening's conversation, my late partner-in-marriage, Barbara Rumscheidt, and I translated two books by the German feminist, radical, social activist theologian, the late Dorothee Sölle, *Against the Wind: Memoir of a Radical Christian* and *The Silent Cry: Mysticism and Resistance*.[2] During our labor of translating, I became aware that I had become quite uncomfortable during that conversation with Lisa with what she called "spirituality" and "spiritual formation" but that I was beginning to change my perception of those concepts as a result of translating Sölle. I had thought that speaking about Bonhoeffer's "spirituality" was tantamount to soiling the profound *theological* significance, value and importance of his work; that to draw on his work as an instrument for "spiritual formation" was reminiscent of what he had to say about cheap grace. But now I recognized and admitted to myself that it was precisely this perception that contributed to my escaping into the perfection of the evening above San Francisco Bay rather than seeing with eyes "from below."

There is an interesting conversation between Dorothee Sölle and her partner-in-marriage Fulbert Steffensky in *The Silent Cry*. I cite an excerpt from it now because it pinpoints precisely what my perception of "spirituality" had been and how it led me to change and subsequently

---

1. "After Ten Years," translated by Barbara [+] and Martin Rumscheidt for the new critical edition and translation of *Letters and Papers from Prison*, in Dietrich Bonhoeffer Works in English, vol. 8, forthcoming from Fortress Press, Minneapolis. See also *Letters and Papers from Prison* (New York: Macmillan, 1971) 17. [Publisher's note: excerpts from Letters and Papers from Prison are reprinted with the permission of Scribner, a Division of Simon & Schuster Adult Publishing Group, from LETTERS AND PAPERS FROM PRISON, REVISED, ENLARGED ED. by Dietrich Bonhoeffer. Copyright (c) 1953, 1967, 1971 by SCM Press Ltd. All rights reserved.]

2. (Minneapolis: Fortress, 1995 and 2001 respectively).

regret my escape and, gratefully, come to a much more appropriate and appreciative understanding of what Lisa Dahill is about in this book.

> Fulbert: Perhaps my skepticism about mystics is not meant so much for them as for a certain craving for mysticism prevalent in the present religious climate. The high regard for categories of religious experience is growing at an inflationary rate. The religious subject wants to experience the self without mediation, instantly, totally, and authentically, in the manner she or he shapes personal piety.... In this craving for experience, everything that occurs suddenly and is direct rather than institution-mediated—everything that's oriented to experience and promises religious sensation—becomes ever so interesting.

> Dorothee: I cannot agree with your covert pleading for the institution.... I think there must be a third entity, next to voguish "religious sensation" and the homespun institutions that are in charge of such things. You are seeking something like that yourself, except that you call it spirituality.

> Fulbert: When I speak of spirituality I always rule out the ideas of particularity and extraordinary experience. It's the name, more than anything else, that makes "spirituality" so alluring. What spirituality itself actually is has much to do with method, order, and repetition. It's a matter of constituting the self, in the midst of banality and everydayness.... Spirituality is not a *via regia*, an elevated pathway, but a *via laborosa*, a labor-intensive regimen for determining one's own vision and life options. And I stick doggedly to the notion that something is important only when it's important for everyone.... [N]o human being ought to be exhausted in sheer survival. Everyone should be allowed to come to the truth. For everyone there ought to be places free of intentionality, places where vision can happen, where the beauty of life is perceived and ... where God is enjoyed.... Is there such a thing as a human right to behold God?
> And this has led us by a circuitous route to your ... concept: resistance. Mysticism is the experience of the oneness and wholeness of life. Therefore, mysticism's perception of life, its vision, is also the unrelenting perception of how fragmented life is. Suffering on account of that fragmentation and finding it unbearable is part of mysticism. Finding God fragmented into rich and poor, top and bottom, sick and well, weak and mighty: that's the mystic's suffering. The resistance of Saint Francis or Elisabeth of Thuringia or of Martin Luther King grew out of the

perception of beauty. And the long lasting and most dangerous
resistance is the one that is born from beauty.[3]

"Spirituality" had seemed to me to be the polar opposite of Bonhoeffer's
"religionlessness" and "spiritual formation" a novel way for the "me
generation" to retreat from "the world come of age" into a "two sphere
reality." Sölle's and Steffensky's connecting mysticism (= spirituality) and
resistance became the key for me to understand and applaud the project
that Lisa Dahill is about in this book: "By contextualizing Bonhoeffer in
terms of gender, . . . my work is intended to make his work more accessible for those . . . for whom Bonhoeffer's widely-taught insistence on a
radically self-denying spirituality does not in fact function as inspiration toward resistance to evil but rather has the opposite effect, namely
reinforcement of or actual participation in the voice of evil itself in their
lives."[4]

Bonhoeffer scholarship has richly explored the meaning of his
interpretation of Christ for the world come of age as "the One for
others" and what that implies for resistance on behalf of others who are
"outcasts, suspects, maltreated, powerless, oppressed, reviled." The resistance offered against apartheid in South Africa, against the military dic-
tatorship in South Korea, a resistance nourished by Bonhoeffer among
others, comes to mind here. In those places as elsewhere where "the cry
of the oppressed went up to God" (Ex 3:7), an ethics of discipleship
ushered in activities nourished by a denial of self precisely on behalf
and for the benefit of the "neighbor." Bonhoeffer called such discipleship "conformation with Christ." Through the lens of feminist-critical
application of gender analysis within the larger social location critique,
Dahill raises the question of "whether and how the heart of Bonhoffer's
spirituality (that is, 'conformation' with Jesus Christ self-sacrificially
active in human life, in community, and in the world) may speak to
those of very different social-psychological locations from his own."[5]

Her probing of that question enriches the scope of what Bonhoeffer
had learned both personally and vicariously about the potential of "the
view from below," the "underside of selfhood," as she calls it. And yet,
however much what she presents enriches our understanding of the

3. *The Silent Cry*, 300–302.

4. Cf. her Introduction, 4.

5. Cf. her Introduction, 6.

view from below, as Bonhoeffer himself understood it, Lisa Dahill does not merely add to that understanding; she challenges prevalent Bonhoeffer interpretation to do what Karl Barth recommended to his interpreters late in his life, namely, to go with him beyond him.

Reading from the Underside of Selfhood: Bonhoeffer and Spiritual Formation shows well that Lisa Dahill knows and appreciates Dietrich Bonhoeffer's work. Her treatment alone of him and his theological reflections is illuminating, but precisely because she carries his connection of spirituality and resistance into a yet unexplored pastoral dimension, having rooted the requisite forms of resistance in a vision of unfragmented beauty, she is faithful to Bonhoeffer in moving beyond him.

—Martin Rumscheidt
Halifax, Nova Scotia
Pentecost 2008

Acknowledgments

OF COURSE, A DISSERTATION IS ALWAYS A GROUP EFFORT, NO MAT-
TER how solitary the hours of its writing. And a revised dissertation
includes further circles of conversation, critique, and feedback. Many
have contributed to the material contained here, whether directly
through discussion, feedback, mentoring, or research assistance, or less
directly but no less significantly through their friendship and support.
My GTU dissertation committee chair, Sandra M. Schneiders, provided
careful and wonderfully clarifying assistance throughout the process of
proposing and writing the work; even more fundamentally, her teaching and ground-breaking leadership shaped my entire course of study
in the discipline of Christian Spirituality. I was deeply honored by the
opportunity to work with her on a project of this scale. Mark Brocker
was part of this research since its inception, through countless hours
of conversation on Bonhoeffer; it was an additional privilege to work
with him in teaching and in the translation project which bears fruit
here in the citations from *DBWE* 16 (which Mark edited and I translated). Diane Jonte-Pace provided resources and insights from her work
in feminist psychology, as well as assistance with methodology in the
use of the psychological material and steady encouragement over the
year of its writing. Gary Pence brought his experience as a practicing
therapist, a key contribution to the discussion, alongside his scholarly
expertise on religion and abuse.

Outside my committee, I am grateful to the members of the
International Dietrich Bonhoeffer Society who gave critical feedback
on this project, particularly Martin Rumscheidt and Wayne Whitson
Floyd in the U.S. and Vivienne Blackburn in the U.K. The gift of a foreword from Martin for this volume is a particular joy. Faculty of the
Christian Spirituality area of the GTU (especially Arthur Holder) and of
the Pacific Lutheran Theological Seminary were invaluable discussion
partners along the way. My work with Martha Ellen Stortz on a GTU
Newhall research grant laid important conceptual groundwork for the

dissertation and for my ongoing thinking about questions of selfhood. In subsequent years, several senior scholars of the Carnegie Foundation for the Advancement of Teaching, where I worked from 2001 to 2005, gave feedback on the project: Charles Foster, Anne Colby, and William Sullivan. And here at Trinity Lutheran Seminary, my colleagues Cheryl Peterson and Joy Schroeder, along with Han van den Blink of our affiliated school, Bexley Hall Seminary, have helped sharpen my thinking as the dissertation moves into further writing. And students Kerstin Hedlund and Derek Hoven provided invaluable assistance with updating and formatting the manuscript.

Pieces of this book have appeared in the following articles or essays (cited in full in the bibliography). Sections from the first five chapters are woven into an essay that serves as an extended abstract of the book: "Reading from the Underside of Selfhood: Bonhoeffer and Spiritual Formation," presented to the Bonhoeffer: Theology and Social Analysis Group of the American Academy of Religion in 2000, then published in *Spiritus: A Journal of Christian Spirituality* (edited by Douglas Burton-Christie) and included in the 2005 anthology *Minding the Spirit: The Study of Christian Spirituality,* edited by Bruce Lescher and Elizabeth Liebert. Parts of chapter 3 appear in the essay, "Probing the Will of God: Bonhoeffer and Discernment," which appeared in *Dialog* (edited by Ted Peters) in 2002. Three presentations in the fall of 2006 gave rise to the two pieces published in *Studies in Christian-Jewish Relations* (edited by Philip Cunningham) and in the *Journal of Lutheran Ethics* (edited by Jim Childs); the published pieces reflect comments from those who attended the 2006 presentations in Boston, Berkeley, and Waterloo, Ontario, as well. Finally, pieces of chapters 4 and 5 appeared in the 2007 essay published in *Currents in Theology and Mission,* edited by Ralph Klein (originally presented at the Lutheran Women in Religion and Theological Education gathering in 2006). The editors of these journals or books provided critical feedback to strengthen each of these pieces of the whole. And I am grateful to Charlie Collier and Patrick Harrison of Wipf & Stock for guiding the present manuscript through its editing process, and to Michael Moore of Fortress Press for his assistance with the intricacies of Bonhoeffer copyright permissions.

In the original writing, Jennifer Peace provided a marvelously clear-eyed reading of chapter 5, while Melinda Quivik asked wonderful, provocative questions; both these friends were treasures of the GTU for me. The entire book is saturated with years of lively conversation, debate, criticism, friendship, and solidarity with my colleagues in the GTU doctoral program in Christian Spirituality, especially Francis McAloon, Maria Bowen, and Timothy Hessel-Robinson.

Special thanks go to Alice Feller, George Murphy, and Elizabeth Ekdale, along with the members of St. Mark Lutheran Church, San Francisco, who have cheered on this project and insisted on its importance for the church of Jesus Christ and those on the underside of selfhood. I am grateful for this lively worshiping community as well as for the Camaldolese monks and oblates of Incarnation Monastery in Berkeley; both communities were healing and transformative spaces of grace for me throughout the years of this project's gestation. Finally, I offer deep thanks to my parents, Richard and Susannah Dahill, whose love and support made the writing possible on many levels. They continue to amaze me.

Thanks to these and to any I have overlooked or been unable to include here. Most of all, thanks to the One whose mercy is at the heart of it all.

—Lisa E. Dahill
Feast of Dietrich Bonhoeffer
April 9, 2008
Trinity Lutheran Seminary
Columbus, OH

Introduction

Introduction to Problem

SHIRLEY IS A BRIGHT, CHARMING WOMAN IN HER EARLY 60'S. SHE IS a member of my congregation and is faithful and active in the life of the church. As chair of adult education, she seeks out opportunities for ongoing learning to nourish her leadership and teaching, and so she enrolled two years ago in a week-long summer course on Bonhoeffer at the Graduate Theological Union. She told me of her experience in that class the day the professor lectured on Bonhoeffer's view of how one is to relate to the neighbor, the other, the enemy. The lecture moved through Bonhoeffer's early writings on the necessity of giving up one's self in favor of the claims of the other, and loving the other instead of the self, and culminated in a reflection on the central Christian stance of loving the enemy, letting the enemy "grasp" a person in a radical claim on one's time and priorities and even one's life.

Shirley had an unsettling reaction to this lecture, and she was assertive enough to go up to the professor afterwards and tell him, "If I had been hearing this theology thirty years ago, I would be dead right now." And she went on to recount how her alcoholic and abusive husband had come home one night extremely drunk and gone on a rampage, finally pinning her against the wall with his hands around her throat, strangling her. She recalled how she had struggled and realized he was truly trying to kill her. In the brief moments of clarity between this terrifying realization and her imminent loss of consciousness, she had a decision to make. Raised in a conservative Christian home and taught to obey the male authorities in her life, she was lucky, she said, that her pastor at that time was not preaching Bonhoeffer's theology, that these words were not filling her head that night. For in that moment, with his hands around her neck, Shirley chose *not* to let the enemy "grasp" her, and surrender her own claims to his absolute demands.[1] She summoned all her strength and was able to claw him off her and run for her life.

Shirley's story continues to move me, and it crystallizes some of the uneasiness I too have experienced in trying to come to terms with aspects of Bonhoeffer's legacy. This uneasiness emerged only gradually. I have been reading Bonhoeffer for many years, since my introduction to him during my year living and studying in Tübingen, Germany, in 1983–1984. That year, the recently-formed congregation I was a part of had come to the point of building their own sanctuary and deciding on a name for the community. After an extensive process of discernment, the congregation chose to call itself "Dietrich-Bonhoeffer-Gemeinde."[2] That decision gave rise to in-depth adult education offerings about the life, writings, and legacy of Bonhoeffer, events that inspired me to read his *Letters and Papers from Prison*.[3] This text moved me deeply,

1. This language of the complete "surrender" of the self and all its claims to the "absolute demands" of the other comes from Bonhoeffer's dissertation, *Sanctorum Communio*, Dietrich Bonhoeffer Works series (hereafter abbreviated DBWE), volume 1. On pp. 31–59 I examine these themes.

2. Notably, this was one of the first times a congregation within the German Protestant Church (*Evangelische Kirche in Deutschland*) was allowed to call itself by Bonhoeffer's name. Prior to that point such requests had been denied by church authorities on the grounds that Bonhoeffer's reputation was still so ambiguous. How, after all, could a Christian church be named after someone who was executed for treason and conspiracy to commit murder? Eberhard Bethge, Bonhoeffer's biographer, mentions a typical example of this reluctance on the part of the post-war church to honor Bonhoeffer when, in the late 1960's, "the council of a large German regional church [forbade] one of its parishes to name a newly built church after Bonhoeffer" (E. Bethge, "Turning Points in Bonhoeffer's Life and Thought," 75). By the early 1980's, however, general perception of Bonhoeffer was beginning to shift in Germany, so that church leaders became more able to recognize in public ways (such as the naming of a congregation) the authentically Christian faith and courage that led Bonhoeffer into the conspiracy against Hitler. Indeed, in 1996, the German Parliament officially overturned Bonhoeffer's indictment of treason, publicly rehabilitating him and the other conspirators.

3. Bonhoeffer, *Letters and Papers from Prison*. Hereafter referred to as LPP. See notes 5 and 18 regarding the new German and English editions of Bonhoeffer's works. The translation of the prison letters for this series (DBWE 8) is forthcoming from Fortress Press in 2009 but is not ready for citation in the present volume. Thus I will continue here to use LPP or my own translation but will provide page citations from the German critical edition (Bonhoeffer, *Widerstand und Ergebung*, Dietrich Bonhoeffer Werke

especially in the beauty of the faith reflected in these letters and their search for new "non-religious" language for the church suitable for its situation in the nearly unrecognizable post-war "world come of age."[4] Since that time, during seminary and my years in Lutheran parish ministry, I continued to read Bonhoeffer and to draw nourishment from his compelling vision of a deeply nourishing and thoroughly this-worldly spirituality. In the doctoral program in Christian Spirituality at the Graduate Theological Union and at Trinity Lutheran Seminary in Columbus, Ohio, I have worked and taught on Bonhoeffer and have had the privilege of serving as translator for volumes 8 and 16 of the new critical edition of his works.[5] In all my work on Bonhoeffer, both in scholarship and in translation, he never fails to move me with the clarity and subtlety of his insight, the human texture of his faithfulness and courage.

Yet in doctoral studies I began to articulate a problem similar to Shirley's with Bonhoeffer's understanding of the relationship between self and other. At the time I was in therapy struggling with a difficult relationship, and I began to realize that the way Bonhoeffer spoke of the self, while congruent with major streams in Christian history, not only failed to name the problems I was experiencing but in fact obscured them. In particular, the language of selflessness, the assertion that holiness, redemption, and the very presence of God are found in turning away from oneself and toward the claims of others, powerfully echoed the language of my Christian and gendered upbringing. While this message bore a nearly irresistible pull of familiarity and perceived rightness, it nevertheless had the effect of blinding me to the long-unmet needs and desires I was discovering in myself, whose articulation in real life required me to renounce precisely the sort of "selflessness" urged upon me by Bonhoeffer and countless others. My immersion in feminist theology had always paralleled my interest in Bonhoeffer; now they came

---

(hereafter abbreviated DBW), volume 8). Because the Fortress Press volume will include the DBW 8 pagination in the margins throughout, readers will be able to find the passages noted here in this new English translation.

4. These themes, which first occur in the April 30, 1944, letter to Eberhard Bethge (LPP 279ff.), become further developed in later letters as well. Cf. DBW 8: 401–8, 435–36, 454–46, 476–82, 503–4, 509–12, 529–38, 541–43, 556–61."

5. DBWE 8 (in process) will be the new edition and translation of *Letters and Papers from Prison*; I am one of four translators on this volume. DBWE 16, published in 2006, is *Conspiracy and Imprisonment: 1940–1945*; here I was the sole translator.

together as I learned to name these problems as in fact gender-based. I decided to try reading Bonhoeffer against the grain, substituting "self" for "other" and vice versa in my reading of him, and was amazed to find previously problematic material coming alive in startling ways. This new reading of Bonhoeffer was novel precisely in giving me a glimpse of an opposite way of seeing reality.[6] And it aroused my hunch that Bonhoeffer's conception of the relative place of self and other, both in brokenness and in the experience of redemption and subsequent spiritual formation, was equally a matter of his own gendered conditioning and social location.

None of this diminished my admiration for Bonhoeffer, whom I continue to see as a great saint and whose living faithfulness to Jesus Christ and to the crucified Jews of his own day led him to a martyr's death at the hands of the Nazis.[7] If anything, my emerging critique allowed me to see more clearly the ways he too was resisting his own traditional German/Prussian gendered upbringing. By contextualizing Bonhoeffer in terms of gender, therefore, my work is intended to make his witness more accessible for those readers, like Shirley, for whom Bonhoeffer's widely-taught insistence on a radically self-denying spirituality does not in fact function as inspiration toward resistance to evil but rather has the opposite effect, namely of reinforcement of or actual participation in the voice of evil itself in their lives.

This is not, of course, the first time women have noticed a disjunction between their experience and the teachings of respected theologians. Since 1960 an impressive line of theological critiques has challenged normative Christian understandings of sin and self as those have developed in highly androcentric ways. Beginning with Valerie

6. For instance, one might read: "*Woman* 'in' and 'after' the fall refer[s] everything to *the other*, puts *the other* in the center of the world, does violence to reality, makes *the other person* God, and [makes] God and *herself the other's* creatures" in place of Bonhoeffer's original, written in English: "Man 'in' and 'after' the fall refer[s] everything to himself, puts himself in the center of the world, does violence to reality, makes himself God, and [makes] God and the other man his creatures" (DBW 10: 425). This against-the-grain reading is useful not least—by its manifest unclarity of reference (what could it possibly mean to speak of "woman" in general?)—in highlighting the extent to which sentences like this reflect unconscious generalizing biases in Bonhoeffer alien to his lifelong rejection of abstract principles. On Bonhoeffer's suspicion of abstraction see, e.g., chapter 2, pp. 32–33.

7. In *Bonhoeffer as Martyr*, Craig Slane traces the complexity inherent in speaking of Bonhoeffer's death as an instance of Christian martyrdom.

Saiving's suggestion of the paradigmatic female sin as self-abnegation rather than self-justification and pride,[8] and continuing with Judith Plaskow's fundamental re-reading of Paul Tillich and Reinhold Niebuhr along similar lines,[9] this feminist challenge to the assumed universal applicability of the regnant tradition (and the normative selfhood of the privileged white male) has opened the door to much more nuanced views of the human self. By taking account of complex dimensions of human social location, including gender, race, class, culture, sexual orientation, etc., these thinkers and many who for decades have built on their work have made possible theological analyses that more accurately describe characteristic patterns of brokenness and holiness experienced by selves in society.[10]

To date, however, such critical application of gender analysis, within a larger social location critique, has not taken place for Bonhoeffer's writings.[11] Interpreters continue to follow Bonhoeffer himself in speaking of "the" person, or of "human" sin, as if these could be understood monolithically. Because most of these interpreters share Bonhoeffer's general social location as educated white Western males it is not surprising that they find his analysis true and compelling, and that they take for granted its similar applicability to others. Yet Shirley points out dramatically that Bonhoeffer's insights on spiritual formation may themselves be shaped by his particularity in ways that make aspects of his vision not merely irrelevant but potentially or actually harmful to others.

Accordingly, a study of Bonhoeffer's significant contributions in the area of Christian formation must first illumine and critique the normative human selfhood he presupposes, rooted in his own experience and articulated in his writings. Who exactly is this human self he envi-

8. Saiving, "The Human Situation." Originally published (with the last name "Goldstein") in *Journal of Religion* 40 (1960), 100–112.

9. Plaskow, *Sex, Sin, and Grace.*

10. See, for instance, the studies cited in note 22.

11. Although a full-scale gender analysis of Bonhoeffer has never been published, several studies have examined questions of social location in regard to Bonhoeffer along the lines of race and class, both in terms of his own relation to the Jews (and the African-Americans he knew in New York), and in terms of the applicability of his witness for those in cultures and situations different from his own. See, for example, Young, *No Difference in the Fare.* Also see Godsey, "Bonhoeffer and the Third World," and the essays collected in Carter's *Bonhoeffer's Ethics: Old Europe and New Frontiers.*

sions needing "formation" in a particular direction, bearing particular capacities and blind spots? Without such critical contextualization his prescriptions, naively universalized, may paradoxically undermine the authentic spiritual growth of those readers who do not share his privileged social location, those who in fact read from what I term "the underside of selfhood."[12] My analysis here is therefore oriented around the fundamental question of whether and how the heart of Bonhoeffer's spirituality (that is, "conformation" with Jesus Christ self-sacrificially active in human life, in community, and in the world) may speak to those of very different social-psychological locations from his own. These are not merely academic questions; as Shirley's story demonstrates, "lives are at stake."[13]

Introduction to Arena of Discourse and Key Terminology

Having surveyed the broad terrain within which this project has materialized, I will now review aspects of its general shape, including an examination of the field of Christian Spirituality; my choice of women in abuse as dialogue partners with Bonhoeffer; and my use of important terms such as "women's experience," "separative/soluble selfhood," and "spiritual formation." In the final section of this Introduction, I will give an overview of the project in its specifics, concluding with a sketch of the book as it will proceed from this point.

Discipline of Christian Spirituality

Christian spirituality as an academic discipline is an inherently interdisciplinary and self-implicating approach to the study of Christian spiritual experience. As Sandra Schneiders asserts, "Christian spirituality as an academic discipline studies the lived experience of Christian faith, the subjective appropriation of faith and living of discipleship in their individual and corporate actualization(s)."[14] That is, this discipline in

12. This language makes intentional use of Bonhoeffer's own assertion of the hermeneutically privileged "view from below" and applies it to the arena of selfhood. See "After Ten Years" (DBW 8:38).

13. Neuger, "Narratives of Harm," 86.

14. Schneiders, "Approaches to the Study of Christian Spirituality," 16. I am making use of Schneiders' hermeneutical approach to this discipline because it provides

the broadest sense examines "the experience of conscious involvement in the project of life-integration through self-transcendence toward the horizon of ultimate value one perceives."[15] This ultimate value takes different forms in different human lives, according to the religious, cultural, linguistic, and social worlds a given person inhabits. In the Christian context, specifically, this "horizon of ultimate value is the triune God revealed in Jesus Christ, and the project involves the living of his paschal mystery in the context of the Church community through the gift of the Holy Spirit."[16] I write as a scholar of this specifically Christian spirituality, attempting to trace the ways Bonhoeffer himself experienced this Christian mystery and the ways particular others continue to experience Jesus Christ present (or not) through Bonhoeffer's legacy.

Working within this discipline, then, my book is an exploration of the spirituality of Dietrich Bonhoeffer, as he experienced the transforming presence of Jesus Christ within the contours of his own particular

---

scope for the sort of interdisciplinary conversation my project requires. See her earlier essay, "A Hermeneutical Approach to the Study of Christian Spirituality," in which she distinguishes her own work in the discipline from those whose focus is more specifically historical or, especially within the Christian world, theological. For consideration of methodology within these latter perspectives, see, e.g., McGinn, "The Letter and the Spirit"; Principe, "Broadening the Focus"; Sheldrake, *Spirituality and History* and *Spirituality and Theology*; and Hanson, "Spirituality as Spiritual Theology." On self-implication as a considered aspect of this discipline, see Schneiders, "Spirituality as an Academic Discipline," 14; and "Hermeneutical Approach," 58–59; Lane, "Galesville and Sinai"; and the essays gathered in Part Two of Dreyer and Burrows' *Minding the Spirit.* Three additional recent additions to the literature on the study of Christian spirituality are the volumes edited by Holder, Sheldrake, and Lescher and Liebert.

15. Ibid.

16. Schneiders, "Study of Christian Spirituality," 6.

experience[17]; as he articulated this life-changing reality in his writings[18]; and as these writings continue to engage the experience of contemporary Christian readers.[19] Those Christian readers whose contemporary

17. Bonhoeffer never wrote an autobiography, and given the high store he set on privacy and discretion did not speak often of his own deepest emotions, longings, and fears; in fact, he considered those who freely poured out their hearts to observers to be shamefully immodest. Further, even if Bonhoeffer were alive today and consented to an interview on these subjects, much of what is encompassed by the category of "experience," especially at the level of ultimacy encountered in the study of spirituality, can only inadequately be disclosed to any listener; some levels remain finally inaccessible even to the subject. Thus when I speak of "Bonhoeffer's experience," I am not claiming to know these depths to which only his closest companions, his own heart, or ultimately only God found access. Rather, I intend with this language to describe the elements of Bonhoeffer's subjective life to which his published and miscellaneous writings point, in conjunction with the remembrances of those who knew him best. Fortunately for the Bonhoeffer scholar, these twin sources provide entrée to a rich and nuanced store of human experience and self-disclosure. And when new questions or categories of analysis are brought to this material, one can speak of tracing new dimensions of his experience, hidden perhaps even from his own conscious awareness. It is in both these senses that I refer to Bonhoeffer's experience: i.e., both his own conscious (and consciously disclosed) and subconscious (but on some level accessible to observers) subjectivity. Still far and away the most complete biography of Bonhoeffer remains that written by his best friend, Eberhard Bethge: *Dietrich Bonhoeffer: A Biography*, revised edition (2000). See also the reminiscences collected in the volume, *I Knew Dietrich Bonhoeffer*. The essay by David Hay in the *Blackwell Companion to Christian Spirituality* provides a useful introduction to the use of the category of "experience" in the study of Christian spirituality.

18. Throughout this book I will primarily be citing Bonhoeffer's writings in the new critical edition. In German, these volumes have appeared in seventeen volumes as *Dietrich Bonhoeffer Werke* (DBW). In English, they are in the process of being translated, appearing as *Dietrich Bonhoeffer Works* (DBWE). This critical edition includes writings Bonhoeffer intended for publication and occasional pieces such as letters, sermons, essays, notes, poems, etc. The only piece of Bonhoeffer's known writings not contained in this series is the prison correspondence between him and his fiancée, Maria von Wedemeyer, published separately in *Love Letters from Cell 92*.

19. These three levels correspond to those Sandra Schneiders articulates in her study of New Testament hermeneutics, *The Revelatory Text*. There, building on Paul Ricouer's work, she speaks to the necessity for adequate understanding of attending to the worlds "behind," "of," and "before" any given text. That is, the biblical interpreter or, as I am using her categories here, the scholar of Christian spirituality more generally necessarily pays attention in critically appropriate ways to the context and/or events that broadly or specifically underlie a given writing (see chapter 4, "The World Behind the Text," 97–131); to the text itself in all its complexity, by close reading (see chapter 5, "The World of the Text," 132–56); and to the potentially transformative world the text opens to readers' own ongoing constructive engagement and appropriation (see chapter 6, "The World Before the Text," 157–79).

engagement with Bonhoeffer I particularly wish to explore are women in abusive relationships, such as Shirley. My ultimate aim is to elucidate elements of Bonhoeffer's spirituality that function in potentially healing or liberating ways for these women (i.e., evoking analogous reactions to the transformation in Christ he himself experienced), as well as those that function in potentially oppressive ways (i.e., where Bonhoeffer's human limits make his writings particularly unhelpful for these women). An exploration of such complex terrain requires the use of various lenses. As Schneiders notes, "Spirituality as an academic discipline is intrinsically and irreducibly interdisciplinary because the object it studies, transformative Christian experience as such, is multi-faceted."[20] Therefore, in addition to close readings of Bonhoeffer's writings and both biographical and historical materials, this interdisciplinary study will make extensive use of feminist psychology to gain access to the complexity of the experience under examination: both Bonhoeffer's own and that of the women through whose eyes I am attempting to read him.

Women in Abuse and "Women's Experience"

As noted, I propose here to examine Bonhoeffer's writings on questions of selfhood and spiritual formation from the perspective of women in abusive relationships. I have chosen this particular audience partly because its perspectives have so long been invisible to mainstream theology, with devastating results; and partly because these women who are present at every level of church and society represent a pole of human experience profoundly different from Bonhoeffer's own. Furthermore, it is specifically around questions of selfhood and its gendered formation that the experience of abused women differs most strongly from Bonhoeffer's and thus offers the greatest possibility of critique. For all his astute and far-sighted sensitivity to issues of race, culture, class, nationality, and privilege as those shape the Christian spiritual life, he was apparently quite blind to gender oppression as a systemic reality.[21] That

20. Schneiders, "Study of Christian Spirituality," 7.

21. Several short studies trace Bonhoeffer's attitudes toward women. These studies in various ways juxtapose his closeness to his mother, sisters, and fiancée, and respectful treatment of female students and acquaintances, with his lifelong unquestioned support of patriarchal social structures. See Siegele-Wenschkewitz, "'Die Ehre der Frau, dem Manne zu dienen'"; R. Bethge, "Bonhoeffer and the Role of Women"; van

is, the experience of those whose bodies and spirits bear the devastating brunt of violently enforced systems of male domination would have been outside Bonhoeffer's theological awareness. Thus these women provide an excellent test case for the wider applicability of his thinking; and a critical and appreciative reading of him from this perspective provides a glimpse of strategies by which Bonhoeffer might be retrievable also for other marginalized groups (especially those whose oppression includes the degradation of selfhood).

This analysis is taking seriously the experience of women *in abuse* and thus does not intend or pretend to speak for all women. Although early feminism did indeed raise the category of "women's experience," precisely as a way to lift up dimensions of human life invisible to those whose frameworks encompassed only the male, in more recent years womanist, *mujerista*, lesbian, and Asian feminist scholars, among others, have recognized that "women's experience" is of course almost infinitely varied according to complex social and personal variables.[22] Thus it is

---

Eyden, "Dietrich Bonhoeffer's Understanding of Male and Female." Note however that Bonhoeffer also from his earliest writings consciously refrains from traditional teachings regarding the shared culpability of women in Eve's sin and the "Pauline" injunction of wifely submission among Christians. He does not actively refute these (although he does explicitly deny the teaching of the sexual transmission of original sin); but he clearly chooses to omit them as widely cited Scriptural "proofs" of the subordination of women. With the exception of the wedding sermon he sent from prison for Eberhard and Renate Bethge's wedding (May 1943, LPP 41–47; DBW 8:73–80), he generally asserts the normativity of patriarchy on sociological and historical grounds rather than scriptural ones. See Siegele-Wenschkowitz, "'Die Ehre der Frau,'" 108–26. The latter essay finds revealing, however, that precisely in the prison period, in which Bonhoeffer's longing for the idealized life of home and family manifests itself in such reactionary-sounding writings as the wedding sermon, he also apparently for the first time recognizes the discrepancy between Christian support of patriarchy and the biblical preference for those on the underside. In his fragment of a novel, a character muses (reflecting on Gal 3:28 in light of social gender inequalities), "I don't understand this. There's some contradiction here" (Bonhoeffer, *Fiction from Tegel Prison*, DBWE 7: 108). Siegele-Wenschkowitz goes on to suggest that this brief signaling of the dilemma could represent Bonhoeffer's "thereby opening the discussion for further later theological reflection," which was of course precluded by his execution (126, my translation).

22. Important studies along these lines include Townes, ed., *Embracing the Spirit*; Gilkes, *If It Wasn't for the Women*; Isasi-Díaz, *Mujerista Theology*; Kyung, *Struggle to Be the Sun Again*; Fabella and Park, eds., *We Dare to Dream*; Heyward, *Speaking of Christ*; and Spahr, *Approaches to the Spirituality of Lesbian Women*. Books that gather a variety of voices include Plaskow and Christ, eds., *Weaving the Visions*; and Ochshorn and Cole, eds., *Women's Spirituality*. For a broad overview of Christian explorations on the varieties of women's experiences, in all their complexity and diversity, see Walsh,

impossible to speak in any critically meaningful way of "female" experience, just as feminists have long asserted the impossibility of rhetoric about "human" experience in the abstract.[23] So this project refrains from speaking of "women's" experience, or "women's" selves, and speaks more specifically of the experience and selfhood of women *in abuse*. Such a category still represents an abstraction, of course, since every victim and survivor of abuse has a particular story and a particular configuration of experience shaped by dynamics unique to her as well as by social or human realities shared by others. Part of the thesis of this book is that it is precisely Bonhoeffer's attention to such particularity as it diverges from and challenges general or abstract or universal "truths" that represents one of his most important contributions for ministry with those on the underside. The field of Christian spirituality is similarly focused on the particular, as each human being's story opens contours of experience of God and reality found nowhere else. Yet within that field the particularity I am interested in here is how the experience of trauma shapes human and female selfhood and God-experience in ways that, taken together across a range of analyses of these phenomena, open new questions for Christian theology and spirituality—and for contemporary appropriation of Bonhoeffer in particular.

And in speaking of *women* in abuse, I am intentionally engaging in a gender-based analysis. Socialized from birth within more or less patriarchal families and cultures, according to pervasive explicit and implicit gender codes and roles, girls have by and large grown up with a different sense of who they are, who they are allowed to be, and what their tasks and goals in life are to be than their brothers. Thankfully, this is changing for both boys and girls, as shifts in parenting patterns and women's work model new options for them. But the fact that brutal and subtle forms of abuse still fill homes just as violence fills the news and popular media means that patterns of domination and submission are still well entrenched, still need naming and challenging. Of course, women can be abusers, and boys and men victims of trauma and abuse, for all people have the capacities for both inflicting and absorbing abuse. But I am tracing the continuities between gender socialization and the psychological problems of domination and submission, which in the

Feminism and Christian Tradition. And for a study of the complexities of gender in the study of Christian spirituality in particular, see Dahill, "The Genre of Gender."

23. Davaney, "The Limits of the Appeal to Women's Experience."

overwhelming majority of cases still means male abusers and female victims.[24] For this reason, I will risk speaking broadly of the experience of *women* who suffer abuse.

But the significance of this reading is not limited to its applicability to abuse victims and survivors. Rather, those who suffer abuse represent an extreme pole of a gendered spectrum around issues of selfhood, making possible a clarity of analysis around gender socialization, including its maintenance by means of power and violence. But many women who never endure physical assault, or men who do, may also find elements of this analysis pertinent to their own experience as well, to the extent that their socialization or subsequent relationships have participated in the same dynamics of silencing and submission.

"Separative" and "Soluble" Selfhood

To introduce some terminology I find helpful in this regard, in 1986 Catherine Keller proposed that Western (presumably especially white) men tend to be socialized into "separative" selves and women into "soluble" selves.[25] The "separative" self, in her terminology, is the traditional autonomous male, whose identity is defined by separation, originally and most primally by being "not mother/female." She writes of this self, "its sense of itself as separate, as over against the world, the Other, and even its own body, endows it with its identity. It is *this*, not *that*."[26] This sense of paradigmatic and all-defining separation is illusion, not reality, since of course no being is in any meaningful sense truly separate from others. Thus this form of selfhood is called "separative," to indicate this desired sense of autonomous independence, held apart from the messy demands of others. It is correspondingly marked by extremely firm, even rigid, ego boundaries set up to defend against all insubordinate claims on one's time or affections.

In contrast, she suggests an alternate shape for the selfhood traditionally conceived as feminine:

24. Statistics repeatedly indicate that "95 to 98 percent of battered spouses are women." Cooper-White, *The Cry of Tamar*, 108. For insight however on situations in which both abuser and victim are women, see Lobel, ed., *Naming the Violence*.

25. Keller, *From a Broken Web*, 7–46.

26. Ibid., 9.

> Let us designate this sort of self, neither necessarily nor essentially but historically embodied by women, the *soluble self.* In the classical dyad, it complements the separative self, which works upon it as a solvent. Women's tendency to dissolve emotionally and devotionally into the other is a subjective structure internalized by individual women, but imposed by the [patriarchal] superstructure. Woman is to wait: for her very self, her self-definition, and the advent of the hero who will bring her joy.[27]

Keller develops her critique of this traditional complementarity between separative and soluble selves, each dependent on the other for those capacities lacking in itself, through a series of mythic-poetic and process-theological chapters. Ultimately, she aims toward the assertion of "connective" selfhood as providing a healthy balance for both men and women.[28]

In my view, her book is marred by its overly simplistic assignment of men's selfhood as separative and women's as soluble. For the reasons outlined above this seems untenable today, its applicability undermined by any number of exceptions in both directions. Nevertheless, I find her terminology itself helpful in describing dimensions of human selfhood, and certainly it can be asserted that normative Western gender socialization has traditionally attempted to push male children toward the separative end of this spectrum and female children toward the soluble, regardless of how particular children may personally develop. Those who end up in the positions of abuser and abused can similarly be seen to inhabit the far ends of the same spectrum: as extremely, if not pathologically, "separative" and "soluble," respectively.

Other terminology can describe this gendered selfhood spectrum as well. For instance, in chapter four we will explore Jessica Benjamin's psychoanalytic model using the language of "dominating" and "submissive" selves, also clearly relevant to the situation of abuse. Yet while I will make use of Benjamin's terminology, I find Keller's language of "separative" and "soluble" selfhood useful more generally as well. It names the experience of each pole on this spectrum differently from either the language of "men's/women's experience" *or* of "dominating/submissive

---

27. Ibid., 13. On this "devotional" stance, she quotes Kierkegaard: "'by devotion (the word literally means giving away) she has lost herself'" (Kierkegaard, *Fear and Trembling/The Sickness Unto Death,* 183). Citation found on p. 12 of Keller.

28. Ibid., 155–215.

selfhood," namely in terms neither primarily of gender nor of hierarchical power but of boundaries and their excessive (separative) or inadequate (soluble) development. On the one hand, this allows for the more expressive language of fluidity, dissolving, permeation, in describing the soluble pole, expressions that characterize the experience of traditional femininity more broadly than the language of explicit "submission." On the other hand, "separative" terminology captures the experience of the rigidly imprisoning ego; for purposes of exploring Bonhoeffer's own experience, it seems to do so more effectively than the language of "domination," however accurate this term is also for him. That is to say, it is the sterile loneliness of his "separateness," the empty isolation of his alienated self, and not the experience of mastery and domination alone, that defines this state as a hell for him.[29]

Finally, Keller's terminology (like Benjamin's) allows for the possibility of different gender locations than is traditionally assumed. That is, while I am interested in the ways gender stereotypes are reinforced by violence, and the toll this takes particularly on female selfhood, nevertheless ultimately both "separative" and "soluble" forms of selfhood are human capacities, not strictly gendered ones. Thus the "separative" selfhood assumed by Bonhoeffer makes his analysis helpful for those in a similar location who in any given situation or social context may be male or female. Similarly, my challenge to Bonhoeffer on behalf of those with "soluble" selfhood, paradigmatically found in victims of abuse, may prove insightful also for others, men and women, who in a particular context find themselves on the underside of selfhood. And finally, my use of this language allows for the possibility of seeing both the separative and the soluble dimensions of one's own complex being: aspects of every person that either dominate other aspects of oneself or are coerced into silence. Seen on this level, this project's attempt to retrieve elements of Bonhoeffer's legacy that are helpful for soluble selves can be viewed as relevant to some extent for all human persons, since there are parts of us all that have been suppressed.

29. See pp. 59–70 of chapter 2 ("The Autobiographical Dimension") for more on how this takes shape in Bonhoeffer's own experience.

Spiritual Formation

The two primary poles of my overall analysis of Bonhoeffer are selfhood and spiritual formation. Of course, the two are essentially related in that any experience of or proposals regarding spiritual formation necessarily depend on the discerned needs, desires, and gifts of the human self being thereby formed. Having briefly examined some terminology around matters of selfhood, then, I turn now to the language of spiritual formation. I understand spiritual formation in a Christian context to refer both to the action of the Spirit of Jesus Christ in creating, redeeming, and calling disciples, and to these disciples' own attending to and growing in this vocation.[30] It is thus a process involving both divine and human action, and its purpose is the disciple's participation in the very form and reality of Jesus Christ as he is encountered through Word and sacrament, church, world, and creation. As a Lutheran, Bonhoeffer asserts that the primary emphasis in the discourse of spiritual formation needs to fall on the formational power of Jesus Christ in us, rather than on the ways we attempt to form ourselves or the world in his image.[31] "Christ remains the only one who forms. . . . [forming] human beings to a form the same as [his] own."[32] I use the language of "spiritual formation" therefore both because of its present-day currency in church and academy and because Bonhoeffer himself views it as the means and goal of the Christian life.

Introduction to Outline of Project

To summarize, then, I will explore the spirituality of Dietrich Bonhoeffer as it took shape in his own life and writings and as it encounters contemporary readers, specifically women in abuse. Although I make central use of the category of selfhood, it is beyond the scope of this study to explore ways the category of the "self" has shifted over the course

30. Cf. Stortz, "Practicing Christians: Prayer as Formation." Of course the literature on the subject of Christian spiritual formation itself is voluminous; a primary focus of such study in recent decades has been around the formation of candidates for ministry and/or religious life (see, e.g., the chapter entitled "Pedagogies of Formation" in Foster, et al., *Educating Clergy*, 100–26).

31. See especially the section of his *Ethics* entitled "Ethics as Formation" (DBWE 6: 76–102). The first place Bonhoeffer develops this material on "conformation" with Jesus Christ is at the end of *Discipleship* ("The Image of Christ," DBWE 4: 281–88).

32. *Ethics* (DBWE 6), 93.

of the twentieth century and as it is used today.[33] Suffice it to say that, despite various attempts within recent post-modern analyses to deconstruct the language of *selfhood*, I find this terminology to have continuing significance especially for women, who for millennia (and since the invention of the modern Cartesian self) have traditionally been denied the privileges and burdens of full human selfhood.[34] Further, although I make primary use of psychology as the non-theological discipline most relevant to my work, I will not be able here to do justice to the full range of psychological and psychoanalytic understandings of the self or subjectivity.[35] Rather, my work focuses specifically on selected theorists in the area of feminist psychology and psychoanalysis, specifically those

33. A plethora of texts from any number of perspectives greets the reader interested in exploring the self in contemporary thought. Some important works tracing primarily the philosophical dimensions of this reality include Taylor, *Sources of the Self*; Schmidt, *The Development of the Notion of Self*; Schrag, *The Self After Postmodernity*; Strauss and Goethals, eds., *The Self*; Colapietro, "The Integral Self"; and Thisleton, *Interpreting God and the Postmodern Self*. For feminist reflection on the self, again primarily philosophical, see e.g., Benhabib, *Situating the Self*; Griffiths, *Feminisms and the Self*; and Meyers, ed., *Feminists Rethink the Self*.

34. In a recent article, Keller writes powerfully of the irony that the "self" is being dismissed philosophically just as women and other traditionally oppressed peoples are claiming their own subjectivity. Despite the playful appeal of much contemporary postmodern thinking and its usefulness in deconstructing traditional patriarchal models of the human person, she urges women not too quickly to dismiss the selfhood only newly available to them but to consider carefully whose interests such philosophies may serve: "Perhaps deconstructive postmodernism can best be approached more or less as feminists are learning to approach pre-modern constructions. The assault on the subject as essentialist, like the classical assault on the self as sinful, must be read as part of the internal dialogue of the malestream. Let us not as women read ourselves uncritically into its terms and its tones" (Keller, "'To Illuminate Your Trace,'" 220f.). Feminists she cites who are attempting to work creatively within the postmodern context include Harstock, "Foucault on Power," and others collected in *Feminism/Postmodernism*; and Johnson, *A World of Difference*, who provides "a promising feminist Derridaism." Cf. also Ferguson and Wicke, eds., *Feminism and Postmodernism*.

35. Of course, in the field of psychology as well as philosophy the topic of the self has generated considerable literature, beginning most prominently here with Heinz Kohut's development of self-psychology, but continuing within a variety of schools. See Kohut, *The Analysis of the Self*; and, *The Restoration of the Self*. For later work in the area of self-psychology, see Kirstein, *Heinz Kohut's Nuclear Self*, and Fosshage, "Self Psychology." An excellent overview of a range of approaches to the self can be found in Lapsley and Power, eds., *Self, Ego, and Identity*; and in Skolnick and Warshaw, eds., *Relational Perspectives in Psychoanalysis*. For a brief overview from the inter-subjective perspective, see Kennedy, "Becoming a Subject," or his more recent *The Elusive Human Subject*.

who attempt in their work to describe both the origins and the effects of the disordered gender relationships that give rise to abuse. Finally, although I rely on the work of historians in locating Bonhoeffer within his tumultuous context, I will not be able here to engage the historical material in great depth, let alone the fascinating questions about gender roles during Bonhoeffer's lifetime in Germany.[36]

Within these limits, then, the project will unfold as follows, proceeding by means of the methodology outlined by Sandra Schneiders: namely, "thick" description (chapters 2 and 3), critical analysis (chapters 4 and 5), and constructive interpretation (chapters 5 and 6).[37] Chapters 2 and 3 will provide an overview of Bonhoeffer's experience and writings on these subjects. Chapter 2 explores his understanding of the human self, both as he (apparently) experienced his own selfhood and as he universalizes on that basis in articulating the problems and needs of "the" person in his writings. Chapter 3 gives a sketch of the liberation Bonhoeffer experienced through encounter with Jesus Christ and some of the over-arching thematic motifs he develops to express this life of ongoing intimacy with Christ. Thus these two chapters attempt to show how his theology of human selfhood shapes his views of the appropriate trajectory of Christian formation. Conversely, they seek to make clear the personal significance for Bonhoeffer of the christocentric spirituality he articulates, one whose whole desire and purpose is conformation (in the heart of this world's struggles and needs) with Jesus Christ himself, the very reality of it all. In these chapters I will move in a broadly chronological manner through Bonhoeffer's major published works. Beginning with an analysis of the categories suggested in his dissertation, *Sanctorum Communio* (1927), I will refer more briefly to *Act and Being* (1931), touching down again in *Discipleship* (1937) and *Life*

---

36. For information on the Nazi period generally, see, e.g., Fischer, *Nazi Germany*; and Barnett, *Bystanders*. On women in the Nazi era, cf. Siegele-Wenschkewitz and Stuchlik, eds. *Frauen und Faschismus in Europa*; Bock, "Ordinary Women in Nazi Germany"; and Thalmann, *Etre Femme sous le IIIe Reich*. On the roles of women in the pre-Nazi period formative of Bonhoeffer's childhood and youth see Mücke, "Lebenssituationen von Frauen in der Weimarer Republik." Finally, on the powerful role of racial and gender images during the entire period, see Briggs, "Images of Women and Jews in Nineteenth-and Twentieth-Century German Theology."

37. Schneiders, "Hermeneutical Approach," 54–57. For more on "thick description" as originally formulated by Clifford Geertz, see his piece on the subject: "Thick Description," in *The Interpretation of Cultures*, 3–30.

Together (1938), and culminating in the major works from the last five years of his life (*Ethics, Conspiracy and Imprisonment: 1940–1945,* and *Letters and Papers from Prison*).

Chapter 4 of the book will present an alternative vision of human selfhood and its appropriate formation based on contemporary feminist psychological insight. Following a sketch of the worldwide statistical realities of abuse toward girls and women, I will describe psychological and psychoanalytic bases for this contemporary feminist construction of the self. Here my research concentrates on intersubjective theories of women's development. Beginning with the work of the Stone Center theorists (Jean Baker Miller, Judith Jordan, et al.), who suggest the distinctively feminine, if to my mind problematic, "self-in-relation" model of selfhood from their work with adult women, I will move into a discussion of the work of the Harvard research team founded by Carol Gilligan and their longitudinal work with adolescent girls. Third, the psychoanalytic theorist Jessica Benjamin provides a complex feminist reading of the development from infancy of gender-linked patterns of domination and submission; her work proves illuminating of both Bonhoeffer's experience and that of women in abuse. Finally, I draw from Judith Herman's encompassing study of the psychological effects of violence to describe further the experiential impact of abuse. The chapter concludes with an examination of the needs of abuse victims for healthy psychological formation. Thus this chapter provides a feminist theoretical alternative to Bonhoeffer's theology of selfhood and will allow me to examine the processes needed for authentic health and growth among women whose sense of self is degraded or blurry. Chapter 4 as a whole, therefore, will parallel the study of Bonhoeffer in regard both to theories of selfhood and strategies or resources for psychological and spiritual formation.

Chapter 5 of the project, next, will create a critical conversation between Bonhoeffer and these feminist thinkers around the theoretical understanding of selfhood and the appropriate formation of the self into greater Christian and human wholeness. This will be a broadly twofold conversation moving in four stages from feminist critique of Bonhoeffer through Bonhoeffer's own challenge to these psychological theorists. On the one hand, I will engage the feminist voices in a critique of Bonhoeffer's theories and prescriptions as those undermine or countermand the movements toward health and spiritual maturity demanded by soluble selves. On the other hand, I will point to life-giving dimensions of Bonhoeffer's witness, some unearthed only by an ongoing "against the grain" reading, but others unambiguous and powerful. In this chapter, then, I will suggest ways central aspects of Bonhoeffer's spirituality can be read in all their liberating power for those who suffer under abuse and sketch possibilities for the appropriation of these motifs. This retrieval takes its impetus from Bonhoeffer's own love of a "polyphonic" spirituality, one that is able in great freedom to listen for and develop themes quite divergent from earlier variations on the *cantus firmus.* Finally, a concluding chapter will summarize my research and findings, suggest broad implications for ministry with women in abuse, and point to the project's significance for Bonhoeffer studies precisely as a psychologically-informed feminist analysis within the discipline of Christian spirituality.

2

Bonhoeffer's Sense of Self: Experienced and Articulated

As noted by its title, this chapter provides an overview of how Bonhoeffer appears to have perceived the mystery of human self-hood, both in his own life's unfolding and as he describes the place of the self in his writings. In order to be able to trace his experience as a self and a Christian, I will first provide a short summary of his biography. Because of space limitations, I am of course unable to develop every interrelation between his biography and writings. Instead, this summary will begin with a more extensive depiction of what is known about Bonhoeffer's family background and dynamics, as these shaped him in obviously formative ways, and will then proceed with a more factually-oriented overview of the major events of his life. The central section of this chapter, following the biography, is devoted to an exploration of Bonhoeffer's writings about the place of the self and his development of a theology of human relationality. This section will include treatment of Bonhoeffer's dissertation, *Sanctorum Communio*, and move into consideration of his views on the human person and the Christian community from various perspectives. Following this (the final section of this chapter and at various points throughout chapter three) I will return to Bonhoeffer's life and develop certain dimensions of his biography more fully in order to show consistently the grounding of Bonhoeffer's experience of self and spiritual formation in the events of his own life, particularly as these were shaped by and in turn affected his social location.

Biographical Overview

Dietrich Bonhoeffer was born on February 4, 1906, along with his twin sister Sabine, as the sixth and seventh children (of an eventual eight) of Karl and Paula Bonhoeffer. Dr. Karl Bonhoeffer was a neurologist and psychiatrist who in 1912 was invited to chair the department of psychiatry at the University of Berlin, Germany's leading post in the field; the family moved from Breslau to Berlin when Dietrich and Sabine were six years old. Their mother, Paula née von Hase Bonhoeffer, was a licensed teacher who devoted herself to her children's early education, so that they entered school well advanced for their years. The family was quite well off, with a staff of ten full-time servants, and moved in the foremost cultural and intellectual circles in Berlin; Dietrich's biographer Eberhard Bethge writes, "From his earliest childhood Dietrich Bonhoeffer was accustomed to being privileged, not the underdog."[1] The children grew up engaging socially with leading thinkers, scientists, artists, and professionals. They were expected to develop sharp critical and verbal skills from a young age, to play musical instruments in frequent family music-making, to read widely and appreciatively, and to prepare themselves consciously for their own eventual place as leaders and contributors to Germany's great cultural and intellectual heritage. Because of Karl's agnosticism, the Bonhoeffer family was not church-going, but Paula instructed the children in the Bible and catechism, and taught them prayers and hymns. The only real connection to a congregation the children had growing up was their eventual confirmation; even their baptisms were conducted privately at home by Paula's brother.

Both parents descended from distinguished forebears: the von Hase family was an aristocratic lineage including a prominent church historian and a pastor to the Kaiser, and the Bonhoeffer line included statesmen and artists, not to mention an independent streak surfacing in Julie Bonhoeffer, Dietrich's grandmother, who in 1933 at age 90 defied the SS by marching through their blockade to shop at a Jewish market. When in 1940 the ban on speaking was imposed on him by the Nazis, Dietrich attempted to defend himself against their accusations of "activity subverting the people" by drawing on his impressive pedigree:

> I reject this charge. My entire outlook, my work as well as my background, make it inconceivable for me to allow myself to be

1. E. Bethge, *Dietrich Bonhoeffer*, 20. Hereafter abbreviated as DB.

identified with circles warranting the stigma of such a charge. I am proud to belong to a family that has rendered outstanding service to the German people and nation for generations. Among my ancestors are Field Marshall Count Kalckreuth and the two great German artists of the same name, the Jena church historian Karl von Hase, renowned in the entire scholarly world of the past century, and the Cauer family of sculptors; my uncle is Major General Count von der Goltz, who freed the Baltics; his son, the state attorney Count Rüdiger von der Goltz, is my first cousin; Major General von Hase, who serves in active military duty, is my uncle; my father has been a full university professor of medicine in Berlin for nearly thirty years and serves to the present day in distinguished public offices; his ancestors lived for centuries as highly esteemed craftsmen and councilors of the then free state of Schwäbisch Hall, and even today their pictures hang proudly in the city church; my brothers and brothers-in-law serve in high government positions; and one of my brothers was killed in the world war. It has been the aspiration of these men and their families to serve the German nation and people at all times and to risk their lives for this service. In conscious affirmation of this spiritual legacy and moral position of my family, I cannot accept the charge of "activity subverting the people." Action corresponding to this charge is foreign to my very nature and is completely out of the question for me.[2]

This argument did not convince the Gestapo to rescind his ban on speaking. But it does give a sense of the self-understanding of the Bonhoeffer/von Hase family in its location among the cultural elite of Germany. The free-thinking and courageous stance manifested by Julie Bonhoeffer, and passed on through her son and daughter-in-law to their eight children, made the Bonhoeffer family one of the centers of the underground organized resistance to Hitler, precisely because they took seriously their position as defenders of the German heritage Hitler grotesquely defiled. As Clifford Green puts it, "A better context than this family for developing the strengths and skills of a strong and healthy ego would be difficult to imagine."[3]

Yet it could also be a lonely place, especially for Dietrich. He was close to Sabine, his twin, and their younger sister Susanne, but separated by many years from his older brothers. As the youngest boy, he felt a

2. Bonhoeffer, *Conspiracy and Imprisonment* (DBWE 16), 75.

3. Green, *Bonhoeffer*, 146.

keen desire to be noticed and accepted by his brothers and by their father; yet his relative lack of interest in the prestigious fields of science, medicine, and the law in which they moved put him at a further disadvantage. This created in him a fierce "ambition and competitiveness"[4] to be noticed by them as a person in his own right: Bethge speaks of Dietrich's "isolation among his brothers and sisters" as formative in the shape of his later life, fueling his "urge to surpass them all."[5] His decision at age 14 to become a theologian thus reflected both his own more speculative temperament and his need to find his own world in which to excel, one deliberately removed from theirs. His brothers' scorn (and his father's unvoiced skepticism) at this decision only reinforced his resolve to prove them wrong.

It is important to note as well that the Bonhoeffers were a model of the patriarchal family. Obedience to the parents, and especially the father, was deeply instilled, and the children were taught from a young age that Karl was never to be disturbed with their squabbles and needs. Nurse, governess, other servants, older siblings, and Paula served as buffers between the children and their father.[6] Karl's attention was on his own terms and was very highly prized. To live and think and express oneself in such a way as to deserve his approval was the child's best reward. If, within this environment, the Bonhoeffer parents devoted their wealth and love to provide the most stimulating, creatively engaging, and well-structured possible home for their children, nevertheless the deeply-instilled emotional reserve left Dietrich, at least, profoundly lonely,[7] desperate for his father's and brothers' approval, let alone comraderie. It was only when he went to Tübingen at age 17 for university

4. Ibid., 144.

5. DB 37; cf. also 20.

6. Paula was the primary mediator between Karl and the children, an interesting role given Bonhoeffer's later development of the category of Christ as mediator (*Mittler*); see pp. 83–87 of chapter 3. Renate Bethge, Bonhoeffer's niece and the eventual wife of his biographer, Eberhard Bethge, writes of the Bonhoeffer family, "The children saw their father much less frequently than their mother, so his worth may have grown by his rarity. And their mother herself cared that the father's image appeared spotless and that things went the way he liked it, that he had peace and quiet for his work" ("Bonhoeffer and the Role of Women," 34f.).

7. DB 37. An example of this reserve within his family shows up in a much later incident, namely his inability to ask his psychiatrist father for help even in a painful later depression, still not wanting to "bother" him. Cf. Glazener, "On Being a Christian Today," 89.

that, "for the first time, he had a circle of friends," but even these did not prove long-lasting bonds.[8]

The painful loneliness of this young man, desperate to prove himself by means of his intellectual prowess and ambition, yet isolated from nourishing, non-competitive or -combative relations with others, shapes his spiritual journey and theology in understandably formative ways, as we shall see throughout this chapter. In 1923, then, he began his studies in Tübingen; after a year there he transferred to Berlin, where he defended his doctoral dissertation, *Sanctorum Communio*, in December of 1927. Following a year as a vicar in Barcelona, Spain, he began lecturing in systematic theology at Berlin University and became a professor following his habilitation (for which he wrote *Act and Being*). Before continuing in Berlin, however, he spent a year of further studies at Union Theological Seminary in New York, where he was stimulated for the first time to consider the power of the Gospel in Christian pacifism, in ecumenical commitment, and in confronting racism, all themes which engaged him the rest of his life.

It is to the period immediately following his year in the U.S. that Eberhard Bethge dates the crucial shift whereby Bonhoeffer the theologian became a Christian.[9] As he himself put it later in life, this was a shift "from phraseology to reality";[10] that is, it was a true conversion in which what had been merely academic truths became cherished personal ones. Trained well in the virtues of discretion and modesty, Bonhoeffer did not trumpet this change. In fact, he almost never spoke of it directly; only a handful of later letters suggest its significance. In January, 1935, for instance, he wrote to his brother, the agnostic physicist Karl-Friedrich,

> It may be that in many things I seem to you rather fanatical and crazy. I myself am sometimes afraid of this. . . . When I first began [in theology], I imagined it quite otherwise—perhaps a more academic matter. Now something very different has come

---

8. DB 50.

9. DB 202–6. For a thoughtful study of the two main "conversions" Bethge delineates in Bonhoeffer's life—the theologian becoming a Christian (1931–1932), and the Christian theologian becoming a contemporary (*Zeitgenosse*), fully engaged in the struggles and calling of his own time and place (1939)—see his essay, "Turning Points in Bonhoeffer's Life and Thought."

10. LPP 275 (DBW 8:397).

of it. I now believe that I know at last that I am at least on the right track—for the first time in my life. And that often makes me very glad.[11]

Back in Berlin in 1931, Bonhoeffer took up his lecturing in theology at the university, was ordained and began some pastoral duties, and was appointed youth secretary for the World Alliance for Promoting International Friendship through the Churches (a predecessor body to the World Council of Churches). At this point in Germany the National Socialist Party was building its strength and beginning to become a dominant force in German politics. By the time Hitler became chancellor (January 30, 1933), Bonhoeffer had already been speaking out actively in church circles and writings regarding the Nazi threat. Two days after this seizing of power, Bonhoeffer gave a national radio address in which he warned that should Hitler "surrender to the wishes of his followers, who would always make him their idol—then the image of the Leader [*Führer*] will gradually become the image of the 'misleader' [*Verführer*].... Leaders or offices which set themselves up as gods mock God."[12] The broadcast was cut off before the speech was finished, but, as one observer puts it, "the speaker was marked; he was not to be lost sight of again."[13]

This interrupted radio broadcast from the very outset of Hitler's power marked the beginning of Bonhoeffer's public resistance to the Nazi government. He was also among the first in the church to present, in April 1933, heated opposition to the Nazis' Aryan Civil Service legislation. Not all pastors were as outspoken as Bonhoeffer, however. Many embraced National Socialism, the Nazi swastika flag, and Hitler. As months went on, it became painfully clear that the state church[14] as a whole would not defy Hitler's attempts to nazify it. Those who re-

11. Bonhoeffer, DBW 13:272–73, trans. from DB 205. See pp. 59–70 below ("The Autobiographical Dimension") for a fuller examination of the significance for Bonhoeffer of his conversion. Chapter 3 will then explore further the faith into which he was drawn, and its contours in his experience, writings, and practice.

12. DB 260; the full text of the radio speech is found in DBW 12:257, 259–60.

13. Casalis, "Theology Under the Sign of Martyrdom," 81.

14. Generally in this paper, references to the "church" in Germany will mean the Lutheran–Reformed state church. For information on the situation within the German Roman Catholic Church in this period, see among others Binder, *Irrtum und Widerstand*. On the developments in the Nazi-controlled state church, see Bergen, *Twisted Cross*.

mained in this body, about two-thirds of Germany's pastors and church members, became known as the German Christians. In September 1933 the dissenting pastors led by Bonhoeffer and Martin Niemöller organized the Pastors' Emergency League and in May 1934, at a synod of pastors and laity, adopted the Barmen Declaration[15] and founded the Confessing Church (*Bekennende Kirche*).

Bonhoeffer himself was not present at Barmen, as he had begun serving a German congregation in London in 1933, a pastorate that opened further ecumenical contacts for him. The two most notable ecumenical events of this period for Bonhoeffer were the beginning in fall 1933 of his friendship and collaboration with Bishop George Bell of Chichester and his active participation in August 1934 at the Ecumenical Conference in Fanø, Denmark, where in addition to having the Confessing Church recognized internationally as the only legitimate Protestant ecumenical partner in Germany he gave an electrifying sermon on the call to peacemaking and unity in Christ.

Following his London pastorate, Bonhoeffer had hoped to spend time learning from Mahatma Gandhi in India, following years of fascination with this great spiritual leader, and had received an invitation from Gandhi to stay at his ashram to observe the techniques and life of pacifist resistance. Before his departure for India, however, he was called to serve the Confessing Church at one of its five newly established (illegal) seminaries, located in Finkenwalde, Pomerania. Here then, from 1935–1937, Bonhoeffer served as director, pastor, and professor of the seminary; this was the experience of Christian community underlying his 1938 book *Life Together*. At Finkenwalde he attempted to create a nearly monastic community of common prayer, meditation, silence, confession, and worship, in addition to lectures, study, games, and engagement with current developments in church and politics. It was in this period as well that he published *Discipleship*, perhaps his most famous book, which calls Christians to lives of "costly grace." After the Finkenwalde seminary was shut down by the Nazis in 1937, he con-

15. This series of six theses repudiating false Nazi teaching was written by Karl Barth. Its thrust was to contest Hitler's claim to be "Führer" of the church, in addition to the state, and to claim lordship for Jesus Christ alone as the church's only *Führer* (leader) and authority. The title "Confessing Church" came out of this declaration that the church can confess only Christ as Lord. The adoption of the Barmen Declaration was an emotional and spiritual high point for the Confessing Church in defiance of Hitler; its anniversary is still celebrated in German church circles.

tinued training Confessing Church seminarians in even more covert situations. Gradually, as the repression of the Jews and Nazi aggression became only more acute, Bonhoeffer moved into active resistance, into the circle of conspirators (including his brother Klaus, sister Christine, and two brothers-in-law) who were plotting the overthrow of Hitler's government.

The process of Bonhoeffer's joining the conspiracy is the second of his life's two major "turning points" outlined by Eberhard Bethge. Here, in Bethge's terms, the theologian and Christian became a "contemporary," one who fully shares the agonies, struggles, and vocation of one's own particular time and place as the only possible arena for faithfulness to Christ. The crux of this second (1939) turning occurred, like the first, in the U.S., where Bonhoeffer had fled at the invitation of American friends, including Reinhold Niebuhr and Paul Lehmann. Having come with the intent of surviving the increasingly nasty times, with war imminent and Bonhoeffer himself the target of tightening surveillance and restrictions by the Nazis, he nevertheless found himself oddly out of place in New York. Unable to share his friends' enthusiasm for his presence there, he struggled to discern God's call for him and, after much prayer, made the decision to the dismay and astonishment of his colleagues to return to Germany. An often-quoted passage from his letter to Niebuhr explaining his decision states,

> I have made a mistake in coming to America. I must live through this difficult period of our national history with the Christian people of Germany. I will have no right to participate in the reconstruction of Christian life in Germany after the war if I do not share the trials of this time with my people.[16]

Once back in Germany Bonhoeffer served the Confessing Church in several appointments before moving full-time into the resistance in 1940. His *Ethics*, written during the period of his conspiracy activity, reflects on the attempt to act faithfully in the midst of a people's guilt. Feeling responsible as a German to stop Nazi atrocities being committed in the name of the German people, and as a Christian for doing

16. Letter to Reinhold Niebuhr, late June 1939 (DBW 15:210). The material from this period of Bonhoeffer's life is fascinating. See his journal from June 8—July 9, 1939 (DBW 15:217–40), of which excerpts are translated in Bonhoeffer, *Testament to Freedom*, 493–501. Letters from the period (many of which are written in English) appear in DBW 15:182–215.

the will of God come what may, he could find no way ahead but to add his efforts to those seeking the end of the Nazi government. He had been unable to persuade the Confessing Church as a body to "become a spoke in the wheel" of state, as he had first urged in 1933, but he himself felt called in Christ now to take that further step.

Officially, Bonhoeffer's war-time role became that of an agent in the Abwehr, the military intelligence branch of the government. Because this unit was independent of the Gestapo and led by high-ranking conspirators, members of the resistance found cover there. Along with his brother-in-law Hans von Dohnanyi, Bonhoeffer was essentially a double agent. Dohnanyi obtained the assignment for him as an escape from the draft, and Bonhoeffer served the resistance through contacts with his international ecumenical partners in the Allied nations. Between 1941 and 1943 he made several trips abroad, meeting among others with Willem Visser't Hooft in Geneva and Bishop Bell in Sigtuna, Sweden. The goal of the resistance was the overthrow of the Nazi government, meticulously organized through covert connections with those opposed to Hitler within the military, government, unions, and other groups.

While opinions vary as to the actual estimated probability of success the resistance may have had,[17] it appears the closest they got to reaching their goal occurred with the failed assassination attempt on Hitler of March 1943.[18] That attempt marked the high point of nation-wide underground readiness to move into an interim non-Nazi government. Following its failure some important generals slid back into

17. For more detailed information on the history and complexity of the German resistance, one may turn to the rich literature and resources in the field. A selection to begin includes Gill, *An Honorable Defeat*; the powerful film by Beller, "Restless Conscience"; von Schlabrendorff, *Offiziere gegen Hitler*; Hoffmann, *History of the German Resistance*; Manvell and Fraenkel, *Canaris Conspiracy*; and, for the often-overlooked role of women in resistance to Hitler, Szepansky, *Frauen Leisten Widerstand*.

18. The fact that Bonhoeffer participated in a conspiracy which included plans for not simply the removal of Hitler but his actual assassination has resulted in vigorous debate among those who evaluate his legacy. It is beyond the scope of this analysis to engage this debate. But for reflections on the principles of non-violence in light of Bonhoeffer's decision to join the conspiracy, see among others, Boesak, "What Dietrich Bonhoeffer Has Meant to Me"; and Larry Rasmussen's comparison of Bonhoeffer's and Daniel Berrigan's positions on resistance, including an extended treatment of the question, necessity, and ethical limits of violence, in the chapter entitled "Resistance" in *Dietrich Bonhoeffer—His Significance for North Americans*, 43–56.

Nazi loyalty, the movement lost momentum, and within six weeks the Gestapo had unwittingly crippled the resistance in a crackdown on the Abwehr: on April 5, 1943, they arrested several resistance members, including Bonhoeffer, his sister Christine, and her husband Hans von Dohnanyi. This arrest came, also, just four months after Bonhoeffer had become engaged to be married to Maria von Wedemeyer, the 17-year-old daughter and granddaughter of a family long known to Dietrich from his Finkenwalde years.

At the time of his arrest, Bonhoeffer was suspected not for any known resistance activity but because of irregularities the Nazis had discovered resulting from the cover-up of an operation that brought several Jews to safety in Switzerland. His trial was connected to Hans von Dohnanyi's, who was higher up in the organization, and was seemingly endlessly delayed. Christine von Dohnanyi was released after five weeks; she was able to play on prevailing gender stereotypes by pretending to know nothing, although in fact she was an insider to conspiracy details and plans, and continued her work following her release. The imprisoned conspirators were successful during their interrogations in concealing their resistance activities and the ongoing work outside from Nazi discovery. Only after the attempt on Hitler's life on July 20, 1944, were documents discovered that made clear their connection to the resistance. The remaining resistance leaders had regrouped to prepare this final plot against Hitler, whose failure effectively marked the end of any organized effort to overthrow the Nazi regime.

Bonhoeffer was imprisoned at Tegel military prison in Berlin from April 1943 until October 1944. After his arrest, he at first suffered shock and even despair but within a short period of time was creating a way of life that sustained him to the end. Ever since consciously becoming a Christian, he had maintained a disciplined prayer life, centered in meditation on Scripture, and while in prison he was able to continue and deepen that practice. His warmth and kindness soon led to respect from the guards and a relaxing of restrictions prohibiting contact with family and friends outside. He was also able to intercede for other prisoners and, after becoming an assistant in the infirmary, to interact with fellow prisoners with some regularity. Both staff and prisoners came to depend on his strength, spiritual wisdom, and care for them.

Bonhoeffer's emotional lifeline during these months, in addition to visits from his family and fiancée, was the system of correspondence he worked out with a sympathetic guard, who smuggled letters in and out for him. A letter-writer all his life, with strong ties to family and close friends, Bonhoeffer wrote eagerly and these prison letters provide powerful glimpses of the faith that sustained him even as hope for survival was fading, and of his lively mind still trying to make theological sense of this "boundary situation" of Christian faithfulness in the face of totalitarian evil.

From Tegel, Bonhoeffer was transferred in October 1944 to a Gestapo prison in Berlin, where letters and visits nearly ceased. In February 1945 he was moved to Buchenwald concentration camp, then to other camps on the way to Flossenbürg where, along with other key resistance figures, he was executed on April 9. Hans von Dohnanyi was killed the same day elsewhere, and Dietrich's brother Klaus and another brother-in-law, Rüdiger Schleicher (Renate Bethge's father), were executed on April 23. At the time he was summoned for imminent execution, Bonhoeffer was concluding a worship service for other prisoners that second Sunday of Easter. He gave his last recorded words to an Englishman, Payne Best, to pass on to Bishop Bell: "Tell him this is the end; for me, the beginning of life."[19] The following morning he was hanged at dawn, having prayed in his cell and before the gallows.[20] At the time of his death, he was thirty-nine years old.

From the loneliness of his youth, then, Bonhoeffer moved quite a distance during his life, becoming a person able to relate deeply to a circle of intimate others, and effectively and pastorally to a wide variety of persons. This move into increasing relationality with others, God, and those who suffer in the world describes a central dimension of the liberation he experienced in Jesus Christ, whose presence in his life through his conversion provided release from the confines of lonely self-imprisonment. The remainder of this chapter will trace Bonhoeffer's descriptions in both academic and more personal writings of this imprisoning selfhood as he seems to have experienced it, beginning with his dissertation. Throughout this exposition, and especially in the concluding section of this chapter ("The Autobiographical Dimension"), I will attempt to show how the events of his life, particularly as his social

---

19. DB 927.

20. On Bonhoeffer's death see Fischer-Hüllstrung, "A Report from Flossenbürg," and the discussion in Slane, *Bonhoeffer as Martyr*, 27–28.

location changes in later years, correlate with the liberating shifts he increasingly experiences in his sense of his own and Christian selfhood.

Theology of Human Relationality: Sanctorum Communio

From the very first of his published writings, Bonhoeffer demonstrated an interest in questions of human selfhood.[21] *Sanctorum Communio*, his doctoral dissertation written in 1927 and published in a somewhat abridged form in 1930, is centrally concerned with matters of theological anthropology and sociology.[22] As the title indicates, his dissertation explores the significance of Christian community (the communion of saints) within a broader overview of human personhood and relationality in general. In an oft-quoted programmatic statement in the very first paragraph of the preface to the published edition, Bonhoeffer writes,

> The more this investigation has considered the significance of the sociological category for theology, the more clearly has emerged the social intention of all the basic Christian concepts. "Person," "primal state," "sin," and "revelation" can be fully comprehended only in reference to sociality [*Sozialität*] (SC 21).

Although it is a very early work, written at age 21, nevertheless this dissertation provides a foundational basis for all of Bonhoeffer's later thought. The form, style, and urgency of his thinking would shift dramatically as the 1930's and 1940's progressed, but throughout these years, and even into his final prison correspondence, the categories he develops here of "person," of the typical forms and shape of human sin, and of the social nature of salvation and discipleship remain remarkably constant. This work, in fact, proved to situate the budding theologian with exceptionally clear and useful intellectual resources for seeing through Nazi ideology and for his prophetic attempts to call the church (both in Germany and abroad) to resistance from the very outset of Hitler's regime. His dissertation's fundamental categories and

21. In addition to Green's volume, *Dietrich Bonhoeffer: A Theology of Sociality*, other important studies of Bonhoeffer's theological anthropology include Brocker, *Community of God, Jesus Christ, and Responsibility*; Marsh, "The Overabundant Self and the Transcendental Tradition"; Dahl, "Bonhoeffer and Human Being"; Griffin, *Self and Jesus Christ*; and Bowman, *Bonhoeffer's Methodology*.

22. Bonhoeffer, *Sanctorum Communio* (DBWE 1). Henceforth I will use parenthetical references (SC). Unless otherwise noted, all italics in SC quotations are Bonhoeffer's own. Citations include material from the original dissertation and the 1930 edition.

presuppositions thus remain crucial to the whole of Bonhoeffer's later thinking and action.

Ethical Personhood and Sociality

One of these fundamental categories is a "Christian concept of person" developed as the topic of his second chapter (SC 34–57), following a brief introductory chapter on definitions of social philosophy and sociology. Here Bonhoeffer is at pains to distinguish his own notions of personhood from the traditions of ethical idealism that had shaped the dominant understandings of human personhood of his day. For the idealists, of whom Bonhoeffer cites Kant, Fichte, and Hegel most frequently,

> one I is like the other. Only on the basis of this likeness is a relation of persons conceivable at all. . . . *It is the destiny of the human species to be absorbed into the realm of reason, to form a realm of completely similar and harmonious persons, defined by universal reason or by one spirit and separated only by their different activities.* (SC 43)

Bonhoeffer however resists the attempt to make "absolute principles" or "universality" governing categories for theology, ethics, or personhood. For him, a Christian understanding of the human person is inherently and necessarily particular:

> we must . . . overcome the idealist concept and replace it with one which preserves the *individual, concrete character of the person as absolute and intended by God.* . . . By person I do not mean the idealists' person of mind or reason, but the person in concrete, living individuality. (SC 44–45, my italics; and 48)

In a summary statement also countering the idealists' subsuming of human being into a disembodied-sounding realm of pure "spirit," he writes, "The Christian concept affirms the whole concrete person, body and soul, different from all others, as ethically relevant" (SC 53).

Although aimed primarily at the tradition of German philosophical idealism, this criticism also marks an early deviation from Karl Barth. In contrast to Barth, Bonhoeffer insists that one loves the concrete other not because that other person is merely a bearer of Christ,[23]

---

23. Here see also SC 50.

unimportant in his or her own being, but rather precisely in and for that person's essential uniqueness and concrete living reality:

> Who gives Barth the right to say that the other is "as such infinitely unimportant," when God commands us to love precisely that person? God has made the "neighbor as such" infinitely important, and there isn't any other "neighbor as such" for us. The other is not merely "parable of the wholly other," a "proxy of the unknown God"; rather, the other is infinitely important as such, precisely because God takes the other person seriously. . . . Should not the other through God's command be infinitely affirmed as a concrete human being?[24]

Note that this emphasis on the particular and the concrete will shape Bonhoeffer's entire theological project right up to the end, as he questions relentlessly any universalizing programs or absolutist ethics that would deny the essential variety and concreteness of human life. What is good or right or the will of God cannot, for Bonhoeffer, be deduced from on high or "formulated as a general principle" (SC 168) to be applied to any and all human contexts. Rather, the good must be discerned over and over for every new circumstance: "With every new day, therefore, the question arises, how, today, here, in this situation, can I remain and be preserved within this new life [of conformation] with God, with Jesus Christ?"[25] For Bonhoeffer, then, the Christian understanding of the human person develops differently from both German idealism and Barth's neo-Kantian theology. He describes his sense of the move from idealism into Christian personhood as follows:

> As long as my intellect is dominant, exclusively claiming universal validity, as long as all contradictions that can arise when one knows a subject as an object of knowledge are conceived as immanent to my intellect, I am not in the social sphere. But this means that I enter this sphere *only when my intellect is confronted by some fundamental barrier [Schranke].* . . . . Only the experience of the barrier as real is a specifically ethical experience (SC 45–46, 47).

24. SC 170, note 28, citing Barth's *Epistle to the Romans*, 452.

25. Bonhoeffer, *Ethics* (DBWE 6), 323. This quote from the *Ethics* is typical of and ubiquitous in Bonhoeffer's later thinking as well as in SC, showing how this emphasis on particularity and concreteness continues throughout his life.

Thus for Bonhoeffer it is running up against some other that shatters the illusion of the all-knowing universal intellect and draws a person into the ethical and social arena where authentic personhood is formed. He describes this experience of encounter with another (divine or human) being using the interchangeable images of barrier *(Schranke)* or boundary *(Grenze)*. This barrier of another person's concrete and separate being confronts the individual with a reality alien to his or her own, drawing the person into what Bonhoeffer calls the state of "responsibility," or of ethical demand for some response.

Such encounter, first and foremost with the divine as creative and confronting Other, is what creates the personhood of the individual:

> It is a Christian insight that the person as conscious being is created in the moment of being moved—in the situation of responsibility, passionate ethical struggle, confrontation by an overwhelming claim; thus the real person grows out of the concrete situation. . . . *For Christian philosophy, the human person originates only in relation to the divine; the divine person transcends the human person*, who both resists and is overwhelmed by the divine. . . . The Christian person originates only in the absolute duality of God and humanity; only in experiencing the barrier does the awareness of oneself as ethical person arise. (SC 49)

He describes this person-forming confrontation as one that necessarily happens over and over, further undercutting Cartesian/idealist notions of the unchanging, timeless self: "[Thus] the person does not exist timelessly; a person is not static, but dynamic. The person exists always and only in ethical responsibility; the person is re-created again and again in the perpetual flux of life" (SC 48). This occurs primally in relation to God, as noted above; but because of the essential and inseparable "interconnection of God, community, and individual" (SC 51), this sort of ethical encounter takes place constantly between persons within the complex networks of human sociality as well. He writes, "In this sense we call the ethical concept of the individual the social basic-relation, since one cannot even speak of the individual without at the same time necessarily thinking of the 'other' who moves the individual into the ethical sphere" (SC 50). In fact, for Bonhoeffer, any given "individual exists only in relation to an 'other'. . . . *for the individual to exist, 'others' must be there*" (SC 51).

The most characteristic language by which Bonhoeffer expresses this is in terms of the encounter between "I" and "You" ("Ich" and "Du"). In his introduction to the volume, Clifford Green points out the analogies of this usage to that of Martin Buber, as well as the ways Bonhoeffer differs from Buber. Although Buber's *I and Thou* (*Ich und Du*) was published in 1923, i.e., well prior to Bonhoeffer's completion of his dissertation, Bonhoeffer nowhere cites the volume. And although both authors would concur in the usage of I and You "resisting the objectification of persons" generally, nevertheless Buber's emphasis is one of intimacy between I and You, whereas Bonhoeffer "stresses the 'other' as boundary and barrier to the self; he emphasizes ethical encounter rather than intimacy."[26]

For Bonhoeffer, then, the "You" is any other self who confronts the "I" as a barrier:

> The You as a reality-form [*Wirklichkeitsform*] is by definition independent in encountering the I in this sphere. In contrast to the idealist object-form, it is not immanent to the mind of the subject. The You sets the limit for the subject and by its own accord activates a will that impinges upon the other in such a way that this other will becomes a You for the I. (SC 51)

> [T]here would be no self-consciousness without community—or better, . . . self-consciousness arises concurrently with the consciousness of existing in community. . . . by recognizing a You, a being of alien consciousness, as separate and distinct from myself, I recognize myself as an "I," and so my self-consciousness awakens. (SC 70–71)

The You meets the I in this encounter as "demand" on the I. The I as a "whole person, who is totally claimless, is claimed by this absolute demand" (SC 54). It is important to note that at this point in his discussion Bonhoeffer is speaking of such absolute demand issuing from encounter not (or not only) with the divine You but explicitly with a human You.[27] In the encounter of human persons, the "totally claimless"

26. Green, "Editor's Introduction," SC 5. Green goes on to note that for Bonhoeffer, "The other transcends the self in ethical encounter—indeed, the human You is a form and analogy of the divine You in precisely this present otherness. This personal-ethical model of transcendence, which is found throughout Bonhoeffer's theology, distinguishes him clearly from Buber" (ibid. 5–6).

27. The very next sentence reads, "But this seems to make one human being the creator of the ethical person of the other . . ." (SC 54).

I is confronted by the "absolute demand" of the other, the You. Coming so soon after his categorical denials of any absolute principles in theology or ethics, this language is interesting; it is the first inkling of a curious blindness to questions of discernment concerning the relation of self and other that I will highlight later. It also reflects the tendency throughout this discussion toward a certain blurriness of antecedent: is the You being referred to at any given point the divine You? The human You? Both/either? This is almost always ambiguous. Bonhoeffer does not pursue questions of discernment between these claims, or any differences in the weight each might be given. In his attempt to emphasize as strongly as possible the essential rooting of Christian life and God-experience within human sociality, he opens himself to the risk of seeming almost to equate the human and divine You and their claims in the experience of an I.

As if anticipating this concern, Bonhoeffer does introduce this distinction although he does not develop it, since the possibility of a radical disjunction between human and divine claims on a person seems never to occur to him. But in response to the perceived objection that his schema might appear to set up one person as the god-like creator of the other's personhood, he states that

> The person-creating efficacy of the You is independent of the personhood of the You.[28] We now add that it is also independent of the will of the human You. One human being cannot of its own accord make another into an I, an ethical person conscious of responsibility. If the I nevertheless arises in relation to the concrete human You, there must be another factor we have not yet considered. In Christian terms that means *God or the Holy Spirit joins the concrete You; only through God's active working does the other become a You to me from whom my I arises. In other words, every human You is an image of the divine You in the reality of our lives.* You-character is in fact the essential form in which the divine is experienced; every human You bears its You-character only by virtue of the divine. (SC 54–55)

---

28. This means for him that *any* human being can be a You for me, regardless of his or her own state of ethical formation as a person—regardless, that is, of whether s/he is an "I" to him/herself. As William Peck points out, even enemies can thus be You for me; they can be agents God uses to form me as an authentic person. Cf. Peck, "Role of the 'Enemy' in Bonhoeffer's Life and Thought," 349.

Thus it is God alone who makes an other into a You for me (in fact it is God's "You" that I am experiencing in that encounter) and who also creates me as a person, an "I," thereby. In this case, one might infer that not every human other, even those who attempt to make "absolute demands" in the face of which I am assumed to be "totally claimless," is in fact a You for me. Rather, only those encounters that reveal God-as-You for me can be claimed to be person-forming in Bonhoeffer's sense or to fall within his schema. Bonhoeffer himself, however, does not draw this inference, nor does he again refer to any such distinction between divine and human You-ness. The point being made then appears to be more academically than concretely relevant for him: a safeguarding of the priority of divine agency in a technical sense in the face of possible objections to its near-submersion in human relationships. Bonhoeffer concludes this digression, in fact, by re-emphasizing his main point, namely that "it is a *Christian insight that God uses the social nature of human beings in order to act among them in every respect. God acts in history;* thus God's claim is mediated for us, essentially and primarily, by other people, and is bound to sociality" (SC 55).

SOCIOLOGICAL CATEGORIES

As one who is making use of sociological categories in a theological study (a daring foray into interdisciplinarity for his day), Bonhoeffer treats this human and Christian sociality using the differentiated language of *Gemeinschaft, Gesellschaft,* and *Masse,*[29] and these categories provide helpful tools for a deeper understanding of the sort of sociality Bonhoeffer intends. These sociological structures are distinguished by both the degree of separateness of the persons involved (i.e., healthy distinction between persons vs. unhealthy fusion or merger of selves) and the "direction" of people's wills within the structure. *Gemeinschaft* and *Gesellschaft* are similar in being founded upon the intrinsic and respectful separateness of human beings; they differ in the direction of will each manifests. That is, in a *Gemeinschaft* (such as a family, a friendship, a congregation, etc.) the members of the community will "reciprocally"; they will one another's being and presence in the community

---

29. SC 86–96. That is, "community," "society," and "mass." These terms were first developed sociologically by Tönnies in *Community and Society*; see especially 37ff. and 64ff. of that work.

in a mutual way. The community may also have some stated purpose (such as, in a congregation, serving the poor), but this is secondary to the mutual pleasure members of the *Gemeinschaft* take in one another's company and, in the case of Christian relational communities, in the presence of Christ in their midst. That such purposes are secondary can be demonstrated by the fact that if the purpose were to come to an end (in this case, if there were no more poverty to alleviate), the community would not cease to exist but would continue in mutual love.

In contrast, in a *Gesellschaft* (e.g., a business, an agency, an army), again the separateness of persons is respected but here their wills are directed in a parallel fashion rather than a reciprocal one.[30] That is, their reason for organizing themselves together is for the accomplishment of some purpose. Once the purpose is fulfilled, the *Gesellschaft* has no further reason to exist.

Finally, the *Masse* is an agglomeration of people whose wills run parallel to one another's toward some external goal or good, as in a *Gesellschaft*, yet "the boundary of personhood is lost, and the individual is no longer a person but only a part of the mass, drawn into it and directed by it. The mass is a unity . . . that is not supported by the separateness of the person and thus cannot last" (SC 93–96). Examples of the *Masse* he provides include "the commissioner of nutrition appearing in a time of famine before a crowd, most of whom are starving; another example is a beating on the street" (SC 93). As a subtype of the *Masse* he mentions the "congregation [as] . . . audience, viewers who feel pleasantly edified by the music and the sermon" yet without significant connection to one another's actual lives. Here a sort of rapture can occur, for the *Masse* "is the simplest social form and creates the most powerful experiences of unity" (SC 94).

Just as the church, the highest form of community in Bonhoeffer's view, can have as a subtype a form of *Masse*, so too can marriage, another key form of community. Bonhoeffer does not mention this, but one might use his categories to distinguish the category of marriage as *Gemeinschaft*, or healthy mutual relations between separate selves, from that of romantic fusion, the marital form of the *Masse*. As a social form distinguished by feelings of euphoric unity, by the blurring of personal boundaries, and by long-term instability and unsustainability,

---

30. On societies, see especially SC 90–91.

this form of relationship fits nicely within the category of the *Masse*. And this distinction between marriage (or long-term relationship) as *Gemeinschaft*, rather than as a form of *Masse*, will assist in the naming of abusive forms of intimacy. In such enmeshed relationships, in which neither party (abuser nor abusee) perceives themselves or the other on a deep level as truly separate, no authentic formation of personhood in Bonhoeffer's sense can occur. In contrast, "the I that has become a person is bonded by experience only with other individual egos [*Ichen*] who have become persons; only to such persons can a category of community be applied. All others belong only *potentially* to this category" (SC 117).[31]

CONFLICT AND HIERARCHY

It is with the category of *Gemeinschaft*, community, that Bonhoeffer is centrally concerned in his dissertation. The following definition concisely summarizes his understanding of what constitutes such community, in distinction from both *Gesellschaft* and *Masse*:

> *Community is a community of wills, built upon the separateness and difference of persons, constituted by reciprocal acts of will, finding its unity in what is willed* [i.e., in mutually willing one another's presence; this does not refer to secondary purposes or goals], *and counting among its basic laws the inner conflict of individual wills.* (SC 86)

This definition highlights not only his emphases on the distinction between persons and the directionality of will but also his characteristic framing of the person-forming encounter in community in terms of conflict. Earlier, I cited comments comparing Buber and Bonhoeffer in terms of their use of I and You terminology, in which Buber's use centers on the creation of I-You intimacy, while Bonhoeffer focuses on the dimension of ethical confrontation as that which forms a person. This

---

31. On 94 he quotes Goethe: "Where is society more pleasantly bound together, where else must people confess their brotherhood [*sic*], than when they hang on the lips and features of a single person and are borne heavenward, all knit together in a common feeling?" These words, though cited in reference to the church as audience/ *Masse*, show obvious affinities also to the experience of romantic obsession with the beloved. von Goethe, *Wilhelm Meisters Lehrjahre*, 1:15. Bonhoeffer makes a similar point, again in terms of the church but using the actual language of romanticism, later in the book (278): "It is extremely dangerous to confuse community romanticism [*Gemeinschaftsromantik*] with the community of saints [*Gemeinschaft der Heiligen*]."

tendency to conceive of human relationality using metaphors of confrontation or conflict is pervasive in Bonhoeffer's early writings. Here is a typical quote, showing the rationale for his implicit and explicit portrayal of personhood in community as fundamentally oppositional:

> Will itself experiences resistance [not from natural barriers but] only in the will of a person who wills something different. Only in strife with other wills, in subjecting these to one's own will or being subjected, is strength and richness of will developed. . . . For when a person encounters a person, a will meets a will, and each one wrestles to overcome the other. . . . Will as an isolated phenomenon is absurd.[32]

Perhaps this focus on conflict derives from his will-centered anthropology (following Reinhold Seeberg, his dissertation advisor). But regardless of its origin this focus is striking; and its hold on Bonhoeffer's imagination is such that he seems unable to conceive of human relations (certainly not person-forming ones) based fundamentally on cooperation, or shared creativity, or mutual affection. Indeed, towards the end of the volume he explicitly denies the possibility of authentic community founded on mutual affection. His commendable purpose in this section is to counter those who attempt to exclude those who are different, who treat Christian community as a homogeneous social club. Just a few years later, of course, such arguments and worse would be used by the German Christians to exclude people of Jewish heritage from the church. But note how his suspicion of human affection also supports his antagonism towards socialist principles (see below) and even contradicts Paul's language of "*neither* Jew nor Greek":

> Isn't the commitment to the church, to Christian love, most unmistakable where it is protected in principle from being confused in any way with any kind of human community based on mutual affection? Is it not precisely such a community that much better safeguards the serious realism of the Sanctorum Communio—a community in which Jew remains Jew, Greek Greek, worker worker, and capitalist capitalist, and where all are nevertheless the body of Christ—than one in which these hard facts are quietly glossed over? (SC 246)

---

32. SC 72. For more on the creative and necessary role of conflict in community and in scholarship, see 60–61 and 84–86.

He never seems to consider the possibility that the Sanctorum Communio may be precisely the place where such "hard facts" (or, rather, the injustice they presuppose) could be addressed or alleviated. In his model, confrontation and demand are what forms persons; love, when it appears, functions *within* this fundamental assumption of basic ethical oppositionalism.

The passages cited above reveal also a related and even more pervasive motif in Bonhoeffer, namely his endorsement of hierarchy as a fundamental structure of human community. Like his pervasively conflict-oriented view of personal formation, his affirmation of hierarchy takes both implicit and explicit forms. The implicit form shows up in his assumption that the conflict of wills results in an outcome of a person's either subjecting the other or being subjected. Tellingly, also, the only two models of communal authority he proposes are both hierarchical: the *Gewaltsverband* (association governed by force) or the *Herrschaftsverband* (association of dominion or rule, defined as service of the subordinated party).[33] Thus his assumption of the hierarchical nature of all human relations shows up implicitly in various ways.

But there are also numerous passages in his dissertation (as in the quote on the previous page) and throughout his writings in which he *explicitly* insists that Christians acknowledge hierarchies as intended by God. While unusually sensitive to matters of racial injustice (he breaks from the traditional Lutheran "orders of creation" theology that Nazi theologians would later use to assert their racial "superiority" as intrinsic to creation itself), he nevertheless argues a parallel position in regard to class distinctions and patriarchy. Here and elsewhere, he excoriates socialism as attempting to wipe out all created distinctions and impose an artificial "egalitarianism" among people God has made

33. SC 91–92. The translators render *Herrschaftsverband* as "association of authentic rule" in order to convey this sense that it is a "ruling" to be marked by service. But the term itself means simply "ruling association" or "association governed by a ruling party." Both terms thus are intrinsically hierarchical. Later (265), he writes, "the spirit of the [*Herrschaftsverband*] has the distinctive structure that it is the one who rules who sets in motion the wills of those who obey, thus serving them." This shows that the translators' attempt to make the *Herrschaftsverband* sound palatable to contemporary American readers must still come to terms with Bonhoeffer's own notions of what such "serving" means on the part of the "ruler": here, this "service" makes no reference to love in any form but is defined simply as stimulating underlings' wills toward obedience. For Bonhoeffer, the question of who is the one to rule in the *Herrschaftsverband* is determined by who has the strongest will (ibid.).

different.[34] And in addition to assuming the patriarchal family as the very basis of society, he even considers it the closest human analogy to the *communio sanctorum* itself. He writes about the communion of saints in the church,

> As far as I can see, *only the original patriarchal structure of the family is a sociologically comparable form*, even if only approximately. . . . *The object of the father's will is community between children and servants, and preserving community means being obedient* . . . It is very significant when Paul in Eph. 3:15 says that all fatherhood on earth derives its name from God's fatherhood. This relation is also the reason why the idea of patriarchalism has played such a prominent role since earliest Christianity. . . . It indeed seems that here we have a structure similar [an earlier draft read, "identical"] to that of the church. (SC 263)

Throughout his life, he speaks of the patriarchal family in glowing terms and explicitly defends patriarchy (which he terms "patriarchalism") as belonging to the very creation itself, prior to the fall. He distinguishes "patriarchalism understood as punishment" (after the fall) from the good and necessary patriarchalism of the primal creation; thus the effect of the fall is not to impose patriarchy but only to make it seem like punishment. For him, the necessary "subordination" of women and children in the patriarchal family model is quite compatible with the "equality" of persons he elsewhere asserts:

> Marriage and family are the most primitive social forms and doubtless willed by God. These forms are of course depraved in the state of sin, by concupiscence and also by patriarchalism understood as punishment; they are restored to sanctity again in Christ. Originally, neither reproduction nor the idea of "subordination" is associated with sin as constitutive forces of the family. Both are good and necessary. . . . Rather, what was created unequal must be accepted as such, and this, in turn, sanctions and introduces the idea of patriarchalism (the same Paul wrote Gal 3:28 and 1 Cor 14:23). (SC 97, 205)

34. On 274, he writes, "Our earlier reflections on the problem already made it clear that the socialist idea of equality is theologically and sociologically untenable. . . . The Christian community is based on the dissimilarity and inequality of persons that is part of creation." Cf. also SC 205–7, and R. Bethge, "'Elite' and 'Silence' in Bonhoeffer's Person and Thought."

Thus, for Bonhoeffer human sociality is the necessary and inextricable web within which human beings as persons are formed. For instance, he writes, "human beings, as spirit, are necessarily created in a community—that human spirit in general is woven into the web of sociality" (SC 65). This is a thesis that would be affirmed by many today, including a great number of feminists. The ways Bonhoeffer fleshes out this thesis however manifest his own blind spots, particularly his blindness to patriarchy as a problem—indeed, an evil undercutting much of the power of his theology here for actual Christian communities (on this see pp. 169–78 of chapter 5). Yet, despite this, his analysis of the interrelationships of I and You in bonds of respectful mutuality still bears considerable power, and can even be expressed in terms that belie his own tendency to focus on conflict rather than on intimacy and love:

> In summary, *human spirit in its entirety is woven into sociality and rests on the basic-relation of I and You.* . . . In infinite closeness, in mutual penetration, I and You are joined together, inseparable from one another forever, resting in one another, intimately participating in one another, empathizing, sharing experiences, bearing together the general stream of interactions of spirit. *Here is where the openness of personal being becomes evident.* (SC 73)

We now turn to his view of the person who is formed in such communities.

Bonhoeffer on the Individual

Alongside his insistence on the "openness of personal being" mentioned just above, Bonhoeffer insists equally emphatically and consistently on its "closedness" as a simultaneously necessary aspect of personal formation.[35] The two are inseparable for Bonhoeffer. A person needs community in order to become aware of separate selfhood; yet only fully

---

35. On the structural "openness" of personal being, see SC 65–73; on "personal being as structurally closed," see SC 73–80. An editorial note comments helpfully on this distinction as follows: "By 'open' Bonhoeffer means the capacity and necessity of a person to participate in sociality with others. 'Closed' refers to the unity, integrity, and irreducibility of the person; it indicates the otherness of the other, guarding against the totalization of idealist thinking. 'Openness' does not mean merged into a supraindividual unity, nor does 'closedness' mean shut off from interaction with other persons" (SC 67, note 19). On the necessity of both moments, see also SC 59, 138.

developed and separate persons can participate fully in community[36] (as noted above). He writes, for instance, not only that *"human beings really know their I only in the You-relation"* (SC 73) but also that "the 'openness' of person demands 'closedness' as a correlative, or one could not speak of openness at all" (SC 74). This "closedness" and "openness" are not conceived as parts of a person; but both are constitutive of the whole person:

> There are not two layers in human beings, one social and one intimate; a human being is a structural unity. . . . People must know themselves as inwardly integrated beings and make decisions accordingly. They must not blindly subjugate themselves to the concrete demands of the [community], but must struggle to reach an integrated decision of their own wills. Ethical community can only be built upon such integrated people. (SC 120)

Because therefore one "cannot speak of the priority of either personal or social being" (SC 75), any relational or social systems that insist on the fusion or merger of selves, or the submersion of individual personhood into the life of a community, are alien to both authentic community and authentic personhood: "God does not want a community that absorbs the individual into itself, but a community of *human beings*. In God's eyes, community and individual exist in the same moment and rest in one another" (SC 80).

This could be inferred already, of course, from his insistence on the foundation of all theology and ethics in the concrete, the particular, as well as from his rejection of forms of philosophy and theology (especially idealism) and of communal life (especially the *Masse*) that require the transcending of such particularity. Yet it is important to make this point clearly on its own terms here as well, if only because Bonhoeffer himself returns to it over and over in his dissertation. For all his pioneering grasp of the social as an intrinsic category of Christian experience and thought, he intends thereby no diminution of individuality, the

---

36. This antithesis is articulated in pithy form years later in *Life Together*, where Bonhoeffer writes, "Only as we stand within the community can we be alone, and only those who are alone can live in the community" (DBWE 5:83). On the same page he makes his point in the negative as well: "Whoever cannot be alone should beware of community. Whoever cannot stand being in community should beware of being alone."

integrity, uniqueness, and mystery of every created person; in fact, he argues that such individuality can be most truly grasped only in community, and vice versa. On the one hand, he repeatedly warns against any dissolving of personhood into relational or mystical "fusion":

> Whatever kind of unity of will exists, one must never conclude any kind of unity of the willing persons in the sense of fusion; this is impossible considering all that has been said.... The person who is united with me in common intention is structurally just as separate from me as the one who is not so united. Between us lies the boundary of being created as individual persons. The Christian notion of [communion] with God can be realized only on the basis of this interpretation of community. Otherwise, [communion] with God becomes unification in the sense of transgressing the boundary of the I-You-relation—that is, mystical fusion. (SC 84)[37]

On the other hand, he also makes numerous positive statements about the distinctness, mystery, and solitude of created persons before God:

> The person arises only in relation to a You, and yet the person stands in complete isolation. Persons are unique and thus fundamentally separate and distinct from one another. . . . In summary, *the person is willed by God, in concrete vitality, wholeness, and uniqueness as an ultimate unity. Social relations must be understood, then, as purely interpersonal and building on the uniqueness and separateness of persons.* . . . no "unity" can negate the plurality of persons. (SC 54–55)

On the heart of this created individuality as an essentially God-directed "solitude," he writes, "The Holy Spirit of the church-community is di-

---

37. Note that for Bonhoeffer, "mysticism" refers to precisely this sort of violation of personhood, in this case within the divine-human encounter. He thus repeatedly asserts the impossibility of such person-annihilating "mysticism" or "mystical fusion" within healthy Christian faith. However, it is interesting to note that Bonhoeffer first refers to this understanding of mysticism (SC 56) in clarifying his own earlier statement that "the Christian person achieves his or her essential nature only when God does not encounter the person as *You* [any longer—i.e., as demand], *but 'enters into' the person as I.*" This is something no human You can do, but only God. He seems to recognize here therefore a point in the spiritual journey at which divine relationality comes to shape the very heart of a person's being, his or her "I"-ness itself. Thus Bonhoeffer's exclusion of "mysticism," understood by him as fusion, should not be read to mean a rejection of the possibility of intimate and transforming personal divine encounter.

rected as a personal will toward personal wills, addressing each person *as a single individual, leading that person into 'solitude'"* (SC 161) before God. This "is the solitude of the individual that is a structure of the created order, and it continues to exist everywhere" as "the Spirit's gift. . . . One's faith and prayer takes place in this singularity and solitude" (SC 162 and 181).

Both negatively and positively, then, he consistently upholds the integrity of the individual as of paramount importance in his view of Christian life. It is important to note as well that for Bonhoeffer, this individual integrity is grounded and preserved by human embodiment, and such bodily individuality continues even into the blessed community of eternity (SC 286–89). This Christian appreciation of the body, like his focus on relationality, represents another departure from the idealist tradition in a way that points toward trends in later twentieth century theology and feminism. It is in line with his emphasis on concreteness as well, the body being, one might say, the very concreteness of the person her- or himself. Thus Bonhoeffer's treatment of the individual person as created and perduring seems quite positive and to present a helpful basis for explorations of human selfhood. Yet this represents only half of the story; for in contrast to his descriptions of the inviolable worth of the "person" or the "individual," Bonhoeffer's treatment of the "self" in the experience of sin and redemption becomes quite problematic.

Bonhoeffer on the Self

Before beginning this examination of Bonhoeffer's views of the self, a few notes on his terminology are in order. At various points in his writings, Bonhoeffer uses the terms *der Mensch* ("the human being" or, more broadly, "humanity"); *der Einzelne* ("individual"); *die Person* ("person"); *das Ich* ("ego", or "I"[38]); and *das Selbst* ("self"). *Mensch*, of course, is the standard German term for a human being, used ubiquitously throughout Bonhoeffer's writings. Although its grammatical gender is masculine, the term does not in and of itself refer only to a male human being. For instance, the sentence, "der Mensch neben mir—*den* soll ich lieben" ("the human being next to me is the one I should love") can as

---

38. Note that this is the capitalized (and therefore nominalized) version of the German first-person pronoun, *ich*, which in distinction from English usage is not capitalized.

easily be understood grammatically to refer to a woman as to a man. Nevertheless, Bonhoeffer's use of the term does reveal an androcentric bias in that he consistently speaks of the *Mensch* for whom he is writing as having a wife,[39] being a father or businessman (or some other professional with a masculine ending), or becoming a brother to the neighbor. Thus he really does at times mean "man" and not simply "person."

Next, throughout his writings, he uses *der Einzelne* with a range of connotations. In the neutral sense, the individual is simply another term for the human being as such (like *Mensch* in that sense); any given *Einzelne/r* may or may not be a "person" in him- or herself, in Bonhoeffer's fully ethical meaning, but is still an individual capable of functioning as a You for me nevertheless. In the positive sense, as noted above, Bonhoeffer has a high regard for the particular concreteness of every given individual. Indeed, far from being "merely" the starting point and *sine qua non* of his spirituality, the full extent of this individuality is experienced only as a fruit of redemption itself: "Even where in Christ all are one, we must not think that the personality intended by God is eliminated, but rather have to conceive of it as reaching its highest perfection at this very point" (SC 203). Significantly, also, the very first sentence of his chapter entitled "Discipleship and the Individual" in his book *Discipleship* reads, "Jesus' call to discipleship makes the disciple into a single individual."[40] The passage continues, "Whether disciples want to or not, they have to make a decision; each has to decide alone. It is not their own choice to desire to be single individuals. Instead, Christ makes everyone he calls into an individual." Later in the paragraph, we see the assumed masculine reference visible not only grammatically but also in reference to the "wife" among those responsibilities behind which a "man" may try to hide from the individual-making gaze of Jesus. I continue in my own translation making this clear:

> he does not want to stand before Jesus face-to-face, to have to decide with [Jesus'] gaze upon himself alone. But father and mother, wife and child, people and history do not hide the one called in this hour. Christ wants to make the person [*Mensch*] solitary; he is to see nothing but the One who called him.[41]

39. We can safely assume he does not have a lesbian audience in mind!

40. Bonhoeffer, *Discipleship* (DBWE 4), 92. The term translated here "single individual" is the German *Einzelne*.

41. Bonhoeffer, *Nachfolge* (DBW 4), 87, my translation.

The term *der Einzelne* can also have negative connotations for Bonhoeffer: sin too claims a person in his or her aloneness. Indeed, in *Sanctorum Communio* he writes, "in the sinful act, the individual spirit rises up against God, thus climbing to the very height of spiritual individuality—since this is the individual's very own deed against God, occasioned by nothing else."[42] On the whole, however, *der Einzelne* (like *Mensch* and *Person*, below) is a neutral or positive term for Bonhoeffer.

As we have seen, *Person* is his term for the human being as authentically formed by encounter with an other: here the "I" comes into being as confronted and bounded by the "You." Bonhoeffer occasionally uses *Person* in a non-technical sense, but because the term is much less common in German than in English (German uses *Mensch* where we often translate "person"), his usage tends to be deliberate and to refer to a "person" more specifically in the conscious sense of oneself as living in ethical community and responsibility.

The term *Ich* is perhaps the most ambiguous of Bonhoeffer's usages. We have seen how the *Ich*, the "I", is the mature self formed in engagement with a concrete "You": it is, in other words, used very nearly as a synonym for the positively-connoting *Person*. Yet Bonhoeffer also uses *Ich* to refer to the self-imprisoned ego. Indeed, *Ich* is the term translated as "ego" in Freud and subsequent German psychoanalytic literature.[43] As one whose own very powerful ego not only showcased his gifts but also caused him great anguish, indeed seemed to him the locus of sin itself (see below, pp. 59–70), he has conflicted feelings about this *Ich*. His repetitive language translated in English along the lines of "surrender of the *self*" almost always refers back to the *Ich* whose imperious demands must be relinquished before the claims of the other. He uses Luther to support this case, finding the root of human sinfulness in the *Ich*, as similarly noted above in reference to individuality: "[Luther] identifies the essence of original sin in the 'will of the ego' ["*Ichwillen*"]

42. SC 115. In the German, this reads, "in der sündigen Tat [erhebt] sich der *Einzelgeist* wider Gott und [steigt] damit auf die höchste Höhe *geistiger Einzelheit* . . . —indem das seine *ureigene* durch nichts veranlaßte widergöttliche Tat ist" (DBW 1:72, my italics).

43. There is no evidence that Bonhoeffer himself read Freud, or was intending a technically Freudian sense for the term, although as the son of an (albeit non-Freudian) psychiatrist he surely knew of Freud's usage and perhaps was making use of it in a general sense. See Green, "Two Bonhoeffers on Psychoanalysis." In *Sociality*, Green explicates his understanding of "ego" on 109.

(SC 113)." And in a paper written in English in 1931 at Union Seminary, New York, Bonhoeffer writes,

> The ego stands in the centre (*sic*) of the world, which is cre-
> ated, ruled, overpowered by the ego. The identification of the
> ego with the ground of everything which has been called God is
> inevitable. There are no limits for the ego, its claim and its power
> are boundless, it is its own standard. Here all transcendence is
> pulled into the circle of the creative ego. . . . Man (*sic*) knows
> himself immediately by the act of the coming of the ego to itself,
> and knows through himself essentially everything, even God.
> God is in man; God is man himself.[44]

This paper, and others like it from that period, demonstrate that Bonhoeffer himself used the language in English of "ego" as well as "I" to translate *Ich*. In general, translation practice from the German has tended to use "ego" or "self" for his negatively-connoted references to *Ich*, and "I" for positive ones. But it is the same term, *das Ich*, in each case: one could as easily speak above of the "ego" that is created in ethical encounter with a You. Thus the term is ambiguous.

Finally, the language of *das Selbst*[45] is the most unequivocally nega-tive term in Bonhoeffer's usage. Places where "the self" or "one's self" appears in English translation, also almost always negative, usually refer either to *das Ich* or to *selbst* as a pronoun. Further there are innumer-able occurrences of "selbst-" as a prefix, as in English usage as well. "Self-love," "self-chosen" discipleship, etc., are phenomena Bonhoeffer decries as inimical to authentic Christian faith. An intriguing twist on this usage appears toward the end of his life. At the height of his resis-tance activity with its unimaginable pressures and looming threat to his and his friends' very lives, he does for the first time find a way to speak positively of self-love. In a 1941 letter to Eberhard Bethge, who he feared was in danger of collapse under all the strain, he quotes approv-

---

44. DBW 10:443–44. Bonhoeffer's English. The reference to humanity's knowing itself "immediately" is Bonhoeffer's translation of the German *unmittelbar*, or "without mediation" (not *sofortig*, or "suddenly"): one might say it's a spatial immediacy he de-plores, not a temporal one. This is an early reference to the theme of Christ as the only Mediator (*Mittler*) of reality, who permits no "im-mediate," or unmediated, relation-ships, a topic that proved to be central for Bonhoeffer after his conversion.

45. Or, much more frequently, *selbst* used as a pronoun. *Das Selbst* is an extremely infrequent usage in Bonhoeffer, in fact may only have been evolving as a term in German at that point.

ingly a term he had recently read, namely "selfless self-love."[46] In the context of an abiding friendship, i.e., of genuine care for the other, he was perhaps able to see the dangers of the uncompromising and even ruthless selflessness he had endorsed for so long. Also, perhaps his and Eberhard's "location" now no longer among the privileged but among the threatened and marginalized allowed him to see the importance of claiming self-care more explicitly. In any case it is interesting that even here he is able to speak only of "*selfless* self-love."[47] In summary, it is in coordination of the more negative meanings of *das Ich* and of *das Selbst* that we are able to speak of Bonhoeffer's conception more broadly of "the self" in English. I will therefore now proceed with the analysis of his views.

For Bonhoeffer, the fundamental locus of sin is the self, specifically the self that sees and acknowledges only itself. He writes,

> the fall replaced love with selfishness.... With this change of direction, the whole spiritual orientation of humanity was altered. ... Human love, instead of being directed toward the other— whether that be God or other people—is now focused on oneself. Everything becomes a means to one's own selfishness.[48]

Self-love, for Bonhoeffer, therefore is sinful because it denotes a love that encompasses only the self, a fall from the "primal community" in which love was directed solely toward God and other human beings. Bonhoeffer intends his theologizing on the "primal state"[49] to be speculative only (his term is "hope projected backward") since after all we have no real human experience of a state somehow anterior to sin. Nevertheless, he does at times write as if its loss were a real event that happens because of a selfish move away from love and into egocentricity. Like Luther, he rejects a biological means of explaining the

---

46. DBWE 16:78, also 84, citing Josef Pieper, *Zucht und Maß*, 16–17. For insight on the complicated Christian history around notions of self-love, see Weaver, *Self-Love and Christian Ethics*.

47. Cf. also LPP 287 (DBW 8: 417), letter dated May 6, 1944.

48. SC 107–8. In an interesting aside, Bonhoeffer also notes that "the will for self-preservation is not evil as such. Sin, therefore, does not enter the community with the individual's will for self-preservation—indeed, community is only possible on this basis" (SC 118). This is an important clarification and is in fact the only place in the book where the term or prefix "self-" is used in reference to something good and necessary.

49. SC 58–106.

transmission of original sin and has a consistently positive view of sexuality; but sin takes hold because of selfish human decisions whose corrosive effects ripple through the entire community:

> Sin in every case is unfathomable, inexcusable defiance of God, arising from free will. . . . We look for the motives leading to the deed not in sexuality, as did the tradition, but in the human spirit bound up in a net of sociality. . . . The original community of love, as mutual harmony of reciprocally directed wills, is essentially destroyed when one will changes from a loving to an egocentric direction. (SC 117)

Indeed, a telling reference to self-love establishes it as the very paradigm of sinful distortion: "We have two infallible points of reference for what the New Testament calls love: the first, defined positively, is the *love of God* revealed in Christ; the second, defined negatively, is our *self-love*" (SC 167). From the former we learn of love's "foundation, depth, and meaning"; from the latter we learn of the harshness [*Härte*] of love as it applies to our own persons. An editorial note speculates that such severe, even "crude intensity" might be explained as "the relentless persistence of egotism's focus on the self" (SC 167, note 126). It is interesting that Bonhoeffer finds such self-love one of only two "infallible points of reference" to the meaning of love, albeit a "negative" one; yet even this apparently supercedes any understanding of love we might glean from other sources, such as from "our love for God or for other human beings. . . . the sacrificial deaths of our brothers [in war], or from personal experiences of love shown to us" (SC 167). For him none of these constitute reliable disclosures of the meaning of love. The only places of utterly trustworthy experience of love are the revelation of grace in Jesus Christ and the relentless and even "brutal" obsession of the sinful self with itself. Between these two poles alone (i.e., by claiming the former in conscious and redemptive refutation of the latter) Bonhoeffer finds the truest revelation of what love means. Bonhoeffer's usage of the term "self-love," throughout this volume and indeed for the rest of his life, thus denotes a painful obsession with oneself, to the exclusion of God and other people. A life bound up in such "self-love" is an extremely lonely life.[50]

---

50. See SC 148–49 on the solitariness of the sinner and the isolating effect of sin.

Given this, it is understandable that his notions of grace and re-demption would involve liberation from this self-enclosed prison. And in fact that is precisely the case. Conceiving of the self as the locus of sin in human experience, Bonhoeffer develops an understanding of re-demption and spiritual growth that involves complete abandonment of this self and all its claims. The following passage illustrates concisely the dynamics of redemption in regard to the sinful self (note here as well the typically denigrating reference to self-love):

> this abandoning of our claims, this giving up of our own will to God's will, is possible only through faith in Christ; apart from Christ all love is self-love. Only through faith in Christ do we understand our love to be the love of God given to our hearts by the Holy Spirit, and our will as conquered by God and obedient to God's will for our neighbor. (SC 168)

For him, redemption and love mean learning for the first time to see the other and to be bound by the other's claims, as we have seen prefigured already in the encounter between the "totally claimless" I and the "absolute demands" of the You (SC 54). In his extended chapter on the *sanctorum communio* itself, where he develops his understanding of what happens in the redeemed community, he writes,

> *Love for our neighbor is our will to embrace God's will for the other person;* God's will for the other person is defined for us in the unrestricted command to surrender our self-centered will to our neighbor, which neither means to love the other in-stead of God, nor to love God in the other, but to put the other in our own place and to love the other instead of ourselves. (SC 171)[51]

This sort of statement abounds throughout the remainder of the volume: surrender [*Hingabe*] to the other person is the mark of the Christian and of the Christian community. Surrender of oneself or of one's will (these are used interchangeably) is the liberation to which grace frees a person, and is also a participation in such grace. God wills such indis-criminate and unrestricted self-surrender in order to free both persons and communities from the scourge of selfish egotism that had poisoned

---

51. The reference to loving "God in the other" is intended again to distance himself at this point from Karl Barth (see above): the neighbor is to be loved for his or her *own* sake, not only as a placeholder for God.

them. Thus the surrender of the self is both the will of God and the basis
for Christian community:

> in speaking about love for the neighbor we said that love gives
> itself up to the other unrestrictedly, seeking nothing for itself.
> But to surrender oneself to the other means obeying God; it is
> based on surrender to God's will. *God's love, therefore, is at the*
> *same time self-surrender and will for community.* ... Community
> of love is based on unrestrictedly surrendering to the other.
> (SC 173)

Or, again, "the You is willed while giving up the I" (SC 176).

Since the self is viewed as the problem, salvation must by definition come from outside oneself. By this Bonhoeffer means not only the
Christus extra nos of traditional Lutheran soteriology. He also considers
the human other, the ethically challenging "You," an equally significant
locus of redemptive encounter, indeed the very means by which the
present Christ is at work. Only by allowing the self with its distorted
and autocratic demands to be silenced at last has one any hope of engaging the redemptive contact that arrives from outside oneself, meeting persons at their boundaries and claiming their entire being with
transcendent authority. Such encounter may feel shattering, forcing
the self out of its familiar *incurvatus*[52] world and into disorienting and
unaccustomed focus on another; but this is the shape of salvation itself,
salvation that is necessarily and solely *extra nos*.

Stellvertretung: The Way of Jesus Christ

"To love the other instead of ourselves"; to "will the You" while "giving
up the I"—these are phrases that for Bonhoeffer mean liberation and
life itself. He spends over a hundred pages, the center and culmination
of his dissertation, spelling out some of the implications of the life made
possible by such redemption. A fundamental category he develops,
which will persist throughout his life's work, is *Stellvertretung* (translated as "vicarious representative action").[53] *Stellvertretung* marks the
action of Jesus Christ, who gave himself vicariously for our salvation. It
is thus also to mark the life of the Christian church-community as well,

---

52. On the ways in which Bonhoeffer picked up Luther's image of the *cor curvum in*
se as typifying the sinful self, see Green, *Sociality*, 122–24.

53. See SC 120, including note 129; also 146–48; 155–57, 178, 184, 191.

which after all *is* "Christ existing as community"[54] in the fullest sense. Just as Jesus Christ lived and died for others' salvation, we too are to live and die for the love of others:

> This being-for-each-other must now be actualized through acts of love. *Three great, positive possibilities of acting for each other* in the community of saints present themselves: *self-renouncing, active work for the neighbor; intercessory prayer; and, finally, the mutual forgiveness of sins* in God's name. All of these involve giving up the self "for" my neighbor's benefit, with the readiness to do and bear everything in the neighbor's place, indeed, if necessary, to sacrifice myself, standing as a *substitute* ["stellvertretend"] for my neighbor. (SC 184)

Later on the same page he details what might be sacrificed in such *Stellvertretung* for the neighbor: first and foremost, our "happiness"; next, "possessions, honor, even our whole lives" if necessary. And finally, Christian self-renunciation must be courageous and selfless enough that, if God were to desire it, we would even sacrifice

> our [communion] with God itself. Here we see the love that voluntarily seeks to submit itself to God's wrath on behalf of the other members of the community, which wishes God's wrath for itself in order that they may have community with God. (SC 184; see also SC 173)

He goes on to give biblical examples of those who heroically offered even their own damnation if it could help to save others. Such are the depths to which Christian *Stellvertretung* (like Jesus who descended even into hell to save its occupants) must and gladly does stoop. In sheer gratitude for rescue from the torment of self-imprisonment, the Christian willingly gives up everything, even grace itself, on behalf of the other—the other whose very alterity is the window to salvation. To give up one's own self for the sake of the other: this is the way of Jesus Christ, the only way to life. This is *Stellvertretung*.

For Bonhoeffer, Jesus Christ is not merely the founder of a religion, nor even only the Lord of Christians, but is in fact, even as God, the first fruits of the new humanity itself. Thus the church, "Christ existing as

---

54. SC 121. "Christus als Gemeinde existierend" is one of the most often-cited catchphrases in later scholars' references to Bonhoeffer's dissertation. He himself does not use this precise language as often in later work but its meaning undergirds Bonhoeffer's lifelong engagement with church identity and integrity.

church-community," is itself nothing more (and nothing less) than the place in the world where this new humanity, the future of all humanity, takes on living form. The Holy Spirit builds up the Body of Christ in the world, making real the salvation accomplished once and for all in Christ "in the personal appropriation of the individual" (SC 143). That is, the Holy Spirit "actualizes" in present human lives the pattern and reality "completed" by and in Christ the *Stellvertreter* and makes him fully present to them. This means that the church, the very Body of Christ, and individual Christians as its representatives must also function as *Stellvertreter* for the sake not only of others in the community but of all those in need.

Christ = Church: On the Need for Discernment

This focus on the church as the actualization by the Holy Spirit of the new humanity achieved and completed in Christ is a sacramental one at home using the language of Christ's "real presence" in and through the church.[55] This sacramental or symbolic sense of Christ's presence, and the church as his living Body, is yet another arena where Bonhoeffer (the Lutheran) is attempting to move beyond Barth's Reformed conception of the church as a mere "witness" to Christ.[56] It is also another example of Bonhoeffer's insistence that redemption is necessarily concrete, real, "actualized" in particular times and places.

It can however at times also lead to a potential blurring or lack of distinction between Christ and the church. For instance, he states, "The church-community is in Christ and Christ is in the church-community (1 Cor 1:30; 3:16; 2 Cor 6:16; 13:5; Col 3:9; 2:17), and '*to be in Christ*' is *synonymous with* '*to be in the church-community*'" (SC 137). Given this, a truth obvious to him, he wonders

> why the direct identification between Christ and ecclesia is made so rarely [in the New Testament] (1 Cor 1:13; 12:12; 6:15; Col 3:11; Rom 13:14), and why quite often the collective person-

55. SC 138, 139. "Christus als Gemeinde existierend" is the more typical way Bonhoeffer articulates this real presence.

56. Hunsinger, "Koinonia Between Christ and His Community." Also: "*The church is the presence of Christ in the same way that Christ is the presence of God*" (SC 138). In other respects, Bonhoeffer's language is clearly derived from or analogous to Barth's; for instance, he writes, "Christ does not represent [the church]; only what is not present can be represented" (SC 157).

ality of the church and Christ are thought of as being in some
kind of relation, and therefore as not identical. (SC 137)

Note that on the previous page he considers that "the Spirit of Christ
and the Holy Spirit must be clearly distinguished since their manner of
operation is not identical" (SC 136); yet between Christ and the church
there is no such distinction, clear or otherwise. On the contrary, he is
asserting their virtual identity. He does once concede that "[a] complete
identification between Christ and the church-community cannot be
made" (SC 140), since Christians' ultimate salvation comes from Christ
and not vice versa. But in terms of Christians' ongoing experience in
the church-community, Christ and the community are assumed to be
virtually indistinguishable: "Community with God exists only through
Christ, but Christ is present only in his church-community, and therefore *community with God exists only in the church*" (SC 158). This latter
quote and many like it are intended not to address the question of the
presence of God in other religions but to deny any solo experience of
Christ, insisting on its communal mediation primarily in Word and
sacrament. While this point is important in its broadest sense of the
social mediation of all reality, and certainly of Christian truth, nevertheless his putting it in these terms obscures the possibility of distinction between Christ and church in the actual experience of individuals.
Further, although he acknowledges formally the distinction between
the *sanctorum communio* and the *peccatorum communio*, granting that
short of eternity the church-community will always still also be the
fallen or sinful community,[57] nevertheless he insists in several places
(often citing 1st Cor 6:15) that "Christ existing as church-community"
remains fully true even where sin has marred communion.[58] And in no
place does he ever suggest the importance of distinguishing between
Christ and the fallible community. Despite the inevitable presence of
sin, Christians are called to have a "faith in the community" as fundamental as their faith in Christ, in fact considered to be another aspect
of the very same faith.[59] Indeed, Bonhoeffer at times has trouble even

57. SC 124, 208, 213, 275.

58. SC 136–37, 138, 190, 200.

59. SC 149 reads, " . . . if faith in the love of God in Christ, faith in the community,
existed, then the church of God automatically existed with it." He here treats these two
aspects of faith in an appositive manner, i.e., as synonymous of the same reality.

conceiving of Christ in distinction from the church at all: "It is not as if Christ could be abstracted from the church; rather, it is none other than Christ who 'is' the church" (SC 157).

Needless to say, this practical inability to discern between Christ and the community gathered in his name can have dangerous implications precisely at those points where the sin of the community masquerades as the command or will of Christ. Bonhoeffer himself would soon run up against the church's own *peccatorum communio* at full force in the German Christian party, and from that point on he does become more attuned to the necessity of this discernment. Yet this particular blurriness can be seen as an instance of that broader lack of distinction between the human You and the divine You noted earlier, in terms of one's experience of and response to any given claim. This underlying confusion, resulting in the potential absolutizing of the claims of any given human other/s, persists in various forms throughout his life and appears to be rooted in his fundamental antipathy toward the self.

This has two levels. First, Bonhoeffer seems throughout his life largely unable to conceive of the possibility that the claims of the self might ever outweigh those of the other; for him, the other as demand and gift always has absolute and transcendent priority.[60] Second, and more importantly, I believe that this stance of categorical theological opposition to the needs and reality of the self is precisely what makes the articulation of such discernment difficult for him. From *Sanctorum Communio* through countless miscellaneous and published writings, continuing into his *Ethics* and even his prison letters, he rails against what he calls "self-reflection" (in the *Ethics*, also "self-knowledge").[61] For him these terms refer to the sort of continuing obsession with the self and its imperious demands and categorical judgments, inevitably

60. Green names this Bonhoeffer's "personal-ethical model of transcendence" (SC 5–6), in distinction from more typical Christian ontological or metaphysical models of divine transcendence. In Green's view (which to my mind overstates Bonhoeffer's position and obscures the distinctions he does make between divine and human other/s), Bonhoeffer finds the transcendence of God *only* in encounter with a human other: "God is not *immanent in* us, but is *present to* us in the social relationship. . . . We do not deal with an invisible God in an invisible world of our wishful fantasies; God is met and heard only in the real world where human, personal wills encounter one another" (*Sociality*, 36).

61. See chapter 5, pp. 200–207, which deals in more depth with Bonhoeffer's aversion to "self-reflection," especially but not only in the context of psychotherapy.

distorting all of reality, from which the ethical encounter with Jesus Christ and other human beings frees a person. His aversion to such self-reflection goes so far that he congratulates himself on *not* being very self-aware[62] in his own estimation and condemns those in the fields of pastoral or psychological counseling who advocate such self-knowledge. To him such endeavors are fruitless and even destructive, for they point the person away from the redeeming Christ who comes always *extra nos*.

Yet the capacity for discernment requires precisely the sort of sustained attentiveness to the movements of the Spirit in oneself that Bonhoeffer disparages. Over the course of his life, he articulates an ethic and spirituality that in fact are highly sophisticated and require just this sort of capacity for mature and prayerful Christian discernment, a capacity which, apparently despite himself, he seems actually to have possessed. Toward the end of his life, he even articulates the significance of discernment for his spirituality in an important short section of his *Ethics*.[63] Not surprisingly, perhaps, this section is devoted to questions of the self's true relation to reality in Jesus Christ as a central focus. Again, when pondering questions of discernment, attention to the self seems to be a natural and necessary concomitant. Perhaps it is not surprising that the two emerge to consciousness in him only together, as questions of personal risk became more acute toward the end of his life. Born in wrestling with extraordinarily complex questions in an extraordinarily disorienting time, the *Ethics* as a whole and this section in particular manifest a broader and more subtle vision than the earlier theology, open to perceiving the leading of God in directions that would have been previously inconceivable. Into such openness, even a new sense of self seems to be on the verge of making itself visible; perhaps the un-yielding armor of the rhetoric of self-sacrifice is gradually developing chinks. Perhaps, in other words, a discrepancy is developing between the *fact* of his increasingly discernment-based experience and spiritual-ity and the long-regnant *theory* of his theological aversion to the self.

But because Bonhoeffer still lives within this theoretical armor, still considers "self-reflection" to be wrong, even in the *Ethics*, he is largely unable to see (let alone articulate or encourage outright) the sorts of

62. See, e.g., LPP 162 (DBW 8:235).

63. Bonhoeffer, *Ethics* (DBWE 6), 320–26. See pp. 87–92 in chapter 3 of the present volume.

discernments that would assist the soluble self in particular in challenging destructive forms of community, precisely on the basis of the call of Christ experienced in oneself. Indeed, in other passages of the *Ethics* he makes statements about the self-other relation that could have come straight from *Sanctorum Communio*.[64] And for all its crucial importance, and its distance from the unnuanced self-suppression of his early theology, the passage on discerning God's will is notable mostly as an exception within the broad sweep of Bonhoeffer's writings. Because of his theoretical aversion to paying attention to the self, he is hindered in the sort of sustained focus on discernment, especially around questions of the self's own claims, that would assist readers in living out his spirituality in all its concrete contextuality. And thus his lingering blindness to the reality of the self, both as the locus for discernment and as a person whose needs and claims deserve weighing alongside those of others in any given situation, brings about that odd exception to his focus on the particular and the concrete, a focus that of course requires a high level of ongoing discernment in each new context. In the case of the self, namely, his commitment to concreteness gives way consistently to the otherwise repudiated "absolute principles": over and over in his writings, the self must always surrender to the will of the other.[65]

The Autobiographical Dimension: *Act and Being*

Having surveyed Bonhoeffer's early theology of Christian personhood, a theology that frames all his later thinking and action, we can now return to consideration of how this framework gives expression to his own experience of human selfhood. In *Bonhoeffer: A Theology of Sociality*, Clifford Green details some of these connections, tracing what he calls the "autobiographical dimension" of Bonhoeffer's thought through most of his major writings. Looking at this "autobiographi-

---

64. See, e.g., *Ethics* (DBWE 6), 259, where he writes, "Vicarious representative action and therefore responsibility is possible only in completely devoting one's own life to another person." In the same paragraph, however, he begins to rethink this: pp. 188–95 of the present volume ("*Stellvertretung* and Responsibility").

65. Of course, the *Ethics* and, needless to say, the prison letters, are fragmentary works, unfinished and written under unimaginably stressful conditions. Perhaps, had he been able to finish his *Ethics* after the war, something with a rather different slant might have resulted, born out of his experience of devastating powerlessness and oppression, the first time in his life he himself lived on the underside of anything.

cal dimension" will help to illuminate Bonhoeffer's characteristic and otherwise puzzling blindness around questions of selfhood.

As a gifted, indeed brilliant, young thinker, Bonhoeffer had garnered himself a great deal of attention and praise for his ground-breaking theological work. He used the considerable power of his gifts, especially his mind, in an attempt to master reality itself, and to prove the supremacy of his insights in academic debate with others. Yet his experience of this drive of ambition and ego was an extremely alienating one. Precisely in this masterful ego, in its ruthless attempt to establish itself as the center of the world, he perceived himself cut off from God and others in their genuine alterity: instead, he came to realize that the dominating self distorts all of reality into a mere projection of itself. In *Act and Being*, his habilitation thesis written at age 25, he expands his description of the pain of the self-enclosed subject, utterly and devastatingly isolated. This quote provides a glimpse into the reality Green convincingly claims was in fact that of Bonhoeffer himself:

> The individual has torn himself *(sic)* out of the community with God, and thus also with other people, and now he stands alone, which is in untruth. Because he is alone the world is "his" world, the neighbor has sunk into the world of things . . . , and God has become a religious object; but he himself has become his own creator, his own master and property. . . . But eventually, under the colossal burden of being creator and bearer of a world, in the cold silence of his eternal solitude, he becomes anxious about himself and begins to dread. . . . the cry of conscience only disguises the mute loneliness of a bleak isolation ['*Bei-sich*'] and sounds without echo in the self-dominated and self-interpreted world. . . . Only when Christ breaks a person's solitude does he know himself placed in the truth.[66]

The pursuit of knowledge and of a prestigious and brilliant academic career thus increasingly appears empty to him:

> The concrete person, including the philosopher, is not in full possession of Geist; to imagine that he *(sic)* needs only to

66. *Act and Being* (hereafter abbreviated AB), 137–41. I am deliberately citing this text (and those following) in the version used in *Sociality*, in which Green actually alters the newly published, inclusive-language translation of *Act and Being* in order to retain the masculine-language pronouns of the German. He does this in order to correspond to his assertion that the "individual" referred to here is Bonhoeffer himself. On the implications of this use of masculine language, however, see below.

come to himself in order to be in God must lead to horrible disillusionment in experiencing the total self-introversion [*In-sich-selbst-gekehrt-Seins*], the self-confinement and isolation of the very loneliest solitude with its tormenting desolation and sterility.[67]

Green locates numerous passages throughout Bonhoeffer's early writing (from *Sanctorum Communio* through *Act and Being* and several later papers and lectures) that echo this description of the painfully isolated ego whose confinement to a self-projected and distorted world is hell itself. These passages use almost identical language and metaphors to describe this alienated reality: "cold" solitude; the dead "echo" of an utterly isolated cry; the objectification of God and neighbor into projections of the ego; the self at the "center" of this empty world, etc.

He asserts that the striking convergence of these passages is not accidental: "it is . . . to a large degree a self-portrait of the theologian himself, whose urgent existential concern is expressed in this theology."[68] Analogously, Eberhard Bethge's comprehensive biography of Bonhoeffer comments, in reference to *Act and Being*:

> This highly abstract discourse, which the uninitiated are hardly able to follow, concealed a passionate personal involvement. Bonhoeffer's deepest feelings were involved in his insistence on the *extra nos* and *pro nobis* of salvation. His own difficulties sharpened his sensitivity to every loophole in the system through which fatal self-reflection might invade his own ego and establish its secret domination.[69]

A comparison with a rare autobiographical fragment of Bonhoeffer himself is helpful here. Written in 1932, around the time of his conversion, this passage reflects in the third person on an experience he had as a high-school student announcing his intention to become a theologian:

> Solemnly he stood in the presence of his God, in the presence of his class. He was the center of attention. . . . The moment swelled into endless pleasure, the classroom expanded into the infinite. There he stood in the center of the world as the her-

67. AB 42. This passage is part of Bonhoeffer's critique of Hegel. Green, *Sociality*, 113, note 17.

68. Green, *Sociality*, 79.

69. DB 134.

ald and teacher of his knowledge and his ideals. . . . What was the meaning of the curious, mistrustful, bored, disappointed, mocking eyes of his classmates? . . . A leaden silence lies over the throng, a dreadful, silent mockery. . . . They have no right to scorn me, they are unjust to me, unjust . . . all of you . . . he prays. . . . God, say yourself whether I am in earnest about you. Destroy me now if I am lying. Or punish them all; they are my enemies, and yours. They do not believe me. I know myself that I am not good. But I know it myself—and you, God, know it too. I do not need the others. I, I, I shall triumph. Do you see how I triumph? Do you see how they retreat? Their consternation? I am with you! I am strong. God, I am with you.

Do you hear me? Or do you not? To whom am I speaking? To myself? To you? To those others here?

Who is it that is speaking? My faith or my vanity?[70]

In commenting on this passage, Green observes, "Even the metaphors— especially the ego in the center, the silence of solitariness—are identical to those recurring in the theological writings. Here is a man with god-like power, ostensibly God's conquering hero on earth but in actuality an egocentric student."[71] This experience of the self as lonely and distorting of reality precisely in its proudest and most ostensibly insightful moments thus intimately shapes Bonhoeffer's descriptions of the fallen self in his writings.

His alienation included another dimension, however, namely the chasm between his professed vocation as a theologian of the church and this inner reality of extreme alienation from God and the church community. To use the Gospel as a means of his own career advancement seemed an increasingly intolerable contradiction to him, one that developed into an existential crisis resolved only by his conversion in 1932. Here the brilliant theologian and ordained pastor actually became a practicing Christian who prayed and experienced the Bible as the Word of God for him, a means of revelation of Jesus Christ who alone was able to break through his terrifying isolation. Further, he found the call of Jesus Christ to be necessarily into the church and into whole-hearted devotion to the church's life and mission. Eventually even sacrificing his academic career in order to devote himself fully to the needs of the church in the growing crisis of the early Nazi years, he

70. Ibid., 40–41.

71. Green, *Sociality,* 120.

experienced in all this a powerful and life-changing "liberation." In a
1936 letter to his friend Elisabeth Zinn, he wrote of his earlier academic
career and conversion:

> I plunged into work in a very unchristian way. An ... ambition
> that many noticed in me made my life difficult. . . . Then came
> something else, something that up to this day has changed my
> life and turned it sharply around. For the first time I came to
> the Bible. Previous to this I had often preached and seen a great
> deal of the church . . . but I had not yet become a Christian.
> . . . I know that to that time I had made the cause of Jesus Christ
> into an opportunity for my own advancement. . . . I had never,
> or hardly ever, prayed. Despite all my abandonment I was very
> pleased with myself. The Bible, especially the Sermon on the
> Mount, liberated me from that. Since then everything has been
> different. . . . It was a great liberation. It became clear to me that
> the life of a servant of Jesus Christ must belong to the church
> and step by step it became clearer to what extent this must be
> so. . . . Christian pacifism, which I had recently combated pas-
> sionately, suddenly became self-evident to me.[72]

Green comments, "In 1932 Bonhoeffer finds the Christ of the Sermon
on the Mount to be a genuine 'other'"[73]; it was a powerfully transforming experience that changed the course of his life. Now the liberating
and authentically person-forming encounter he had hypothesized and
toward which he had struggled in his dissertations had become reality
for him. Now he had been drawn out of his lonely ego and into real
communion with Jesus Christ and, for the first time in his life, with
other human beings in his Body; this presence of real, face-to-face others with whom to be in genuine relationship in Christ was an awesome
gift for Bonhoeffer, the gift of his own humanity and salvation. Green
notes Bonhoeffer's statement in 1932 that

> A man *(sic)* first becomes human and first rightly asserts himself
> "when he understands himself not as the lord over his own life,
> but when he understands his life as responsible to the brother:
> [the other] human being. Then he does not live alone, but he
> lives essentially through and for the other, co-ordinated to him
> in responsibility."[74]

72. Letter of January 27, 1936 (DBW 14:112ff; translation from DB 204–5).

73. Green, *Sociality*, 142.

74. Ibid., 132, citing DBW 11:222–23 ("The Right of Self-Assertion," lecture, February
1932).

Thus we see the extent to which Bonhoeffer's attitude throughout his life to the self is shaped by his early experience of the self as a place of lonely, empty isolation, of terrifying boundlessness, and of distorted projections out of touch with reality itself, a reality that can encounter a person only from outside in the shattering and redemptive experience of touch. Of course, the obvious implication of this "autobiographical" dimension of Bonhoeffer's theology of the human self is that its applicability would be greatest for those whose experience is similar to his, and potentially less for those whose experience diverges from his. Green unwittingly reinforces this point by his deliberate decision to use masculine language throughout both his cited quotations of Bonhoeffer's writings and his own analysis (even, as noted above, altering recent inclusive-language translations in order to return to forms of masculine usage).

The effect of this decision, which in a book published in 1999 is of course jarring, is to call immediate attention to the androcentric bias of Bonhoeffer's analysis. In Green's telling, this is the theology of a particular "man" whose experience is explicated in terms and language that are intended to address other "men," his "brothers" in sin and faith. Understood in that sense, the decision to maintain Bonhoeffer's masculinist bias even in translation, rather than attempting to mask it with contemporary inclusive-language English, has the ring of intellectual honesty and is a helpful linguistic device showing the relative (and thus more limited) range of applicability of Bonhoeffer's thought. To the obvious question occurring to readers of Green's book, "What about the *woman* of faith?" the answer would seem to be that Bonhoeffer's writings on the self do not directly address her: they are intended not for her, not thus for "all people," but for his "brothers," those whose experience of selfhood may more closely correspond to his.

Yet this is precisely the inference Green avoids drawing. He asserts the highly experiential nature of Bonhoeffer's writings in the most pointed terms possible, playing on the archaic ambiguity of the English word "man" to want to refer both to "humanity" or "human being" in general (as the German *Mensch* indicates) *and* to the particular man Dietrich. Yet in the same breath he claims to be showing thereby Bonhoeffer's "catholicity" and applicability to the entire human condition. A typical explanation reads, "Where masculine language appears in these quotations, it appropriately indicates the autobiographical reference, though without denying the wider import of the analysis."[75] Thus he wants to have it both ways: highly particular, thus also androcentric, and simultaneously all-inclusive. What might initially appear an act of intellectual honesty is not only emptied of its denotative power but revealed to be a further universalizing of male experience.

It is a fundamental unstated tenet of Bonhoeffer studies that his writings are indeed to be read as revelatory of contemporary Christian experience, with no apparent exceptions. Despite Bonhoeffer's insistence on the concreteness of revelation, I know of no previous study that suggests any potential limitation of his works' relevance based on his gendered particularity. Most interpreters assume Bonhoeffer's universal applicability rather passively, behind their inclusive language, simply by failing to consider human experience that might relativize his analysis at crucial points. Green brings this contradiction into unmistakable view by simultaneously asserting (verbally) and denying (linguistically) Bonhoeffer's universality of reference. The fact that Green assumes Bonhoeffer's "catholicity" is demonstrated not only by his explicit assertions of this point (as noted above) but even more so by his sweeping and repeated references to "*the* soteriological problem"[76] and to "the anthropological problem *in general.*"[77] I am struck by the irony of Green's highlighting Bonhoeffer's particularity and concreteness while making a "general principle" out of the experience of this most contextually-oriented Christian.

Yet let us assume, along with Green's apparent subconscious realization that inclusive language just doesn't *sound right* for many of Bonhoeffer's utterances, that indeed Bonhoeffer is writing for other men from his experience as a man. In that case, we have a valuable record of a particular man's sensitive, ongoing, living interpretation of male experience as traditionally socialized: the powerful, even dominating, self-imprisoned ego moving toward humanity and salvation through

75. Green, *Sociality*, 113, note 17. Bonhoeffer's "notably catholic appeal consists in his being a twentieth-century man whose problems, struggles, discoveries, and insights are recognized by his contemporaries as their own problems and possibilities" (292–93).

76. My italics. This usage occurs on almost every page. Here is a typical example: "Bonhoeffer consistently defines the personal side of the soteriological problem as that of the powerful ego and its violation of the essential sociality of a person with others and with God." *Sociality*, 125.

77. Ibid., 116. My italics.

encounter with Jesus Christ and other human beings. For such a man, a "separative self" in Keller's terms, whose self puffs itself up to dominate and distort all of reality, the divine and human "other" *is* thus as we have seen the locus of salvation in its alterity and in providing a redemptive boundary to the self in reality. And the "surrender" of such a violently inflated "self" would indeed open the space necessary for real intimacy, for risk and vulnerability and life itself.

Indeed, Bonhoeffer's descriptions of the inner life of such a man are replete with the violence inflicted upon reality by the isolated ego intent on maintaining its own dominance. He uses several variants of the German *Gewalt*, or "force," in heightening intensification of the effect of such violence: the *Bewältigung* (overpowering)[78] of another person or of reality itself with sheer *Gewalt*,[79] issuing ultimately in the *Vergewaltigung* (rape, violation)[80] of that other. Neither Green, nor the translators or editors of *Act and Being* (or any other volume of Bonhoeffer's works, as far as I have seen), has commented on the significance of this latter word choice. It and its verbal and adjectival cognates are universally translated with terms of "violation" or "doing violence to." Of course, these are not inaccurate translations, and they convey an element of the brutal force denoted here. But nevertheless the word *Vergewaltigung* simply *is* the German word for "rape" as well, investing the word with a shocking horror beyond the less graphic "doing violence to." Any reader of the German would hear this double meaning[81]: Bonhoeffer chooses language that not only connotes but ac-

78. *Akt und Sein* (AS, DBW 2) 36, 58, 61.

79. Ibid., 71, 144–45, 149.

80. Ibid., 36, 89–90, 136, 152. Note that on page 36, Bonhoeffer uses *Vergewaltigung* also to refer to the violation people suffer, in his view, precisely when they encounter the redemptive "other" shattering the illusion of the self-enclosed world. He distinguishes this from their own confident desire for *Bewältigung* of the world. It is telling that for Bonhoeffer even the person-forming encounter that alone leads to life is experienced by the powerful ego as *Vergewaltigung*: as violation or even rape. This is an extreme example of his tendency noted earlier to conceive of even liberating engagement with the other in terms of combat or confrontation.

81. In his *Ethics* Bonhoeffer uses the term in both senses: i.e., both in reference to bodily rape (*Ethik* (DBW 6), 179, 212–13, 296) and in its metaphorical sense of extreme violation (among others, see *Ethik* 107, 134, 168, 178, 217, 258, 268, 342); at 168 he refers also to the *Vergewaltiger*, the rapist/violator. *Ethik* 168, 178, and especially 134, including note 37, are examples where the literal and metaphorical meanings are nearly indistinguishable. I cite here from the German, rather than the English translation,

tually denotes the violent *rape* of others, of God, and of reality itself on the part of the sinful "man's" ego. And the fact that, as Green has gone to such lengths to demonstrate, such passages in *Act and Being* and other texts are not merely theoretical for Bonhoeffer but disclosive of his own inner life means that Bonhoeffer chose this term because it accurately described the violence so terrifyingly present within his own self. This suggests that Bonhoeffer is charting, and experiencing liberation from, the stance not merely of a "powerful ego,"[82] which has rather positive connotations in our masterful culture, but in fact that of an aggressor.

Thus I suggest that, far from being a universal ethic, let alone one that would apply indiscriminately to the *abused*, in fact Bonhoeffer writes a theology and ethics from the *aggressor's* experience of selfhood. That is, he charts the path of escape by grace from within a male socialization that, at its extreme, issues in violation and abuse. The self as the center of the world; the forceful imposition of his own reality on others; the metaphors of violence and rape; the sterile isolation from genuine intimacy; the experience of God as "himself" also inflicting violation or as merely a projection of the self's own controlling fantasies: these describe *not* "human sinfulness in general" but specifically the problems typical of abusers.[83]

I do not mean to suggest by this that Bonhoeffer actually enacted consistently abusive behavior in his personal relationships, let alone that he was guilty of rape in any form. To be sure, he was an extremely con-

---

so that the reader can see Bonhoeffer's actual use of this term; those who do not read German can find the relevant passages in English through the German parallel pagination provided in DBWE 6.

82. This is Green's central metaphor for "the" anthropological and soteriological problem Bonhoeffer is describing. He acknowledges that Bonhoeffer does not ever state this himself; but like me he is inferring this from Bonhoeffer's choice of metaphor and images. While I would not dispute Green's impressive evidence on the problem of dominating power for Bonhoeffer, nevertheless it does not go far enough, in my view. "Power" is essential for life itself; its absence, as in the case of oppressed people in a variety of contexts, is a mark of sin as pernicious as its abuse (although neither Green nor Bonhoeffer recognizes or refers to the sins of powerlessness). The "powerful ego" too can of course be a force for good as well as evil. "Aggression," on the other hand, names the problem in an unmistakably destructive manifestation of power, particularly important as well in light of the dynamics of abuse.

83. See for instance Brooks and Silverstein, "Understanding the Dark Side of Masculinity." The section of chapter 4 devoted to Jessica Benjamin's work will explore further this experiential dimension of socialization into aggression.

fident (at times arrogant and condescending) thinker and had a violent streak. On his intellectual arrogance, Green notices "signs of an attitude of superiority, and of aggressiveness, competitiveness, and ambition";[84] this was manifested clearly, for instance, in his dismissive opinions toward his American peers while studying in New York. On his capacity for violence, which was an aspect of his personality he struggled hard to overcome, a letter he wrote to Eberhard on the occasion of his own birthday, February 4, 1941, is instructive. In enumerating the gifts Eberhard's friendship had provided him over the years, he writes,

> You have . . . patiently withstood the severe tests of such a friend-
> ship, particularly due to my violent temper (which I too abhor in
> myself and of which you have fortunately repeatedly and openly
> reminded me), and have not allowed yourself to be made bitter
> by it. For this I must be particularly grateful to you.[85]

Also, there are hints of both intellectual condescension and patriarchal bias in his relationship with Maria. For instance, in regard to his deploring of her literary tastes, he writes in a November 28, 1943, letter from prison to Eberhard Bethge:

> I would very much like that my wife be conformed to me as
> fully as possible in such matters. But I think this is only a matter
> of time. I don't like it at all when wives and husbands are of dif-
> ferent opinions. They must stand together like an unassailable
> bulwark. Don't you agree? Or is this perhaps another aspect of
> my "tyrannical" nature that you know so well?[86]

This quote is revealing both in his assumption that "[his] wife" should "conform" to him at all, let alone that he would want also to dictate her literary tastes, and in his perceptive awareness that perhaps this demand on his part is not in fact a matter of course but an aspect of his sinfulness, that Eberhard as his confessor would indeed know well. Given his developed theology of Christian conformation to Jesus Christ alone,[87] it is striking that he here expects Maria to "conform" to him rather than to Christ!

---

84. Green, *Sociality,* 147, note 93.
85. DBWE 16: 136 (I/68, letter of February 1, 1941).
86. DBW 8: 214, my translation.
87. See pp. 92–100 in chapter 3.

Yet by all accounts he was a warm, sensitive, and appealing human being. For instance, in the "Portrait" that opens his biography, Eberhard Bethge writes,

> Dietrich's smile was very friendly and warm. . . . In conversation, he was an attentive listener, asking questions in a manner that gave his partner confidence and led him (*sic*) to say more than he thought he could. Bonhoeffer was incapable of treating anyone in a cursory fashion. He preferred small gatherings to large parties, because he devoted himself entirely to the person he was with. . . . [His ability to work with great focus] was accompanied by a willingness to be interrupted, and even a craving for company when playing music. . . . He liked talking to children and took them seriously.[88]

Further, significantly, there is no indication that he struggled with, let alone acted out, violent impulses toward women. His existential struggles with violence and egotism appear not to have shaped his behavior in manifestly destructive ways. Rather, his very sensitivity to the dynamics inherent in his strict German male upbringing may have helped to make him such a perceptive lifelong observer and reporter of their inner reality, which he experienced as deadly bondage. His honesty and courage in leaving behind this tyranny, and his capacity to receive grace as a deeply humbling and liberating reality, allow him to serve as a powerful witness to redemption for men caught in such destructive isolation. His experience of transformative, living intimacy with Jesus Christ shaped him for a life of gratitude, faithfulness, and self-sacrifice in the face of the worst evils, which he recognized and resisted with such clarity of vision perhaps precisely *because* of their continuity with his own inner demons.

Thus to claim that Bonhoeffer is writing a self-implicating spirituality from a perspective of patriarchal dominance is in no way to disparage him as a human being or a Christian. It is simply to specify more precisely than usual the particular shape of the sin he describes within himself and the "man" for whom he writes, as well as the contours of the liberation he experiences in Christ. This more precise naming of Bonhoeffer's social location then also opens up space for a feminist reading that will both mark those aspects of his spirituality inappropriate for application to the abused and retrieve liberating elements he

88. DB, xvii–xviii.

explores. I suggest that this is preferable to the usual uncritical reading that attempts to force all of human experience into his, with potentially disastrous results. Before moving to the feminist analysis of soluble self-hood that will make possible this dialogue with Bonhoeffer, however, we must first explore his vision of spiritual formation itself, keeping in mind its formulation in the terms emerging from his own experience.

3

Bonhoeffer and Christian Spiritual Formation

IN THE PRECEDING CHAPTER WE EXAMINED ELEMENTS OF BONHOEFFER'S conception of the human self as derived from his own experience and articulated in his major writings. This chapter will contain an overview of his vision of the spiritual formation of such a self.[1] I will begin with a treatment of his widely-read volume, *Discipleship*, as that provides the basic shape and imagery of his understanding of ongoing life with Jesus Christ. Following that exposition, I will expand on four important elements of his spirituality that continue into later works as well (his articulation of a self-effacing christocentrism, Christ as mediator of reality, discernment of reality, and christological formation); these are developed in distinctive ways in the period of conspiracy and imprisonment. Finally, I will delineate the primary arenas in which this christological formation occurs for Bonhoeffer (engagement with Scripture, friendship/confession, and public life).

Post-Conversion Period and *Discipleship*

Following an introduction to the context from which *Discipleship* emerged, I will give a brief overview of its structure, followed by an examination of the shape of the encounter with Jesus Christ for Bonhoeffer. In the Gospel stories he interprets, Bonhoeffer hears the clarion call of Jesus as the summons and power to a new life. Jesus' voice breaks through the sterile isolation of the *incurvatus* self and ush-

1. There have been various studies of Bonhoeffer's spirituality that inform my work indirectly, though to my knowledge nothing on spiritual formation per se. See, e.g., Kelly and Nelson, *Cost of Moral Leadership*; Godsey, "Dietrich Bonhoeffer and Christian Spirituality"; Kelly, "Prayer and Action for Justice"; Pelikan, *Die Frömmigkeit Dietrich Bonhoeffers*; Zimmerling, "Die Spiritualität Bonhoeffers in den Gefängnisjahren"; and the studies contained in Mayer and Zimmerling, eds., *Dietrich Bonhoeffer*.

ers in the encounter with reality in the shape of the divine Other. He characterizes this encounter with Jesus through the recurring use of several key terms: *Ruf* (call), *Blick* (gaze), *Bindung an Jesus* (attachment to Jesus), *Gehorsam* (obedience), *Bruch* (break with former life), and *Nachfolge* (discipleship). I will treat these briefly, as a means of sketching the contours of the spirituality Bonhoeffer experienced and that shaped the rest of his life.

Discipleship and Conversion

Following his conversion (summer 1932, i.e., six months before Hitler's rise to power), things shifted for Dietrich. No longer did he experience himself caught in inner self-imprisonment or in self-accusing contradiction between his professed vocation and his deepest reality. Although he left almost no direct written documentation of his experience of this conversion, it is clear from his later descriptions of the overall shape of his life and from revealing changes in his published and miscellaneous writings that something decisive happened at that point. The grace he described in *Sanctorum Communio* had become real for him personally:

> The fact that my claim is met by the other I who loves me—which means, of course, by Christ—fulfills me, humbles me, frees me from bondage to myself, and enables me—again, of course, only through the power of faith in Christ—to love the other, to completely give and reveal myself to the other. (SC 166)

His book *Discipleship*,[2] published in 1937, gives evidence of the shape of this conversion and the life unfolding from it. Some clear contrasts from his earlier works present themselves immediately: first, this is a book for the church, not primarily for the academy. Its language is simple, clear, and direct, a remarkable shift from the dense and highly abstract language of his dissertations, especially *Act and Being*, that is nearly inscrutable at times. This is manifested, second, in that the discourse of the work has shifted from the philosophical to the exegetical. While he assumes and uses the conceptualities developed in his earlier work (the self as imprisoning and sinful, the formative effect of personal encounter, the christological focus, the centrality of *Stellvertretung*

---

2. Bonhoeffer, *Discipleship* (DBWE 4). Hereafter referred to in parenthetical references as *D*, with page citations.

for christology and discipleship), here they are articulated within the context of the Gospels' portrayals of Jesus and his disciples rather than in philosophical categories and scholarly debate with other thinkers. Finally, the book carries a political edge that is scarcely less powerful for having to remain cloaked in publishable "religious" language in Hitler's Germany. Emerging from the upheavals of the Nazis' sweeping encroachment into all that Christian Germany once held dear, including the soul of both Protestant and Catholic churches,[3] this book's uncompromising call to discipleship of Jesus Christ alone was spiritual dynamite. Its powerful transparency to both its author's own deepest spiritual needs and liberation, and to his church's and society's continuing bondage to the "Antichrist,"[4] makes for compelling reading indeed.

Discipleship (and its 1938 companion volume from the Finkenwalde years, *Life Together*) presents a clear vision of Bonhoeffer's perspectives on spiritual formation. Emerging following his conversion and over the course of his London pastorate (1933–1935) but written primarily during those years leading the underground Confessing Church seminary community at Finkenwalde (1935–1937), the book lays out a spirituality marked by transformative encounter with the person of Jesus Christ. It includes an introductory excoriation of the "cheap grace" that had "poisoned" the very heart of German Protestantism, numbing individuals and the church against living discipleship of Jesus and enfeebling their resistance to Nazi ideology;[5] an extended consideration of the Gospels' call narratives and their implications[6]; exegesis of the Sermon on the Mount, which had been so important in Bonhoeffer's own experience of conversion[7]; a treatment of Matthew 9 and 10 on

---

3. On the church struggle, see Barnett, *For the Soul of the People*, and Scholder, *Requiem for Hitler*. A series of probing essays on the range of Protestant and Catholic responses to Hitler can be found in Erickson and Heschel, eds., *Betrayal: German Churches and the Holocaust*. See especially Barnes' essay in that volume entitled "Dietrich Bonhoeffer and Hitler's Persecution of the Jews," 110–28.

4. *Discipleship* (DBWE 4), 103, 247, 276.

5. See "Preface" (*Discipleship*, 37–40) and "Costly Grace" (ibid., 43–56).

6. See "The Call to Discipleship" (ibid., 57–76), "Simple Obedience" (77–83), "Discipleship and the Cross" (84–91), and "Discipleship and the Individual" (92–99).

7. This includes "Matthew 5: On the 'Extraordinary' of Christian Life" (ibid., 100–145); "Matthew 6: On the Hidden Nature of the Christian Life" (146–68); and "Matthew 7: The Community of Disciples Is Set Apart" (169–82).

messenger and harvest themes[8]; and finally a section on the church and discipleship.[9] I will focus primarily on the material in the second of these headings (the Gospel call narratives). For Bonhoeffer himself, the encounter with Jesus Christ took place initially, and throughout his life, through meditation on Scripture, especially the Gospels. Thus these reflections in *Discipleship* on stories of Jesus calling disciples carry great personal significance for him.[10]

Here Bonhoeffer examines selected stories of disciples being called by Jesus and the life that follows. He makes recurring mention of Peter leaving his nets (Mark 1:16–18; D 46, 62, 64, 77) and, later, being called out onto the water (Matt 14:29; D 63, 66–67, 69, 77). In addition, he pays attention to the call of Levi (Mark 2:14; D 57–58, 62, 77), the accounts of three unsuccessful vocations (Luke 9:57–62; D 60–61), the rich young man (Matt 19:16–22; D 69–74, 78), the lawyer whose question introduces the parable of the Good Samaritan (Luke 10: 25–29; D 74–76), Jesus' prediction of his passion (Mark 8:31–38; D 84ff.) and prayer in Gethsemane (Matt 26:39, 42; D 90–91), and his call to leave everything of one's old life in order to follow (Luke 14:26; D 92ff.). These stories and teachings provide the narrative framework within which Bonhoeffer draws out the meaning of costly grace, the faithful obedience he sets forth in the book's opening chapter.

Encounter with Jesus: Ruf, Blick, Bindung

The call (*Ruf*) of Jesus is the first act of grace for Bonhoeffer. Jesus comes to persons in the midst of their actual life: mending nets, collecting taxes, engaged in ordinary relationships. There his call comes as the inbreaking voice of God, announcing the possibility of a new form of life in radical discontinuity with the old. Bonhoeffer makes extensive use of sensory metaphors to explore this relationship with Jesus. The primal one, for Bonhoeffer as a good Lutheran, is aural: call, voice, listening, responding.[11] The voice of Jesus creates a new reality in which people

8. On Matthew 10 (ibid., 183–98).

9. Ibid., 199–288.

10. Clifford Green demonstrates clear connections between Bonhoeffer's exegeses in *Discipleship* and his own personal struggles and faith experience. Green, *Sociality*, 163–66.

11. The primary image by which "voice" metaphors are expressed for Bonhoeffer is that of the "call" (*Ruf*) of Jesus. See for example *Discipleship* 57–76, 201–4, and through-

are invited to live. It is powerful, the very Word of God, and is able to evoke both the desire and the capacity for response. The call of Jesus brings the fullness of his being as *logos* of God into compelling personal interior engagement with the human being; it is an address to which one must somehow respond.

But Bonhoeffer makes widely-recurring use of visual metaphors as well. Jesus truly sees each person: his gaze (*Blick*) rests on each one, perceives their needs and hopes, and loves them. The metaphor of gaze is significant for Bonhoeffer, permeating *Discipleship* and his later writings and letters.[12] Like Jesus' voice, his gaze invites a person into a new reality, and Bonhoeffer repeatedly develops the implications of this: abiding within the gaze of Jesus, learning to let one's own gaze rest on him alone, avoiding all "sidelong glances" that might distract one from him. The face-to-face intimacy and power of this metaphor is clearly of central redemptive significance for Bonhoeffer as he himself here experiences for the first time in his life the transformative mercy of loving gaze. The concluding chapter of the book, entitled "The Image of Christ," develops this language of gaze and transformation most fully. There he writes,

> The image of Jesus Christ, which is always before the disciples' eyes, and before which all other images fade away, enters, permeates, and transforms them. . . . Those who behold Christ are being drawn into Christ's image, changed into the likeness of Christ's form. . . . This is the indwelling of Jesus Christ in our hearts.[13]

Both Word and image claim believers' hearts, drawing them into exclusive orientation to Jesus.

His repeated use of the language of *Bindung* and its cognates demonstrates this on the level of touch as well, a third sensory metaphor

---

out. His prison letters play also with the metaphors of polyphony and *cantus firmus* as revelatory of Christian life (see pp. 98–100). Perhaps then one might speak more broadly of the "aurality" of faith for Bonhoeffer.

12. *Discipleship* (DBWE 4), 57, 72, 86, 92, 107–8, 149–50, 281–88. See also, e.g., *Ethics* (DBWE 6), 66–67, 293, 325.

13. *Discipleship*, 281, 286. An editorial note on p. 281 indicates that the Greek term underlying the Luther translation of Romans 8:29, on which Bonhoeffer relied for his use of "image" language, was *symmorphous*. This has obvious resonance with the "conformation" motif Bonhoeffer develops (see pp. 92–100). See also *Discipleship* 283–86 on "form."

developed in this treatise. The term itself means, literally, "attachment," and is variously translated "commitment," "bond/being bound," "adherence," or "allegiance" as well. Through this language of touch or connection, Bonhoeffer is developing a spatial metaphor of proximity to Jesus. The center of discipleship for Bonhoeffer is precisely this *Bindung an Jesus*. He states repeatedly that there is no "program" or agenda apart from this: the only call of the disciple is proximity to Jesus, to commit oneself to him and remain with him wherever he might lead.

> [Discipleship] is nothing other than being bound to Jesus Christ [*Bindung an Jesus Christus*] alone. This means completely breaking through anything preprogrammed, idealistic, or legalistic. No further content is possible because Jesus is the only content. There is no other content besides Jesus. He himself is it. So the call to discipleship is a commitment [*Bindung*] solely to the person of Jesus Christ.[14]

And it is an attachment of love, stopping short of explicitly erotic overtones but full of the language of devotion and heartfelt trust. In the embodied metaphors of voice, gaze, and touch, then, the disciple learns to focus attention on Jesus alone: here is where love is found, a love that draws the disciple into radical commitment.

Implications of such Encounter: Gehorsam, Bruch, Nachfolge

This invitation into the new reality of Jesus, described metaphorically in terms of voice, gaze, and touch, obviously has implications for one's former life. Writing in a church context that to his mind had utterly caved in to "cheap grace," Bonhoeffer repudiates all theological attempts to hold on to one's previous existence in the face of Jesus' call. For him there is simply no such thing as faith without obedience (*Gehorsam*), nor obedience without faith: "*only believers obey, and only the obedient believe.*"[15] They are the same reality, described, for convenience's

---

14. Ibid., 58–59. For further instances of *Bindung* imagery, see pp. 62, 74, 85–87, 89, 116, 118, 125, 127, 133–34, 150, 153, 170 (actually translating *Verbundenheit* here), 215. For the German citations, see *Nachfolge* (DBW 4), 47, 51, 65, 78–80, 82, 90, 116, 119, 126, 128, 135–36, 155, 157, 229. Also, note *Discipleship* 95 for "ties" (*Bindungen*; *Nachfolge* 90) that draw a person away from Christ.

15. *Discipleship* (DBWE 4), 63. Bonhoeffer's italics. This entire chapter ("The Call to Discipleship") develops the theme of obedience to the Christ who appears as a commanding figure from the outset. In the section following this summary statement

sake, if you will, internally (faith, trust) and externally (obedience). As his exegeses make clear, the idea of somehow being able to live in this highly developed sensual and spiritual orientation toward Jesus while nevertheless changing none of the patterns of one's *life's* voice/hearing, sight/intimacy, and touch/attachment is ludicrous, impossible. On the contrary, he asserts, the capacity for the sort of spiritual connectedness to Jesus that is alone redemptive comes only by letting him free us from those blockages of voice, gaze, heart, and touch that mark our former life in the world. And such release necessarily and obviously takes real, concrete form in our real, concrete lives. Far from being merely a "spiritual" liberation, Bonhoeffer sees Jesus' call and desire for a whole-life attachment as having radical and disruptive consequences in the real world we inhabit.

This point comes through clearly in his insistence on a clear *Bruch* (break) with one's former existence.[16] Jesus' goal is not to make Levi a holier or more grace-centered tax collector. He wants to call Levi away from the tax booth entirely, to live an entirely new life of freedom in following him. The same is true for Peter, James, and John with their fishing nets and the rich young man with his wealth. Bonhoeffer makes clear that Jesus isn't interested in merely being added to already configured lives as an appendage. Christ wants to be the center of people's lives, forcing them to let go of all that previously occupied them. Bonhoeffer's language is stark and relentless; Green even considers it violent[17] in its unsparing depictions of the upheavals caused by such a clarion call. Family of origin, spouse and children, livelihood and identity—all are to be left behind in the unquestioning, nonnegotiable "immediacy" of response to Jesus.[18]

---

on faith and obedience (i.e., on pp. 63–69) he explains how these two propositions interpret one another, making sense of them within a context of Protestant theology and pastoral care before then providing two biblical applications of these principles (rich young man and lawyer asking about his neighbor: pp. 69–76). Chapter 3, "Simple Obedience" ("Der einfältige Gehorsam"), pushes even more strongly the necessity that this obedience avoid all obfuscating questions or exceptions and simply obey the clear word of Christ heard in Scripture.

16. Ibid., 58, 61–69, 77–79, 92–99.

17. Green, *Sociality*, 173.

18. Note that this immediacy is a spatial one, not a temporal one, as noted earlier. But the language nevertheless carries the insistent urgency of both meanings of *immediacy*: one is to be immediately, non-mediatedly, joined to Jesus, and is to do so now, without reservations.

All these elements—call, gaze, attachment, obedience, break with former life—thus comprise the totality of what Bonhoeffer intends by his central image, the one for which the book is named: *Nachfolge* (discipleship). As readers have known for decades, his is a vision of discipleship that holds a strong punch. It is often read as uncompromising, impossible, even condemning in its repudiation of any lukewarm or accommodationist form of discipleship. Yet for Bonhoeffer personally and for the church context he was addressing as he perceived it, this urgency of the Gospel, far from being a crushing demand, was a lifeline of grace. It meant that God in Jesus Christ was powerful enough to break through all the self-erected barriers of personal ambition and control, all the theological dithering and suspicion of works-righteousness, all the political capitulation of a frightened and beleaguered church. For him, *Nachfolge* meant simply following after (*folgen . . . nach*) the One whose call and love make all things new, and in comparison with whom the rewards of personal success or political maneuvering had little appeal. "Uncompromising obedience" was no burden; it was the only sane response. For him there could be no other way to life in all its fullness, the pearl of great price.

And because for him this movement into life itself means an escape from the sterile isolation of the dominating self, the *Nachfolge* he envisions is replete also with imagery of self-denial. For instance, he excoriates those described in Luke 9:57–62 (three unnamed potential disciples who are unsuccessful in following) for presuming to dictate to Jesus the terms of their discipleship—for setting up a "self-chosen" way as an alternative to the obedience Jesus commands. In passage after passage, he makes use of this contrast between the self-chosen life and the life of discipleship.[19] Further, he conceives the entire movement of attachment to Jesus as necessitating a concomitant detachment from the self: the *Bindung an Jesus* is made possible only by *Ent-bindung* from oneself.[20] And so the language of self-denial represents the conscious

19. See, e.g., *Discipleship* 48, 59–61, 70–72, 81, 83, 87–88, 93.

20. Note that Bonhoeffer himself does not use the language of *Entbindung* from oneself; I am suggesting the word-play to show the connection between detachment from oneself and *Bindung an Jesus*. However, *Entbindung* does not mean only "release" or "detachment"; it also means "delivery," as in childbirth. So I create this wordplay as a way of reading Bonhoeffer's "self-denial" here a bit more creatively as well, on another level: that *Bindung an Jesus* requires and makes possible not merely the suffocation of the self (as self-denial is often intended and interpreted to mean) but the *Entbindung*

negation, toward oneself, of all the broader metaphors of attachment now focused on Jesus alone. He writes,

> Just as in denying Christ Peter said, "I do not know the man," those who follow Christ must say that to themselves. . . . Self-denial means knowing only Christ, no longer knowing oneself. It means no longer seeing oneself, only him who is going ahead. . . . Only when we have really forgotten ourselves completely, when we really no longer know ourselves, only then are we ready to take up the cross for his sake.[21]

What is new in *Discipleship*, therefore, is not its stance toward the self, since in continuity with earlier works it views the self as the shape of sin's prison, and release from sin thus entailing escape from the self. What is new is, instead, the experience of such liberation tasted in the person of Jesus Christ. In the call, gaze, and touch of Jesus, Bonhoeffer experiences a new reality; indeed, he will say, he encounters reality itself. And this new reality eventually begins to fill and shape even his view of that longtime object of fear, his own self.

Continuing Central Motifs

Although the central christological dimension of *Discipleship* remains of lifelong importance to Bonhoeffer, his experience and articulation of this reality becomes increasingly complex in later years.[22] In this section I will sketch some of the ways his spirituality develops during the period of his conspiracy involvement and imprisonment. While none of these emphases is foreign to *Discipleship* (indeed, they can all be seen as central implications of the encounter described there, explicitly or implicitly present already), the ways Bonhoeffer develops them in later years are more nuanced than was possible for him in the earlier text.

—the delivery into reality—of the true self in Christ. See the material on conformation with the Incarnate One on pp. 92–100 of this chapter, as well as that on self-awareness in chapter 5, pp. 203–7.

21. *Discipleship*, 86.

22. In prison he actually pulls back somewhat from the comparatively simplistic, either/or framing of *Discipleship*, though he notes that he still stands by what he had written. See LPP 369 (DBW 8: 542).

Self-Effacing Christocentrism

Discipleship provides access to some of the central dynamics of Bonhoeffer's vision of Christian spiritual formation. As we have seen, this volume reflects the highly christocentric nature of his own spiritual experience in conversion and beyond. Although it has received rather less critical attention than the writings from the end of his life, *Discipleship* is a crucial text of Bonhoeffer's, providing a glimpse into the spiritual experience that shaped the rest of his life and thought.[23] The fact that the heart of his spirituality resides in intimacy with Jesus Christ (articulated in the same central metaphors of voice, gaze, and attachment) can be seen in clues his letters provide of this reality up to the end of his life. Clearly the spirituality articulated in *Discipleship* continues to describe central aspects of his experience.

One example will have to suffice as a glimpse of how this christocentric spiritual experience continues to take shape in both familiar and novel ways in later years. From the years of his conspiracy involvement, in June of 1942, Bonhoeffer writes to his friend Eberhard a reflection on the figure of the Beloved Disciple in the Gospel of John.[24] This text demonstrates both a deepening of the intimacy with Jesus described in *Discipleship* and a new appreciative validation of the contemplative vocation as a central dimension of Christian spirituality. The fact that this reflection is written within the context of a letter to Dietrich's own best friend makes the descriptions of the mutual transparency between Jesus and the Beloved Disciple all the more interesting. It leads me to wonder whether it was the experience of this abiding intimate friendship that both reflected and invited Bonhoeffer more deeply into the experience of contemplative friendship with Jesus himself.[25] The Beloved Disciple, for Bonhoeffer,

23. Green is one who has devoted significant attention to *Discipleship*, although he too tends to see it as, at best, merely a "partial resolution and a compromised solution" to Bonhoeffer's underlying problem of the powerful ego (*Sociality*, 284). Rather than viewing *Discipleship* as an "unnecessary attempt to suppress the strength of [Bonhoeffer's] own ego" (ibid.), however, I see this book as the record of an essential step forward for him, the way to life. His later capacity for more subtle discernment in no way invalidates this work's presentation of the all or nothing character of conversion and discipleship. Indeed, I would assert, it was his years of learning to pay unreserved attention to the call of Jesus that made possible that mature capacity.

24. This text is found in *Conspiracy and Imprisonment* (DBWE 16), 314–15.

25. Mark Brocker has suggested that perhaps Bonhoeffer intended this meditation as a reflection of Bethge's quieter and more contemplative spirituality. In this case, per-

does not aspire to anything but to be the disciple whom Jesus loved, to whom Jesus gave his friendship, . . . who reclined on Jesus' breast at table. Thus John becomes a witness of the experienced love of Jesus, of the most intimate proximity and communion with him.[26]

He writes, "To be content in Jesus' love—I would see that as the conclusion and significance of everything that is to be said about John."[27]

It may seem surprising to hear Bonhoeffer, martyred and enshrined for attempting to push the church fully into the contemporary public and political sphere, assert so clearly this utter contentment in the love of Jesus as, in and of itself, rich and abundantly sufficient discipleship. Yet at the same time this is also simply a more Johannine way of expressing the devotion outlined in *Discipleship*: that the goal of Christian following is never any program or agenda but simply *Bindung an Jesus*—that the gift and pleasure of unreserved intimacy with him and those he loves, wherever he might lead, is itself always the entire content of discipleship. Bonhoeffer defends "[t]he all-encompassing nature of Jesus' love (John 3:16!) . . . against every pietistic narrowing."[28] Yet he goes right on to assert that "this is the very place where the utterly personal must also be expressed, that we too belong to those whom Jesus loved and loves and will love, that Jesus' love is not a private affair but is the center of the world."[29] Toward the end of the reflection he ponders what this means, this reclining as beloved in Jesus' arms. And his answer picks up again some of those sensual metaphors first sketched in *Discipleship*, emphasizing here however more clearly the experience of rest:

> What does it mean to recline at the breast of Jesus (John 13:23)?
> To be sheltered in him, guarded by him, protected from tempta-

---

haps Bonhoeffer intends to place himself in the "Simon Peter" figure the text presents, yet one who himself also finds solace in and desire for "the experienced love of Jesus." See also the later material on the significance of friendship for Bonhoeffer's spirituality (pp. 105–6).

26. Bonhoeffer, *Conspiracy and Imprisonment* (DBWE 16), 314. On the matter of Jesus' friendship he adds the note, "this is analogous to how the Greek reads; somewhere, John 20:2."

27. Ibid., 315.

28. Ibid. Bonhoeffer's exclamation point.

29. Ibid.

tion and fall, held, drawn into trust? To be allowed to question him (John 13!), to receive an answer, to lie at the heart of God? Jesus with wide-open eyes that behold suffering and evil, while the other person sleeps like a child?[30]

This experience of rest in the love of Jesus Christ, an intimacy and trust that embraces beloved disciples throughout all dimensions of their life in him, interestingly does not immediately translate here into an increased regard for one's own selfhood. Just the opposite, in fact, appears to be the case. For one of the main insights Bonhoeffer is exploring in this reflection is his sense that what makes the figure of "John," the fourth Gospel's Beloved Disciple, distinctive and so transparent to this fullness of Jesus' love is precisely his own absence of personal temperament or characteristics that, for the rest of us, merely get in the way. For Bonhoeffer, this vision of discipleship is one of being progressively taken up into Jesus, with a concomitant fading away of all that would keep us separate from him, all that would keep us locked into our own form or identity or personality rather than his. This reflection is full of the language of dissolving, of utter self-effacement.[31] For example, he writes,

> John seems to have nothing of his own: none of his own colors or temperament. Everything vanishes on closer examination. And tellingly, he is characterized only by a purely passive description. . . . in this Gospel his name is not mentioned even once! So fully effaced is his own personality. It does not read, "the disciple who loved the Lord"; even that would be too much of himself. . . . The love of the Lord is enough.[32]

A German term that appears often throughout this essay is *ausgelöscht*. In most places in this reflection, I translated this term *effaced* or *self-effaced*, which I believe captures precisely what Bonhoeffer is talking about: the blurring of John's own distinctive identity or features or *face*. In some cases, "dissolved" seems to work better and also carries interesting resonances to the "soluble" selfhood described by Keller as characteristic of female socialization. In a literal sense, *ausgelöscht* means "extinguished" or "put out," like a fire or a light. Because Bonhoeffer

---

30. Ibid. Bonhoeffer's exclamation point.
31. " . . . he is the one sheltered in the love of Jesus, entirely effaced in it." Ibid., 314.
32. Ibid.

is not referring to direct and outright self-*annihilation*, that language seems too strong here. But nevertheless the literal meaning does give these terms a considerable edge. The goal of this path of discipleship is, in fact, to lose not only our own "face" but even our very "form" as these dissolve completely in union with Jesus:

> John abides with Jesus and his form disappears in communion with Jesus. . . . Everything of our own is effaced and consumed: sin, virtues, unfaithfulness, and faithfulness. The redemptive love of Jesus is sealed through death and resurrection. It abides forever and we abide in it.[33]

Thus I have named this a "self-effacing christocentrism" and see it as a central element of Bonhoeffer's broadly-stroked vision of the Christian life. In the later sections on discernment and christological formation we shall see some ways this "self-effacement" is nuanced or even apparently contradicted. But nevertheless, the self-effacement made explicit here is of a piece with the "unrestricted self-surrender" advocated in *Sanctorum Communio;* with the detachment from oneself in *Bindung an Jesus* in *Discipleship*; and with his lifelong insistence that the Christian, like Jesus, must be a "person for others" (*Letters and Papers from Prison*), practicing self-sacrificial *Stellvertretung* in love for others. For Bonhoeffer, relinquishment of the loud coercive demands of the ego was the blessed way forward into life, i.e., into ever fuller friendship with and transparency to Jesus Christ himself, the reality of all that is.

Christ as the Mediator of all Reality

The centering in friendship with Jesus Christ throughout Bonhoeffer's life is, I would assert, the personal analogue to or experiential dimension of his equally lifelong insistence on Christ as the mediator of all reality. He develops this in two primary ways. In *Life Together,* his entire

---

33. Ibid., 315. This passage actually begins, "Martyrdom is foretold for Peter, but John abides with Jesus . . ." Earlier Peter is described as "the confessor, . . . the man of strong faith, . . . the denier who is later received again, . . . the rock, . . . the one called to pasture the congregation of Jesus (John 20)." Peter is the one with a "story of his own," unlike John; he is also the one who "loved the Lord more than any other disciple did" (314), in presumed reference to John 21. If on some level in fact Bonhoeffer saw himself more in the active, storied figure of Peter, then this reference to martyrdom as well is interesting. The suggestion of Dietrich as "Peter" and Eberhard as "John" (see note 25) is speculative, however.

conception of Christian community derives from the claim that even in the closest spiritual community we do not have immediate access to one another, but all relationships take place only through the mediation of Christ who stands "between" each person and every other.[34] This corresponds to his earliest conception of the human person as an "I" created by encounter with the *Schranke* or *Grenze* of the "You," the barrier of whose alterity Bonhoeffer defined as a running up against the divine Other. Thus what he first conceptualized in philosophical terms he is now able to articulate in the personal language of spiritual experience: that I relate to any other person only through or by means of Christ who is the living boundary between us. This reveals that his conversion has moved him into much clearer focus on the Living One, the divine Other, who mediates and makes possible the relationships between human beings. The philosophical concept of the boundary, partaking of divine alterity in its person-forming power, has taken on flesh and shape as Jesus Christ himself, the one whose voice and gaze and touch Bonhoeffer now knows personally. And so he writes, "Discipleship is bound to the mediator, and wherever discipleship is rightly spoken of, there the mediator, Jesus Christ, the Son of God, is intended."[35]

And this Christ-mediation of all reality means that the only *immediate* relationship a person has is with Jesus himself. In the section of *Discipleship* entitled "Discipleship and the Individual," Bonhoeffer describes how the radical call of Christ severs a person from his or her immediate relations, those bonds in which the person's created individuality was submerged, i.e., in which social enmeshment made free personhood impossible. In commenting on Luke 14:26 ("Whoever comes to me and does not hate father and mother, spouse and children, brothers and sisters, yes, and even life itself, cannot be my disciple"), he writes,

> Jesus' call itself already breaks the ties with the naturally given surroundings in which a person lives. It is not the disciple who breaks them; Christ himself broke them as soon as he called. Christ has untied the person's immediate connections with the world and bound the person immediately to himself. No one

34. Bonhoeffer, *Life Together* (DBWE 5), 41, 43–44. Hereafter referred to as LT. Note that Bonhoeffer uses the terms *Mittler* and *Mitte* nearly interchangeably in reference to Christ's role in mediating (or at and as the center of) reality.

35. *Discipleship* (DBWE 4), 59.

can follow Christ without recognizing and affirming that that
break is already complete.[36]

Throughout his life Bonhoeffer insists that Christ alone is the one
through whom we encounter reality: God, one another, the world, even
ourselves. Thus for him Jesus Christ functions both as the means of
healthy individuation and, simultaneously, as the bridge or link opening
persons in all directions to reality, as Christ reveals it. "*He is the mediator*, not only between God and human persons, but also between person
and person, and between person and reality."[37] And this fact of Christ's
mediation of all relations has consequences for how communities are
structured and the concrete ways their members treat one another:

> So people called by Jesus learn that they had lived an illusion
> in their relationship to the world. The illusion is immediacy. . . .
> Anytime a community hinders us from coming before Christ as
> a single individual, anytime a community lays claim to imme-
> diacy, it must be hated for Christ's sake. For every unmediated
> natural relationship, knowingly or unknowingly, is an expres-
> sion of hatred toward Christ, the mediator, especially if this re-
> lationship wants to assume a Christian identity.[38]

In his *Ethics* then he develops this mediatorial role of Christ further, positing Christ *as* the reality of both God and the world, the one
in whom both God and world are truly known. Notions of the world *or*
of God that attempt to consider these in separation from one another,
or without taking full account of the other and of their union in Christ,
are "abstractions."[39] And the only truly "concrete" or accurate grasp of
reality is that which begins with Jesus Christ, who reveals both the heart
of God's redemptive desire and the stark and beautiful and agonizing
reality of the divinely encompassed world just as it is:

> In Christ we are invited to participate in the reality of God and
> the reality of the world at the same time, the one not without
> the other. The reality of God is disclosed only as it places me

36. Ibid., 93. This entire section of "Discipleship and the Individual" (92–96) develops this theme of Christ's mediation of reality.

37. Ibid., 94.

38. Ibid., 94–95.

39. *Ethics* (DBWE 6), 54. For more on Bonhoeffer's understandings of "concreteness" and "abstraction," see Brocker, *Community of God, Jesus Christ, and Responsibility*,
199ff.

> completely into the reality of the world. But I find the reality of
> the world always already borne, accepted, and reconciled in the
> reality of God....What matters is *participating in the reality of
> God and the world in Jesus Christ today,* and doing so in such a
> way that I never experience the reality of God without the real-
> ity of the world, nor the reality of the world without the reality
> of God.[40]

In Christ one need not flee the reality of either God or the world but
can truly perceive both only in their necessary and inseparable interconnection. This clarity of vision gives rise to capacities for compassion, for embrace of the real, and for responsible action in the world
grounded in a lucid perception of what is. Thus Bonhoeffer names "accordance with reality" as one of the touchstones of responsible ethical
action.[41] Because of Jesus Christ, Christians need not fear reality but in
their movement deeper into him are invited ever more deeply into all
that is: God and world, *one* reality.[42]

   Thus an authentically Christian spirituality, for Bonhoeffer, is necessarily highly concrete. The interconnections between God and world
that for him define "concreteness" are manifested always and only in the
particular. In the previous chapter we saw that already in *Sanctorum
Communio* his critique of German idealism was rooted in just such a
focus on the particular over against any sorts of universal principles.
And this suspicion of abstractions, generalizations, and universal truths
continues to characterize his thinking, and his spirituality, throughout
his life.[43] For Bonhoeffer, what is most real is what is most particular—a
given person, or situation, or context—precisely in its uniqueness, not
only its continuity with or "generalizability" from other persons, situations, or contexts. And thus for him the will of God as well is highly
concrete, reflecting the well-discerned and inseparable realities of God
and world as those converge in highly particular, never predictable
ways in any given circumstance, for any given person or community.

40. *Ethics* (DBWE 6), 55.

41. Ibid., 261–69.

42. Ibid., 54–62, esp. 58.

43. Note that, for instance, his well-known critique of "cheap grace" is formulated as
precisely an attack on "grace as doctrine, as principle, as system.... forgiveness of sins as
a general truth." As such, it is the "denial of God's living word, denial of the incarnation
of the word of God." *Discipleship* (DBWE 4), 43; cf. also 53, 59, 81.

In order to gain a true understanding of Jesus Christ as he truly is, one must be open to perceiving the world itself as it truly is, in all its alterity, and respect its diversity and otherness on its own terms from the very outset.[44]

Discernment of Reality[45]

Because the will of God, or the good, thus cannot ever be defined in advance by means of general theological, ethical, or spiritual principles, Bonhoeffer's lifelong emphasis on concreteness necessarily fosters a spirituality radically dependent on discernment, practiced anew in every new situation. This is implicit throughout his life, but it becomes much more explicit in the years he spends in the conspiracy, where a reliance upon mature discernment makes possible new ventures of public responsibility that would surely have seemed incredible to him in earlier years of his life. I am also suggesting that the move into the conspiracy deepened Bonhoeffer's capacities for discernment on another level as well. That is, as he here renounced his position of secure dominance and moved for the first time in his life into a situation of genuine vulnerability (learning now the "view from below"), he began at the same time to recognize the worth and sacredness of the self, now truly at risk. This allowed him then, I believe, to begin to become conscious of and describe processes of ongoing discernment that, in his earlier situation

44. All this emphasis on concreteness and particularity could open Bonhoeffer to charges of relativism, of envisioning a universe in which there are no ultimate truths, but always only merely conditional or provisional ones, different for each individual, shifting over time or in different relational or historical settings—a world unable to hear the Word of God as that echoes through the centuries from an impossibly alien time and place. How then does the concrete relate to the universal? On this see his extensive treatment of the relation of the ultimate to the penultimate (*Ethics* [DBWE 6], 146–70). In brief, he correlates the realm of the ultimate with *justification* and that of the penultimate with *sanctification*. The justifying Word of God in which (or whom) we and the world are created, named, loved, redeemed, and borne desires always to be made flesh in the penultimate realm of time and space. Without its concrete embodiment in the penultimate (sanctification), it remains an abstraction; yet without that ultimate vision (justification), there is no hope or animation for the penultimate realm on its own. To merely expect people to break free by themselves, without the Word of grace, is condemning and despairing law, while to preach merely ultimate vision without its concrete embodiment in real situations of brokenness is cheap grace and an abandonment of people to their misery in real life.

45. The material in this section appeared in edited form as "Probing the Will of God," 42–49.

of privileged disregard of the self, had been invisible to him. Thus here, and particularly in those sections of the *Ethics* concerned with discernment, he not only assumes but actually articulates for the first time a place for the self *within* the realm of faithfulness.

Thus in his primary explication of discernment, which he terms *prüfen*, that is, "probing" or "examining" the will of God, he writes,

> [The will of God is] not a system of rules that are fixed from the outset, but always new and different in each different life circumstance. . . . Heart, intellect, observation, and experience must work together in this discernment . . . knowing the will of God is not at our human disposal, but dependent entirely on God's grace; and indeed, because this grace is and wants to be new every morning. [That is why] this discernment of the will of God is such a serious matter.[46]

Here he describes a process of discernment obviously requiring clear and focused attention upon one's own "heart, intellect, observation, and experience."[47] Far from distracting a person from divine reality, these aspects of the self now function for him as the indispensable context within which this crucial process daily occurs. Discernment, for him, means coming to perceive reality in all its fullness; now this is beginning to include the self. Bonhoeffer actually makes this explicit in a remarkable passage on *selbst-prüfen* (self-discernment or -examination). Note that this is one of the few instances in Bonhoeffer where *selbst-* (self-) is used in an unambiguously positive sense. He means by *selbst-prüfen* our own deepening self-knowledge in Jesus Christ, as well as our discernment of our true vocation; and he distinguishes this sort of authentic self-knowledge from the distorted and harmful (whether grandiose or shame-filled) self-evaluations that otherwise clutter up our hearts. Far from being a selfish indulgence, this *selbst-prüfen* is at the center of mature Christian life as the very means by which we come to know ourselves in reality, i.e., in Jesus Christ.

> The reason why this exercise of self-examination is not superfluous, however, is the very fact that Jesus Christ really is and wants to be in *us*, and because this being-in-us of Jesus Christ does not simply occur mechanically, but again and again takes place and

46. *Ethics* (DBWE 6), 321.

47. Ibid. Two pages later he writes, "Intellect, cognitive ability, and attentive perception of the context come into lively play here" (323–24).

proves true precisely *in* this self-examination…so Jesus Christ
is completely in us in the very event of our examining ourselves
ever anew in Christ.[48]

Because discernment means accurate perception of reality, it is
inextricably tied to the One who for Bonhoeffer *is* the reality of both
God and the world, namely Jesus Christ. Ultimately then Christian
discernment means learning to perceive the real as that is revealed by
and in Jesus and as his call opens to us our particular vocation in every
new day, every concrete situation. "Only on the basis of Jesus Christ,
only within the realm defined by Jesus Christ, only 'in' Jesus Christ is
it possible to discern the will of God."[49] This means that an important
aspect of the practice of discernment for Bonhoeffer is simply learning
to live "in" the space Jesus Christ creates for us: to pay attention to where
and how he reveals himself to us (see "Loci of Formation" at the end of
this chapter), to learn to distinguish his voice from others' voices and
remain within earshot, to turn "toward" him and not be distracted by
competing demands, etc.

One of the most insidious forms of distraction from the living
presence and discerned call of Jesus Christ is, for Bonhoeffer, the tendency of religious people in particular to think in terms of their own
judgments of "good" and "evil." From his 1933 lectures on *Creation and
Fall* through his *Ethics*, he over and over insists on the inapplicability for
the Christian life of such categories of evaluation. In fact, the very first
lines of his *Ethics* center precisely here:

> Those who wish even to focus on the problem of a Christian
> ethic are faced with an outrageous demand—from the outset
> they must give up, as inappropriate to this topic, the very two
> questions that led them to deal with the ethical problem: "How
> can I be good?" and "How can I do something good?" Instead
> they must ask the wholly other, completely different question:
> what is the will of God?[50]

Further, he describes the attempt to categorize reality into moral spheres
as the primal temptation itself. This is the voice of the serpent promising
"*sicut deus eritis*," "you shall be like God" precisely in knowledge of good

48. Ibid., 326.
49. Ibid., 323.
50. Ibid., 47.

and evil. The role of Christian ethics and reflection is not to place such labels on ourselves, one another, or aspects of reality itself, according to some abstracted system of evaluation. Rather than judgment, the faithful Christian stance is one of discernment and obedience to the voice of Christ who alone reveals what is real and who alone is the content of the good.[51] This frees the Christian from both arrogation to oneself of the divine capacity for judgment and slavish subservience to social, religious, or self-imposed rules and moral systems.

In his explication of discernment, Bonhoeffer thus not only asserts that one can discern the will of God "only within the space which is defined by Jesus Christ," as noted above, but he now defines that "space" more clearly. That is, Christ himself "occupies the very same space in them that had previously been occupied by their own knowledge of good and evil."[52] Thus for Bonhoeffer "the space defined by Jesus Christ" is his image for the relinquishing of *a priori* categories of evaluation of oneself or others and letting reality be defined for us by the living voice of Christ. In his *Ethics* he does not give this new "space" any more content than this, defining it here primarily negatively, i.e., in relinquishing of judgment. But in a lovely essay written in the same period, he seems to be proposing gratitude as a positive criterion of discernment. He writes,

> That for which I can thank God is good. That for which I cannot thank God is evil. But the determination whether I can thank God for something is discerned on the basis of Jesus Christ and his word. Jesus Christ is the limit of gratitude. Jesus Christ is also the fullness of gratitude; in him gratitude knows no bounds. It encompasses all the gifts of the created world. It embraces even pain and suffering. It penetrates the deepest darkness until it has found within it the love of God in Jesus Christ. To be thankful means to say yes to all that God gives "at all times and for everything" (Eph 5:20). Gratitude is even able to encompass past sin and to say yes to it, because in it God's grace is revealed—o felix culpa (Rom 6:17).[53]

51. He develops this insistence on the priority of discernment of the actual will of God, as opposed to judgment according to schemes of good vs. evil, especially in *Ethics* (DBWE 6), 261–69.

52. Ibid., 325.

53. "On Gratitude among Christians," *Conspiracy and Imprisonment* (DBWE 16), 490.

One might say that Bonhoeffer considers gratitude a (if not the) mark of the well-discerned Christian life, as discernment of and faithfulness to one's actual, constantly-evolving, concrete vocation allows a person to rest continually in gratitude even in the midst of evil and suffering. It is a fruit of that immersion in Christ alone that gradually releases people from the habitual human tendency toward placing categories on reality: "good" or "evil."

Of course in ordinary circumstances our familiar religious evaluations of good and evil based on the Ten Commandments and the Sermon on the Mount, for instance, may well be indistinguishable from the voice of Christ, may in fact be places in which Jesus addresses us in our concrete situation. But in extraordinary situations, those in which the magnitude of evil or trauma threaten to devastate the very foundations of life itself, mature faithfulness to Jesus Christ can require the disciple to move outside of accepted human or even divine laws in discerning the responsible course of action. This discernment calls upon the best possible use of one's intellect, judgment, and conscience[54]—it is in no way an abrogation of these—and places them in the service of prayer and faithfulness, trusting that the call of Christ is power enough for even risky and morally condemnable action in highly ambiguous situations.[55] For Bonhoeffer, this freedom made possible his participation in the wartime plot to assassinate Hitler and form a new non-Nazi government, a plan centering on an attempted murder whose sinfulness (especially to himself as a pacifist, for whom Jesus' words on nonviolence were paramount) he did not whitewash or justify. In the section of the *Ethics* that in necessarily veiled terms treats his reflections on

54. Bonhoeffer develops his understanding of the conscience primarily at *Ethics* (DBWE 6), 276–83. This is an interesting section positing the conscience as "the call of human existence for unity with itself" (276, also 282), that can be disregarded only at the cost of "the destruction of one's own being, a disintegration of human existence" (277). As such, it is an invaluable tool of discernment and, significantly, it is specifically *not* to be surrendered in service to others. Rather, "the call of the conscience to *unity with oneself* in Jesus Christ" in any and all concrete situations remains of paramount importance (282, emphasis added).

55. Like most Bonhoeffer scholars, I focus here on the christological dimension of his thinking on these subjects. For a marvelous exploration of Bonhoeffer's scattered writings touching on the role of the Holy Spirit, and how these texts (dealing primarily with questions of hermeneutics and of discipleship) contribute to our understanding of Bonhoeffer's view of discernment, see Kelly and Nelson, *Cost of Moral Leadership*, 51–82.

tyrannicide,[56] he makes clear that, again, he is not attempting to arrogate to himself the power of divine judgment and absolution of his and the other conspirators' actions but to place their best gifts at the service of complex and self-implicating discernment. Confinement of moral thought to pre-determined categories of good and evil makes such complex and living discernment impossible and may, by for instance ruling out from the outset the elimination of Hitler, contribute to the entrenchment of even greater evil.

In conclusion to this section on discernment, I would mention the question that for many has become characteristic of Bonhoeffer and that continues to inspire the church in new situations, namely, "Who is Jesus Christ for us today?"[57] Given Bonhoeffer's notions of Christ as the mediator of all reality, this would indeed seem to be *the* central question of Christian discernment for him. This discernment and the vocation and action that sprang from it allowed Bonhoeffer to challenge the church of his day to a much more radical and contemporary understanding of Jesus and to develop notions of *Stellvertretung*, especially in the person and church for others, that have functioned as an ongoing litmus test to Christians in many subsequent contexts.

Conformation with Jesus Christ

Finally, this material on living discipleship of Jesus Christ, including all the complexity of faithfulness, allows us to see some of what Bonhoeffer intends with his language of the christological formation of the believer, or *Gleichgestaltung* (conformation) with Christ. This term is introduced at the end of *Discipleship* and developed in Bonhoeffer's *Ethics*. As such, it represents a deepening of the "following after" of *Nachfolge* into outright conformation with, or transformation into, the being of Jesus.

> Formation occurs only by being drawn into the form of Jesus Christ, *by being conformed to the unique form of the one who became human, was crucified, and is risen*. This does not happen

56. The material in the *Ethics* that attempts to reflect theologically (although of course covertly) upon the conspirators' plans to usurp the Nazi government and assassinate Hitler is found most pointedly in the section of "History and Good" that treats the ethics of the extraordinary situation (*Ethics*, 272–76). See Green's helpful analysis of this material in his section entitled "Christian Ethics, Coup d'Etat, and Tyrannicide," *Sociality*, 304–21.

57. LPP 279 (DBW 8: 402).

as we strive "to become like Jesus," as we customarily say, but as the form of Jesus Christ himself so works on us that [*so auf uns einwirkt, daß*] it molds us, conforming our form to Christ's own (Gal 4:19).... To be transformed into his form is the meaning of the formation that the Bible speaks about.[58]

This for him is not the same as *imitatio*; its focus is not on action that mimics that of Jesus but on one's ever-deepening immersion into the reality of one's own life, whose center and meaning, like that of all reality, is Jesus Christ. Also, Bonhoeffer is trying to free the term of its connotations of spiritual heroics accomplished in striving to conform ourselves to Christ or, alternatively, to transform the world. In contrast, he notes that authentic formation is not something we "do" with elaborate plans, however holy, but it is done by Christ in and through us, shaping the world into his own form of justice and mercy. For Bonhoeffer, "Formation happens only from and toward this form of Jesus Christ."[59]

As noted in the passage cited above, Bonhoeffer develops this process in three stages. A person grows into *Gleichgestaltung* with Jesus in all three dimensions of Jesus' own being: as the Incarnate, the Crucified, and the Risen One. Conformation with the Incarnate One means to be completely oneself, as one is, just as Jesus himself is truly human and truly himself.

> To be conformed to the one who became human means that we may be the human beings we really are [*in Wirklichkeit*]. Pretension, hypocrisy, compulsion [*Krampf*], forcing oneself to be something different, better, more ideal than one is—all are abolished. God loves the real human being. God became a real human being.[60]

This passage seems to reflect a more positive conception of the self than Bonhoeffer's typical views. Struggling here against both forms of Nazi distortion (both the idolization and the degradation of human beings) he sees in the Incarnation a resource for the affirmation of created humanity, including one's own self, "the human being one really is."

58. Bonhoeffer, *Ethics* (DBWE 6), 93–94; emphasis Bonhoeffer's. Here Bethge added the following scriptural citations: 2 Cor 3:18; Phil 3:10; Rom 8:29; and 12:2 (see note 75 of the *Ethics*, p. 94). See also the material on "participation" in the being and reality of Jesus Christ in his section on "Christ, Reality, and Good," especially pp. 53–55.

59. Ibid., 97.

60. Ibid., 94.

Perhaps, faced with these savage idolatries of Nazism so intent on the destruction of human beings and human life, he begins to recoil from the aggressive energy of his own self-condemnation and to insist on the created goodness of that which they blindly and viciously despise. In any case, from within his by now ten years of relationship with this Incarnate One, Bonhoeffer is increasingly able to affirm in powerful Christian terms not only *others'* reality as good, in and of itself, but his own as well. Conformation to Christ depends on participation in his Incarnation precisely in one's own flesh and reality. Thus Christian formation is not separation or abstraction from our reality or that of the world into something different, "better," more "spiritual." It is instead Jesus' becoming flesh in us and drawing us ever more fully into our reality, and his own. "Christ does not abolish human reality in favor of an idea that demands to be realized against all that is real. Christ empowers reality, affirming it as the real human being and thus the ground of all human reality."[61] That is, we are conformed to Christ precisely in becoming more truly who we really are.

Here Bonhoeffer seems to be struggling toward language for affirmation of some sort of true or authentic self, as opposed to the innumerable false selves he sees glorified or condemned in and around him.[62] If conformation with the Incarnate One is the affirmation of the true self, however, then the immediately following section on conformation with the Crucified might be seen as his way to speak of the condemnation of the false self. Because he does not have language for this distinction, this second section reads like a sudden reversion to the image of the self as deserving only divine rejection, jarring in that it follows so closely

61. Ibid., 99.

62. The language of true and false self has been developed in various contemporary psychological and spiritual discourses to allow for the naming of just this sort of healing and deepening self-discovery. The terminology emerged first in the work of Karen Horney, and was then picked up by D. W. Winnicott in the psychological arena, and by Thomas Merton in the area of spiritual formation. See Horney, *Neurotic Personality of Our Time* and *Neurosis and Human Growth*; Winnicott, "Ego Distortion in Terms of True and False Self"; on Merton, see Carr, *A Search for Wisdom and Spirit*. For a contemporary psychoanalytic perspective, see Mitchell, "True Selves, False Selves, and the Ambiguity of Authenticity." Mitchell's essay and many others make clear that this terminology is not intended as a simplistic or dualistic assigning of favorable/unfavorable traits to the respective true/false selves; to use Jungian language, the true self always includes those aspects of the psyche feared, hated, and suppressed into one's "shadow" as well: the stuff of dreams, longings, obsessions, wounds, and desires.

on his statements about the sheer goodness of the self. In any case, this section represents his awareness that we do not live as fully incarnate "true" selves. Still haunted by sin and illusion, we bear these distortions in our own being, and until these are named as such we cannot hope for true freedom. Thus, although the facing of sin evokes shame and suffering, it is a means of God's liberation of human beings. Here, then, he explores bearing the marks and judgment of sin "knowing that it serves them to die to their own will, and to let the justice of God prevail over them."[63] This condemnation to death is duly accepted because those in conformation with the Crucified "recognize themselves as the greatest of all sinners. One can forgive the sins of others, never one's own."[64]

This reflection on conformation to the crucified Christ produces therefore a sort of negative meaning; that is, it means the divine negation of all that distorts human life. Mark Brocker has suggested, however, that a more substantive content for this aspect of conformation may be found in Bonhoeffer's later prison letters, namely in his desire to explore and abide within the place of the Crucified One in a broken world.[65] In these letters, Bonhoeffer is tracing in new ways the place of God in the apparently "godless" *mündige Welt* (world come of age). The omnipotent "God" of Christendom, the one the world is learning to do without, is an illusion, a *deus ex machina* whose increasing irrelevance in the contemporary world is, he argues, a gift opening space at last for the real God, the biblical God of the cross. Jesus Christ "lets himself be pushed out of the world on to the cross. He is weak and powerless in the world, and that is precisely the way, the only way, in which he is with us and helps us. . . . The Bible directs [us] to God's powerlessness and suffering; only the suffering God can help."[66] Living in conformation with such a God means, then, learning to see the face of God, and the sufferings of God, in all the sufferings of the world. And it means that the Christian being conformed to Christ, far from being preserved from pain, is drawn ever more deeply into those sufferings of God in the concrete lives and bodies and needs of those who live on the underside: "the outcast, the suspects, the maltreated, the powerless, the oppressed, the

63. *Ethics* (DBWE 6), 95.
64. Ibid.
65. Brocker, "Sharing in the Sufferings of God."
66. LPP 360–61 (DBW 8: 534).

reviled . . . those who suffer."[67] Although he does not explicitly use the term "formation" here, these letters are very much concerned with how Christians develop: "It is not the religious act that makes the Christian, but participation in the sufferings of God in the secular life."[68] Thus one might say that in prison he deepens his earlier understanding of con-formation with the Crucified One to be able here to state that "we throw ourselves completely into the arms of God, taking seriously, not our own sufferings, but those of God in the world—watching with Christ in Gethsemane."[69]

This understanding of conformation with the Crucified would then include also Bonhoeffer's understanding of Jesus as the "person for others" to the point of suffering and death and our conformation with him encompassing our "being there for others" too. Because our formation into Christ is essentially and necessarily ecclesial as well as personal, this "life for others" is a true mark of the church, in its own conformation with the Crucified: "The church is the church only when it exists for others."[70] To summarize, then, I have drawn material from both Bonhoeffer's *Ethics* and *Letters and Papers from Prison* to argue that his developing understanding of conformation with the crucified Christ includes three elements: submission to God's judgment of our distorted humanity; participation in the sufferings of God in the world; and life lived "for others," as Jesus himself did.

But our conformation is not completed here in the cross of Jesus; it moves on into his resurrection. In the *Ethics*, Bonhoeffer sees Christians' conformation with the Risen One as a "hidden" participation in Christ's resurrection: it is life, holiness, and new humanity lived in the midst of death, sin, and all that is yet unredeemed. Thus it is not yet fully seen or revealed to others. The Christian conformed with the Risen One does not call attention to his or her own holiness or withdraw into glory but lives in the world. What is actually most visible outwardly is not the radiance of resurrected life but the person's lifelong, ongoing partici-pation in the Crucified One. "Transfigured into the form of the risen one, they bear here only the sign of the cross and judgment. In bearing

67. Ibid., 17 (DBW 8:38), from the essay, "After Ten Years," written before his impris-onment, at New Year's, 1943.
68. Ibid., 361 (DBW 8: 535).
69. Ibid., 370 (DBW 8: 542).
70. Ibid., 382 (DBW 8: 560).

them willingly, they show themselves as those who have received the Holy Spirit and are united with Jesus Christ in incomparable love and communion."[71] Once again, the material only briefly developed here in the *Ethics* receives a fuller treatment in the prison letters, as we shall see; but I wonder if Bonhoeffer's reflections on the figure of John (see above), written at approximately the same time as his *Ethics*, might be an attempt to flesh out this vision of life "united with Jesus Christ in incomparable love and communion." Certainly it represents one way Bonhoeffer may have envisioned such a life.

I see two different ways conformation to the Risen One is explored in the prison letters. First, analogously to how Bonhoeffer rethinks the place of the suffering God in a "godless" world, he makes a similar move with regard to the resurrection. Far from seeing the hope of resurrection as merely a promise of release someday from this doomed world, he calls that a "mythological" view in contrast to the Christian one:

> The difference between the Christian hope of resurrection and the mythological one is that the former sends a person back to life on earth in a wholly new way. . . . The Christian, unlike the devotees of the redemption myths, has no last line of escape available from earthly tasks and difficulties into the eternal, but, like Christ himself . . . must drink the earthly cup to the dregs, and only in doing so is the crucified and risen Lord with him or her, and s/he crucified and risen with Christ.[72]

The resurrection, then, is not an "escape," not just another case of God meeting people as *deus ex machina* only at the limits of their experience. For Bonhoeffer, over and over, God is to be found at the center of human life, transforming us and the world from within, from deep in the flesh and the heart of struggle and ordinary worldly life. So, too, Jesus' resurrection does not somehow rescue us from reality but draws us ever more deeply into it, "in a wholly new way." Here and now we participate in and embody the new humanity itself; this is what taking on the form of Jesus Christ risen means.

A second dimension, in this case an image, of Bonhoeffer's conception of conformation with the Risen One comes from within the

---

71. *Ethics* (DBWE 6), 95 (translation slightly altered: "communion" [*Gemeinschaft*] for "community."

72. LPP 336–37 (DBW 8: 500–1). Translation altered for inclusivity.

broader strain of his vision of the fullness of life.[73] Far from being ob-
sessively focused solely on the "cost" of discipleship, his whole life a stoic
journey toward martyrdom, Bonhoeffer in fact loved and celebrated the
created world in many dimensions throughout his life, most poignantly
of course in his prison letters. One especially significant aspect of life
in all its fullness for him was music: his family and friends made music often, eagerly, for hours on end. Bonhoeffer himself was a skilled
pianist, and his love of hymns and music comes through clearly in the
prison letters, where remembered stanzas or not-quite-overheard radio
broadcasts evoke profound depths of emotion, comfort, grief, or joy. He
often quotes deeply loved poetic lines from hymns, and even sketches
out musical notations to remind his readers of a piece he has in mind.[74]

Thus it is not surprising, perhaps, that an image Bonhoeffer develops to evoke this fullness of life into which the resurrection of Jesus
Christ bears us is that of polyphony. Reflecting in delight on the sensu-
ality and passion of the Song of Songs, and on the Hebrew Scriptures'
great and unrestrained love of this-worldly life in general,[75] he makes
use of this musical metaphor to describe the ways he sees all our loves,
all our fully "secular" passions and vocations, taking their place in relation to God as *cantus firmus*:

> God wants us to love [God] eternally with our whole hearts—
> not in such a way as to injure or weaken our earthly love, but to
> provide a kind of *cantus firmus* to which the other melodies of
> life provide the counterpoint.... Where the *cantus firmus* is clear
> and plain, the counterpoint can be developed to its limits. The
> two are "undivided and yet distinct," ... like Christ in his divine
> and human natures. May not the attraction and importance of

73. Once again I am indebted to Mark Brocker for developing this motif of the fullness of life, although in a somewhat different context. See also Wüstenberg, *A Theology
of Life*.

74. For musical notation in the letters see DBW 8: 213, 247, 261, and 368. For mention or quotation of lines from hymnody in general, see DBW 8: 52, 57–58, 60, 72, 199,
304, 316, and 390; for reference to the hymns of Paul Gerhardt in particular, see DBW
8:44–45, 69, 99, 187, 206, 208, 265, 343, 446, 449, 515, 525, 541, 549, and 571.

75. For more on Bonhoeffer's views regarding divine and human love, eroticism,
and desire, see Zimmerling, "Gottesliebe und irdische Liebe"; and Reynolds, *Coherence
of Life Without God Before God*.

polyphony in music consist in its being a musical reflection of
this Christological fact and therefore of our *vita christiana*?[76]

This image emerges from a Lutheran spirituality profoundly nourished
over centuries, from Luther to Bach to Distler, by hymns and their musical settings. For Bonhoeffer, the image of polyphony evokes our participation in Christ whose resurrection draws us into the heart of the
world, and whose being in us is that *cantus firmus* in relation to whom
our lives' own "counterpoint has a firm support and can't come adrift or
get out of tune, while yet remaining a distinct whole in its own right."[77]
This musical metaphor proves resonant for Bonhoeffer and emerges
(not coincidentally, I believe) at just that point, namely spring of 1944,
at which his letters begin their remarkable and creative opening into
new theological territory as well. In this initial letter the metaphor of
polyphony first serves as a means of comforting Eberhard in the face
of his imminent return to the front lines ("rely on the *cantus firmus*"!)
and then re-emerges in Bonhoeffer's prayer and in later letters as well,
gradually coming to describe his joy in the multi-dimensionality of
faith.[78] Just as each contrapuntal line has its own relative independence
and musical integrity, even as it resounds over against other lines and
the *cantus firmus* itself in surprising, hidden, or revelatory ways, so too
the various innumerable aspects of our lives in the world take on their
true significance only in their ultimate relation to the One "firmly sung"
by God, namely Jesus Christ. This is, I believe, a lovely and authentically
Lutheran image of Christian conformation to the Risen One.

---

76. LPP 303 (DBW 8: 440–41). In musical terms, the *cantus firmus*, literally "firm/
solid song," refers to a melody (usually a hymn melody, carrying the consciously or
unconsciously evoked resonances of that hymn's texts as well) used as the basis of a
complex composition in many voices (*polyphony* = more than one voice). The earliest polyphonic compositions tended to have the *cantus firmus* in the tenor voice, but
by the Baroque period composers experimented with putting this central harmonic
line in all different voices. For organ compositions, very often the pedal line came to
take the *cantus firmus*, whereas many choral cantata arrangements gave the melody to
the sopranos. Regardless of the particular voice expressing it, however, in all cases the
cantus firmus functioned as the harmonic center of the composition, that in relation
to which all the other voices took their places. This is the sense in which Bonhoeffer is
using the metaphor. For more information on *cantus firmus* and polyphony see, e.g.,
Harvard Dictionary of Music, edited by Willi Apel.

77. LPP 303 (DBW 8: 441–42).

78. See DBW 8: 444–45, 453.

To summarize this material on conformation, then, in the *Letters and Papers from Prison* Bonhoeffer gives flesh in powerful and personal ways to the three-fold christological formation he first outlines in *Discipleship*. In these last written fragments from a life straining toward its fullness of conformation with the incarnate, crucified, and risen Christ, we catch glimpses of the freedom and radiant trust opening up in Bonhoeffer even as the threat closing in on him loomed ever more certain. The highly theoretical language of his early years has now fallen away completely. The fragments that escape from prison are almost exclusively written either in the second person—in personal letters or prayers—or in the form of new genres: fiction, drama, and, as the end approached, poetry. What had once been conceptual, phraseological, has become real. In prison, even the language of "conformation" of the *Ethics* now gives way to that of outright participation in Jesus' own being. Such "participation in this being of Jesus (incarnation, cross, resurrection)"[79] is for him the only authentic experience of transcendence. In one of his last letters, for Eberhard's birthday, he writes:

> The key to everything is the "in him." All that we may rightly expect from God, and ask [God] for, is to be found in Jesus Christ. ... If we are to learn what God promises, and ... fulfills, we must persevere in quiet meditation on the life, sayings, deeds, sufferings, and death of Jesus. It is certain that we may always live close to God and in the light of [God's] presence, and that such living is an entirely new life for us ... that danger and distress can only drive us closer to [God]. It is certain that we can claim nothing for ourselves and may yet pray for everything; it is certain that our joy is hidden in suffering, and our life in death; it is certain that in all these we are in a fellowship that sustains us. In Jesus God has said Yes and Amen to it all, and that Yes and Amen is the firm ground on which we stand.[80]

79. LPP 381 (DBW 8: 558). On the move from the "phraseological" to the "real," which is Bonhoeffer's way of describing the process that began in his conversion, see LPP 275 (DBW 8: 397).

80. LPP 391 (DBW 8: 572–73). He is meditating on 2 Cor 1:20, the NT verse appointed for Eberhard's birthday the following week.

Loci of Formation

The preceding quote serves as an introduction to this final section of this chapter. Here I will sketch briefly three major arenas I find in which Bonhoeffer both experienced and described christological formation taking place; all three of them are drawn together in this paragraph to Bethge. They are the Word, the Christian community (specifically the experience of friendship), and public life in the world.

Word

"If we are to learn what God promises, and . . . fulfills, we must persevere in quiet meditation on the life, sayings, deeds, sufferings, and death of Jesus." For Bonhoeffer, Scripture was the central means of grace. His conversion took place through learning to read the Gospels, and particularly the Sermon on the Mount, in a new way—that is, as personally implicating. It was here that he came to experience Jesus himself as a living presence and his Lord and that he learned to pray for the first time. From the fall of 1932 on, the language of his academic lectures and writings moved from the philosophical to the exegetical, and he began engaging in unprecedented conversations with students about their own experience of Bible study, prayer, and Jesus.[81] At Finkenwalde, he instituted two primary disciplines of scriptural prayer for the community: both communal *lectio continua* of longer sections of Scripture in morning and evening prayer (as well as extensive use of the Psalms, which he especially loved)[82]; and extended daily personal meditation on short passages. The latter practice involved the use of the *Losungen* published by the Moravian community, daily verses selected from both the Hebrew and Christian scriptures on which Bonhoeffer encouraged his seminarians to meditate for thirty minutes each day.[83] Here they were to put aside professional or exegetical concerns and ponder the texts as Word of God for them, personally, and as opening up into personal

81. See DB, 202–6, especially 204, where a student recalls Bonhoeffer describing "Holy Scripture as a love letter from God directed very personally to us."

82. See LT 51–65 on communal prayer, including both Psalms and lectio continua. In addition, see *Prayerbook of the Bible* (DBWE 5), 141–77.

83. See LT 84–89. An edition of the *Losungen* published in this country that makes explicit reference to Bonhoeffer's use of them is Mount Carmel Ministries, *Daily Texts: Bible Verses & Prayers for Each Day of the Year.*

prayer and intercession. This was a practice Bonhoeffer himself, as well as the Finkenwalde seminarians in their later dispersal during the war, found deeply sustaining.[84]

Bonhoeffer practiced a surprisingly naïve christological reading of the Bible in both Hebrew and Christian scriptures. Although he was well read in the historical-critical scholarship of his day,[85] he preferred to teach and write about Scripture in a way that emphasized its significance as Word: as making known the living Word himself, Jesus Christ. Because of his high view of the Bible as a bearer of the Word of God to human beings, he emphasized the centrality of the church's diligence in deep, personal meditation on that Word as well as in courageous proclamation of it, especially in situations of complacency or hostility. Bonhoeffer considered the Scriptures and their Lord subversive and powerfully life-giving; and fearless proclamation of the Word was thus of the utmost importance for church and world.

84. The following is an extended quotation from a circular letter written in March of 1942 to Finkenwalde seminarians and other Confessing Church members, many of them on the Russian front of the war. This quote shows the significance for Bonhoeffer of the practice of meditation on Scripture: "the silent daily reflection on the word of God as it applies to me . . . tends to become for me the crystallization of all that brings inner and outer order to my life. With the interruption and dissolution of our previously ordered life that the present age has brought about—with the danger of losing our inner order through the profusion of events, through the all-consuming claims of work and service, through doubts and moral conflicts [Anfechtung], battle and unrest of all kinds—meditation gives our life something like constancy. It preserves the connection with our former life, from baptism through confirmation to ordination; it sustains us in the healing community of the congregation, of our brothers and sisters, our spiritual home; it is a spark of the hearth fire that the congregations at home want to tend for you; it is a fountain of peace, of patience, and of joy; it is like a magnet directing all the available powers for ordering our life toward its pole; it is like pure deep water in which the heavens with their clouds and sun are radiantly mirrored. But it also serves the Most High, in that it opens for God a space of discipline and quiet, of healing order and contentment. Do we not all have a deep longing, however unacknowledged, for such a gift? Could it not become a healing power promoting renewal for us?" (Bonhoeffer, *Conspiracy and Imprisonment* [DBWE 16], 254–55) We see this throughout his time in prison, as the *Losungen* for any given day (such as the verse from Second Corinthians assigned for Eberhard's birthday) continue to nourish him and unite him with others praying with the same texts.

85. See, for instance, DBWE 16: 260–61, 277, 347, and 359 for correspondence regarding the furor evoked by Rudolf Bultmann's publication of "Neues Testament und Mythologie."

An additional aspect of this emphasis on the Word might be overlooked today. In the Nazi era, the "German Christian" state church was attempting to create a nazified Christianity purged of all Jewishness. In this milieu, where powerful forces were attempting to promote a Marcionite Bible, revisionist church history and theology, and an Aryan Jesus, Holy Family, and apostles, even something as simple as embrace of the Hebrew Scriptures was a highly political act. Thus, as naïve or oddly christocentric as its reading might appear to contemporary eyes, for Bonhoeffer to publish in 1940 a book on the Psalms, entitled "Prayerbook of the Bible," was a defiant attempt to counter such propaganda by asserting the supreme christological significance of the Psalms. Not coincidentally, the Gestapo's ban on his writing appeared shortly after this book was published. In later years, as repression and control tightened into the outright persecution, ghettoization, and annihilation of the Jews and all things Jewish, Bonhoeffer found himself drawn more and more into the Hebrew Scriptures, praying them in solidarity with Jews and finding in those chapters important resources for his own embrace of a this-worldly spirituality and resistance.[86]

In these ways, then—personally, ecclesially, and as itself a political act—Bonhoeffer found the pondering and proclamation of Scripture an essential arena of Christian spiritual formation. Here, primally and daily, we are continually being invited deeper into encounter with the Living Word, the One who is reality itself. In "quiet meditation" on all the Bible's texts and stories, and especially on "the life, sayings, deeds, sufferings, and death of Jesus," Christians find holy ground on which to stand.

Christian Community

". . . it is certain that in all this we are in a fellowship that sustains us." Throughout his life as a theologian, Bonhoeffer was centrally concerned with the church. His visit to Rome at age 17 first stirred his awareness of the church as a global reality, as opposed to the smaller regional or national churches of his acquaintance. In *Sanctorum Communio* he developed a theological sociology of the Christian church-community, and in Barcelona, New York, and London he grew to love very different

86. See, for instance, DBW 8:70–72, 188, 196, 415, 226–27, 408, 441, 499–501, 536, 548–49.

faces of the church and became a leader in the nascent ecumenical and international Christian peace movements. But it was at Finkenwalde that he experienced Christian community at its most sustained, and this community proved fertile ground for the growth of his spiritual vision.

Already in his conversion Bonhoeffer found himself consciously drawn more deeply into the church; his was always an ecclesial faith. He writes in 1936 (i.e., several years later) about the "great liberation" he experienced:

> It became clear to me that the life of a servant of Jesus Christ must belong to the church, and step by step it became clearer to me how far that must go. Then came the crisis of 1933 [i.e., Hitler's coming to power]. This strengthened me in it. Also I now found others who shared this purpose with me. The revival of the church and of the ministry became my supreme concern.[87]

These "others" were the members of the Pastors' Emergency League and later of the Confessing Church. The Finkenwalde seminary thus provided an opportunity for full-time immersion in community with these "others" who shared his vocation. In innumerable passages in later personal and circular letters, as well as in his book *Life Together*, he describes the treasure such community was and continued to be for him.

> The physical presence of other Christians is a source of incomparable joy and strength to the believer. . . . A human being is created as a body; the Son of God appeared on earth in the body and was raised in the body. In the sacrament the believer receives the Lord Christ in the body, and the resurrection of the dead will bring about the perfected community of God's spiritual-physical creatures. Therefore, the believer praises the Creator, the Reconciler and the Redeemer, God the Father, Son and Holy Spirit, for the bodily presence of the other Christian.[88]

In the circle of committed believers, living under the Word of God and knit together by means of mutual intercession, service, and respect, Bonhoeffer found new access to the incarnate life of Jesus Christ: precisely in the faces and needs and gifts—even, or especially, in the peculiarities and shortcomings—of those he loved as brothers.

---

87. E. Bethge, DB, 205. See DBW 14:112ff.
88. LT 29.

This had profound significance for him, all the more so as it made possible the surpassing gift of a truly intimate friendship. Eberhard Bethge was initially one of Bonhoeffer's students, but their relationship grew into that of one another's confessing partner and ongoing confidante. Thus within the experience of Christian community, as essential as that is, I see friendship as a further deepening of the grace and trust that Bonhoeffer experienced as so healing and revelatory.[89] And perhaps the most central aspect of this friendship and his vision of Christian community more broadly (the center of these concentric circles, one might say) is the experience of mutual confession. This practice, which Bonhoeffer introduced at Finkenwalde to incredulous seminarians, made possible a relationship of radical truth-telling and authenticity such as he had never experienced, an authenticity that for him shone of the astonishing and transforming love of God for real human beings. "God wants you as you are, not desiring anything from you—a sacrifice, a good deed—but desiring you alone."[90]

With Eberhard, Dietrich for the first time experienced the liberation of honest and mutual self-disclosure and the awesomeness of the trust and freedom this brings. This process of full self-revelation to another Christian (and to God in and through him) stirs up enormous shame and terror for him as he speaks aloud to Eberhard not merely some vague outline of his general human sinfulness but actual, concrete words, deeds, or impulses that threaten to condemn him: "By confessing actual sins the old self dies a painful, humiliating death before the eyes of another Christian."[91] And what a relief it is. Here at last is the place where that "old self" that felt so excruciatingly imprisoning for so many years can over time, confession by confession, be opened to the healing power of love. Here, I believe, is the central arena where the movement toward a new grasp of his own self, a new desire for self-knowledge and even self-love that slowly begin to make their way into his writings, was born and made possible for Bonhoeffer. Here at last, for the first time in his life, he experienced non-judgmental presence simultaneous with

89. E. Bethge, "Bonhoeffer's Theology of Friendship." See also *Conspiracy and Imprisonment* (DBWE 16), 134–36, 138–42: these four letters written between Dietrich and Eberhard for Dietrich's birthday, February 4, 1941, provide moving reflections from each of them on their abiding pleasure in this friendship.

90. LT 108.

91. Ibid., 111.

the most vulnerable self-disclosure he had ever attempted; in fact, he realized that such self-disclosure before God and a trusted other was profoundly healing.

> In the presence of another Christian I no longer need to pretend. In another Christian's presence I am permitted to be the sinner that I am, for there alone in all the world the truth and mercy of Jesus Christ rule.... Every pretense [comes] to an end in Christ's presence.[92]

Of course, it was not only in being deeply heard by Eberhard that Dietrich found consolation but also in the privilege of receiving Eberhard's confession and trust, learning the rich pleasure of listening to a friend at that level as well. The Finkenwalde community produced many abiding bonds for Bonhoeffer, not only the one with Bethge. As these skills of self-opening and of listening bore fruit in him he found his loneliness easing and the goodness of human community deepened for him, to the point that he risked his life in 1939 to return to just this community, leaving the safety of New York to share the fate of his people, his church.[93] To be a Christian, to be himself, meant to be with the church that was his home. For him, there can be no solitary Christian formation; the life of the church is constitutive of the Christian.

Public Secular World

"...danger and distress can only drive us closer to [God]." For Bonhoeffer, living in the "world come of age," the days of a separate church sphere pure and preserved from the world's sinfulness were over. He saw this gratefully as the end of an un-Christian, indeed idolatrous illusion. If we take seriously that Jesus Christ *is* reality, there is no need to separate church from world, sacred from secular, spiritual from political; the church is called not to otherworldly purity but to the messy worldly, political activity of proclaiming and embodying the justice and mercy of God;[94] for his time this was revolutionary. His is a fully worldly vision

92. Ibid., 109.

93. This may have contributed as well to his emotional readiness for engagement to marriage. For more information about Maria von Wedemeyer, including her own reflections on her relationship with Bonhoeffer, see Schindler, "Verhaftet und verlobt"; and Wind, "'Es war eigentlich nur Hoffnung.'"

94. For more on Bonhoeffer's developing views of an utterly this-worldly spirituality, see Wüstenberg, "'Religionless Christianity.'"

of Christian spiritual formation as well. "Ethics as formation, then, is the venture of speaking about the form of Christ taking form *in our world* . . ."[95] And in his sermon for the baptism of his new godson, Dietrich, Eberhard and Renate Bethge's firstborn, he writes from prison that the task of the church in this new era (today often called "post-Christian") is simple, deceivingly modest: "prayer and doing justice in the world."[96] This action for justice, like the conspiracy against Hitler, is meant to be carried out in creative partnership between all people of good will, not only Christians. The church's task here is not its own self-promotion but in the most ordinary, "secular," or political ways promoting the mercy and justice of God revealed in Jesus Christ.

All this adds up to an embrace of the "this-worldliness" of Christianity for Bonhoeffer: "it is only by living completely in this world that one learns to have faith. . . . By this-worldliness I mean living unreservedly in life's duties, problems, successes and failures, experiences and perplexities. In so doing we throw ourselves completely into the arms of God, taking seriously, not our own sufferings, but those of God in the world."[97] In particular as those accustomed to privilege learn to view history "from below," from the perspective of those on the underside of history, the secular world of real personal, social, economic, and political relationships becomes in and of itself an arena for profound Christian formation. Here is where Christians exercise their daily-discerned vocations; here they let their gifts find faithful and responsible use; here they learn to love and be loved across religious, social, and cultural barriers, in the midst of ambiguous and challenging circumstances. This is the world from which Christianity provides no escape hatch, but *in* which Jesus Christ encounters and forms people in reality. The living call of Jesus Christ encountered in the Word, nurtured and discerned in prayer, tested and lived out in community, is meant for the world and for its redemption. And the experience of such daily, usually un-heroic action for justice opens Christians to reality, and thus to their Lord, in unexpected, "unchurchy" encounters. In hidden or dra-

---

95. Bonhoeffer, *Ethics* (DBWE 6), 102. Emphasis added.

96. Translation altered from LPP 300. The German reads, "im Beten und im Tun des Gerechten unter den Menschen" (DBW 8: 435). Geffrey Kelly's essay on Bonhoeffer's spirituality takes this phrase as its point of departure: "Prayer and Action for Justice."

97. LPP 369–70 (DBW 8: 542).

matic ways, the self-effacing church well nurtured in secret[98] meets and embodies this Lord in the world.

The Word of God, the Christian community especially in radical truth-telling in friendship, and vocation in the public world are for Bonhoeffer the three primary arenas of Christian formation, as I see them. Without any one of these, his spirituality would have lost something essential to its very being. But in them, all three held together in a living unity, he offers the church a spirituality simultaneously personal, ecclesial, and worldly.

Conclusion

From his conversion through the end of his life, Bonhoeffer experiences, articulates, and attempts to live out an increasingly expansive Christian vision. By the end of his life, he has moved quite a distance from *Sanctorum Communio*'s heady and self-constricted perspective. Yet the fundamental overarching contours of that work and worldview accompany him in both liberating and narrowing ways throughout his life. His love of Christian community and insight into the fundamental sociality of the human person evidenced in *Sanctorum Communio*; his great respect for the mystery of human individuality; his insistence on the essential particularity and concreteness of truth; and his longing for a christocentric liberation from the loneliness and illusion of distorted selfhood—these will continue to guide and shape his spirituality in life-giving ways all his life. Yet simultaneously, his fundamental blindness to the problem of patriarchy and the pervasive ways in which his gendered social location shapes and hampers his analysis of the self/other relationship will likewise persist, undermining the direct applicability of many of his categories for those in less privileged circumstances.

The following quote from *Sanctorum Communio* provides an early glimpse of the vision that animated Bonhoeffer's whole life: his particular (and therefore also limited) vision of redeemed selves in a redeemed community.

> Whereas even in the church the I and the You still encountered each other as strangers . . . here [i.e., in the blessed community]

98. On the *disciplina arcana*, see DBW 8: 405, 415, 435. Also see Pangritz, "Aspekte der 'Arkandisziplin' bei Dietrich Bonhoeffer" and Poole, "Bonhoeffer and the Arcane Discipline."

the revelation of one heart to the other is fulfilled in divine love. *The community of love becomes visible in hearts who, filled with the Spirit, reveal themselves to one another.* "I and I seek and find one another, and pour themselves into each other. . . . reality and truth become the same. . . ." Here we see love is completed, that is, that we only attain our "self" when we no longer see our own person. And this takes place precisely in the most intimate community with the other, a community that may be described as blessedness. . . . *It is the most powerful expression of personal life itself.*[99]

His vision of the community of redeemed blessedness is also simultaneously the ultimate fulfillment of human personhood, the full attainment of the new humanity inaugurated by and in Jesus Christ. It is a lovely picture he presents, one where the ceaseless ethical confrontation of his earlier view of community has given way to the deep rich intimacy of mutual self-revelation. It is here at last, then, that Bonhoeffer is able to speak of the "self" (*Selbst*) as a positive good, though only when one no longer sees one's own "person" (*die eigene Person*). As always for him, the gaze is directed away from oneself, toward God and the other. Thus, not surprisingly, even in his vision of redemption his orientation toward the relative positioning of God, self, and other is preserved.

Bonhoeffer's spirituality is powerful, opening him to life in the effacement of the false self that imprisoned him. He articulates a vision whose heart is the discernment of reality as that is concretely encountered and mediated by Jesus Christ, and life lived in the world in correspondence with that reality. It gains its greatest and most direct authority from its applicability to others of similarly privileged social location and, given its particular contours, is particularly destructive when naïvely applied to those whose selves are already effaced. In the next chapter we will encounter a radically different approach to the mystery of human selfhood, one that begins with and derives its authority from the experience of women, particularly women in abusive relationships.

---

99. *Sanctorum Communio* (DBWE 1), 288. Bonhoeffer's italics. He is citing Reinhold Seeberg, *Ewiges Leben* (1915), 33.

4

Gender, Selfhood, and Abuse

Introduction

DESPITE THE ADVANCES FEMINISM HAS CREATED FOR WOMEN IN IN-numerable areas in contemporary society, the reality of violence against women persists. Worldwide, at least one-third of all women are beaten or forced into non-consensual sex at some point in their lives, and one woman in four has been abused during pregnancy.[1] Additionally, "at least 60 million girls who would otherwise be expected to be alive are 'missing' from various populations, mostly in Asia, as a result of sex-selective abortions, infanticide or neglect."[2] Millions of women are tricked or sold into sexual slavery around the world, and "honor kill-ings" claim thousands annually, usually murdered by members of their own families.[3] Even in the U.S., where feminism has made great strides, similar patterns hold true. According to statistics from many sources, a woman in the U.S. is beaten every 15 seconds in the home,[4] and at least

1. United Nations Population Fund, *Lives Together, Worlds Apart*, 25. Hereafter ab-breviated "UN Report." On the next page, the document also lists selected statistics of intimate physical assault by country. In India, for instance, 40% of women report such abuse; other countries' percentages include South Africa (20); Ethiopia (45); Bangladesh (47); Cambodia (16); Papua New Guinea (67); Mexico (27); Nicaragua (28); Egypt (34); Canada (29); U.S. (22); and Switzerland (21). See also the powerful accounts collected in *Women Resisting Violence: Spirituality for Life*, edited by Mary John Mananzan et al., regarding gender, violence, and cultural patterns in many worldwide contexts (Latin America, Africa, India, and North America).

2. UN Report, 25.

3. Ibid., 29.

4. National Coalition Against Domestic Violence, *National Coalition Against Domestic Violence Fact Sheet*. Online: http://www.ncadv.org/files/domesticviolencefacts.pdf. And: http://www.ncadv.org/resources/FactSheets_221.html. Accessed March 29, 2008.

four women are killed every day by their partners.[5] By some estimates this adds up to two to four thousand women per year.[6] Domestic violence is far and away the primary cause of injury to women and a leading cause of death: the overwhelming majority of women murdered are killed by men they know, 80% of them in their own homes.[7] Domestic violence is also a leading contributing factor in women's depression and suicide.[8] Nearly half of all women will experience at least one incidence of rape or battering in an intimate relationship,[9] compounded by the dynamics of verbal, emotional, and psychological abuse (which brutalizes women even in relationships where physical violence is minimal). Fifty percent of all homeless women and children are refugees from domestic violence, as overflowing "safe houses" and shelters are forced to turn many away.[10] The list of "crimes" for which women are routinely attacked and tortured is eerily similar around the world: "not obeying the husband, talking back, refusing sex, not having food ready on time, refusing to care for the children or home, questioning the man about money or girlfriends, or going somewhere without his permission."[11]

The experience of selfhood for women who have suffered such injuries, especially over the course of years or decades in the home, takes on a very different cast than that experienced and reported by Bonhoeffer from his position of privilege. This chapter will examine several contemporary psychological perspectives exploring the effects of traditional gender socialization on girls and women, with particular attention to how patterns of domination and submission are perpetuated psychologically and socially, and how these patterns (especially when manifested in abuse) degrade women's selfhood. The fundamental questions guiding this chapter are:

5. Fiorenza, "Ties That Bind," 40; this statistic comes from the National Coalition Against Domestic Violence. She cites here Bean, *Women Murdered by the Men They Love*, 6.

6. Cooper-White, *Cry of Tamar*, 102, citing among others Stout, "Intimate Femicide," 3.

7. Women's Action Coalition, *WAC Stats*, 56.

8. UN report, 25, 28–29.

9. Cooper-White, *Cry of Tamar*, 108, citing the California attorney general. On this statistic, see also Walker, *Battered Woman Syndrome*, ix; and Straus et al., *Behind Closed Doors*.

10. Fiorenza, 40.

11. UN Report, 26.

1. What factors in gender socialization and psychological development make women vulnerable to abuse (and men prone to violence)?

2. What happens to women psychologically in abuse?

3. What do survivors of abuse need in terms of healthy psychological formation?

In the past thirty years or so female psychologists and theoreticians have begun to examine and re-think fundamental assumptions of human psychology, arguing that from its outset in the groundbreaking work of Sigmund Freud, psychoanalytic theory has allowed the experience of traditionally socialized males to define what is normatively "human."[12] In Freud's work itself, centered on the growing boy's experience and resolution of the Oedipal crisis, the world is cast in a decidedly patrilinear mode. Jessica Benjamin notes,

> What is extraordinary about the discussion of authority throughout Freudian thought is that it occurs exclusively in a world of men. The struggle for power takes place between father and son; woman plays no part in it, except as prize or temptation to regression, or as the third point of a triangle. There is no struggle between man and woman in this story; indeed, woman's subordination to man is taken for granted, invisible.[13]

Power resides in the father and is transmitted, however painfully, via the father-son relationship. The goal of the boy's development is disentanglement from the world of women and lust for the mother, and the capacity to take his place in the world of men. Though Freud considered the adult man's capacity for healthy intimacy with women to be an important feature of mature psychological development, he unquestioningly assumes that such relationships will take place within and perpetuate patriarchal family structures. Furthermore, he rarely leaves

12. This re-claiming of the Freudian and post-Freudian tradition has taken various forms within feminist critique more broadly. In addition to those psychologists who will be the primary contributors to this chapter, see for a broader overview of this conversation Diane Jonte-Pace's review of five key feminist theorists in "Psychoanalysis after Feminism." For an overview of feminist contributions to the psychology of religion in particular, see also her "New Directions in the Feminist Psychology of Religion," and Miller-McLemore, "Shaping the Future of Religion and Psychology."

13. Benjamin, *Bonds of Love*, 6–7.

the boy/man world long enough to consider women as subjects of their own development rather than simply as "objects" of the male world.[14] Freud's forays into explanations of observed phenomena of women's psychological experience either recoil sharply from the horrifying implications of such observation (as in his early work with those suffering from "hysteria")[15] or merely describe the effects on girls and women of life in a world inexorably ruled by men (as in his theory of "penis envy").[16]

Despite Freud's assumption of a broadly androcentric reality, however, women in the fields of psychology and psychoanalysis have begun to name and question the male normativity regnant in the field and to develop alternative models of psychological development that attempt more adequately to reflect the actual experience of girls and women.[17] Some of the most popularly-read thinkers in this area include Jean Baker Miller and the Stone Center theorists[18] and Carol Gilligan and her team of Harvard researchers.[19] Both research collectives have made

14. Benjamin writes, "The mother stands as the prototype of the undifferentiated object. She serves men as their other, their counterpart, the side of themselves they repress" (ibid., 77). From this primal developmental matrix evolves a psycho-social system whose hallmark is the "assignment of subject status to male and object status to female" (ibid., 81). In fact, she asserts, "[f]or Freud, woman's renunciation of sexual agency and her acceptance of object status are the very hallmark of the feminine" (ibid., 87). In this section she is drawing on Freud's "The Dissolution of the Oedipus Complex," *Standard Edition of the Complete Psychological Works* (hereafter SE), 19: 173–82; "Some Psychical Consequences of the Anatomical Distinction Between the Sexes," SE 19: 43–58; "Female Sexuality," SE 21 (1931): 7–174; and his lecture "Femininity" in *New Introductory Lectures on Psycho-Analysis*, SE 22 (1933): 3–182. On this motif of woman as the "object" in traditional psychoanalytic theory see Benjamin 7f., 23–24, 60–61, 76, 81, 89, 99, 109. See also Burgin, "Object."

15. See Herman, *Trauma and Recovery*, 17–20, on Freud's discovery (and later repudiation) of memories of incest among those suffering from hysteria.

16. Mitchell, *Psychoanalysis and Feminism*, was an early advocate of the feminist retrieval of Freud, including such theories as penis envy, precisely because Freud elucidates so clearly what actually happens to women in patriarchy. On penis envy, see the works of Freud cited above (note 14).

17. See pp. 10–11 of chapter 1 on the adequacy of language about "women's experience."

18. Many of the Stone Center's *Works in Progress* have been gathered into two anthologies. See Jordan, et al., *Women's Growth in Connection*, hereafter abbreviated *WGC*, and Jordan, ed., *Women's Growth in Diversity*.

19. In particular, I will make use of Brown and Gilligan, *Meeting at the Crossroads*. See also Gilligan, et al., *Making Connections*; Gilligan, et al., *Women, Girls, and*

substantial contributions toward their shared goal of pushing psychologists to speak more precisely about *whose* experience underlies their theories and simultaneously whose experience is being discounted or overlooked. They have initiated lines of questioning that have then created space for even more far-reaching explorations of gendered psychological development. Thus I will give an overview of both research teams' work as that relates to my project, but my central focus will be the psychoanalytic work of Jessica Benjamin, which addresses at this more fundamental level the formation of psychological structures of domination and submission and their perpetuation in society over time.[20] These feminist approaches will provide a theoretical basis on which to understand the complex psychological factors shaping many girls and women in ways that make them vulnerable to abuse. Specifically, these theorists illuminate aspects of the formation of soluble selfhood; and Benjamin in particular will be helpful in showing the radical distinction between such soluble or submissive selfhood and the complementary formation of separative or dominating selfhood, such as that which was characteristic of Bonhoeffer.[21]

Following this developmental overview of contemporary feminist approaches to the formation of selfhood in girls and women, I will look at the second primary question of this chapter, namely "What happens to women in abuse?" This section will rely on the work of Judith Herman, a prominent psychiatrist in the emerging field of trauma studies.[22] It will examine the psychological devastation that takes place under conditions of sustained abuse, such degradation of selfhood both exemplifying and exacerbating the submissive or masochistic stance described

---

Psychotherapy: Reframing Resistance; and Taylor et al., *Between Voice and Silence: Women and Girls, Race and Relationship*.

20. This section will center on Benjamin's ground-breaking study, *The Bonds of Love*. More recent texts that further develop aspects of her thinking are *Like Subjects, Love Objects*; and *Shadow of the Other*.

21. Note that Benjamin herself does not use "soluble/separative" language. Nevertheless, this terminology grounded in Keller's mythic-theological world describes well the respective shapes of the submissive and dominating selves Benjamin carefully delineates, as well as the distinctions between stereotypical patterns of female and male behavior noted by Miller and Gilligan, et al. See pp. 12–14 of chapter 1 for more on this terminology. For an analysis of the contemporary category of gender and its fluidity, see, e.g., Davis et al., *Handbook of Gender and Women's Studies*.

22. Herman, *Trauma and Recovery*.

by Benjamin. Finally, the chapter will conclude with an exploration of the relevance of this psychological material for the spiritual formation of women, especially women in abuse.

Feminist Perspectives on Psychological Development

Stone Center

The publication in 1976 of Jean Baker Miller's *Toward a New Psychology of Women*[23] marked a watershed in contemporary psychological thought. Here, for the first time, was a theorist who attempted to understand women in terms of their strengths and important human gifts rather than only as defective deviations from male-normed definitions of psychological health. In subsequent years, Miller was joined by other similarly interested researchers at the Stone Center for Developmental Services and Studies at Wellesley College, formed in 1981. In a series of *Works in Progress*, these researchers (whose core includes besides Miller also Judith V. Jordan, Alexandra G. Kaplan, Irene P. Stiver, and Janet L. Surrey) have for decades been expanding Miller's project of reclaiming women's psychological strengths, validating as assets those characteristics of women previously dismissed as defects. Rather than condemning women for being, e.g., "too dependent on outside feedback," the Stone Center researchers affirm women's capacities to pick up on others' feelings or needs and their deeply rooted desire to address those. They deconstruct the regnant image of the autonomous Lone Ranger as the model of psychological health and the goal of development; instead, they assert, women model a different image of healthy selfhood, one that is actually constituted in relationship by means of skills of empathy, compassion, and nurture. This project of exploring and reclaiming women's relationality has had the effect of naming and validating these skills as psychologically and culturally invaluable. Yet, as we will see, these researchers often seem to idealize how women are socialized to behave in relationships rather than looking critically at what is healthy and life-giving for them. Thus I cite the Stone Center research in part because of its ground-breaking nature in opening up the field of women's psychology to actual women's experience and gifts, yet

23. Miller, *Toward a New Psychology of Women.*

also because it illustrates some of the problems of women's traditional (and idealized) socialization into "relational selves."

The Stone Center theorists suggest that this "self-in-relation"[24] (or, even more fluidly, "being-in-relationship")[25] is formed by girls' early being taught skills of listening and care by their mothers. Here the mother, by teaching the daughter to care for her and to grow in addressing the mother's emotional needs, initiates her daughter into a sense of self whose well-being depends on the simultaneous thriving of others for whose care she feels responsible. Janet Surrey writes,

> Through the girl's awareness and identification with her mother as the "mothering one" and through the mother's interest in being understood and cared for, the daughter as well as the mother becomes mobilized to care for, respond to, or attend to the well-being of the other. . . . In fact, part of learning to be a "good enough" daughter involves learning to be a "good enough" mother or "empathic relator" *to one's mother* and later to other important people. This ongoing process begins to allow for experience and practice in "mothering" and "relational caretaking."[26]

Thus, in their view, women's relationally oriented selfhood, whose boundaries extend broadly to encompass the well-being of many others,[27] is no liability but in fact a desperately needed antidote to the

24. Many of the essays in the volume *Women's Growth in Connection* contain capsule summaries of this perspective. For more in-depth surveys, see Miller, "The Development of Women's Sense of Self," *WGC* 11–26; and Surrey, "The 'Self-in-Relation': A Theory of Women's Development," *WGC* 51–66.

25. Miller comes to find the term "being-in-relationship" preferable to "self-in-relation," since the latter still implies a level of distinction between self and others, while the former attempts to capture in language the ambiguous, participial (is it a verb? is it a noun?) self-immersion in relationship that her theory describes: "a 'being-in-relationship'. . . . [is] a sense of 'self' that reflects what is happening *between* people" (Miller, "Development of Self," 13). Emphasis Miller's.

26. Surrey, "Self-in-Relation," 56–57. Emphasis added.

27. The following quotes are typical. "[F]or women, the primary experience of self is relational, that is, the self is organized and developed in the context of important relationships." Surrey, 52. "Being in relationship, picking up the feelings of the other and attending to the 'interaction between' becomes an accepted, 'natural-seeming' way of being and acting. It is learned and assumed; not alien or threatening. Most important, it is desired; it is a *goal*, not a detraction or a means to some other end, such as one's own self-development. . . . The girl's sense of self-esteem is based in feeling that she is a part of relationships and is taking care of those relationships." Miller, "Development of Self," 15–16. Emphasis Miller's.

ruthless individualism to which male-normed Enlightenment culture
and mainstream twentieth-century psychology have contributed.

The Stone Center writers are careful at times not to let this relational diffusion lead into a fatal "solubility." Judith Jordan's work on
empathy insists that authentic empathy requires the existence of a
stable and well-boundaried self in reference to which the listener can
truly experience the story of another.[28] And in their clinical examples
(which universally describe women for whom the diffused selfhood
they and the culture promote in fact leads to relational entrapment,
career floundering, and/or major depression) the Stone Center writers describe their therapeutic insistence on learning new skills of *self*-
empathy, boundaries, and the ending of harmful bonds. Surrey, in fact,
who in her theoretical work ("Self-in-Relation") focuses on the development of women's idealized relational capacities with others and explicitly dismisses categories of separation or individuation for women,
includes in a short description of *clinical* work, in the very same volume,
subsections on learning to attend to oneself, the necessity of separating,
and differentiation.[29]

Yet these laudatory clinical emphases rarely translate into theoretical assertions. With the exception of occasional caveats, as in Jordan's
work on empathy and boundaries, Surrey's re-definition of relationship
as necessarily mutual rather than exploitative,[30] or Miller's later study
of relational violence,[31] by and large these authors insist that women's
relational strengths and other-inclusive experiences of selfhood are
psychological assets needing only to be validated and embraced by the
culture at large. They continue to aver that women's socialization for primary focus on others is ultimately "empowering," as women experience
such care from one another. And despite the centrality in their clinical
examples of precisely these needs for women in depression or abuse, in
their theoretical writings they consistently dismiss values like "separation," "individuation," or "autonomy" as patriarchal and unhealthy for
women (or men).

28. Jordan, "Empathy and Self Boundaries," *WGC*, 67–80.

29. Surrey, "The Relational Self in Women," *WGC*, 35–43. See also Miller,
"Development of Self," 22ff., for an extended clinical example.

30. Surrey, "Self-in-Relation," 61–63.

31. Miller, *Connections, Disconnections, and Violations.*

> What this new model emphasizes is that the direction of hu-
> man growth is not toward greater degrees of autonomy or indi-
> viduation and the breaking of early emotional ties, but toward a
> process of growth within relationship, where both or all people
> involved are encouraged and challenged to maintain connec-
> tion and to foster, adapt to, and change with the growth of the
> other.[32]

The viewpoints expressed in this sentence are repeated over and over in
these writings: the dismissal, on the one hand, of focus on "autonomy
or individuation," along with the emphasis, on the other hand, on relationality and connection as the highest positive values. What is chroni-
cally omitted from this exposition, however, is the ability to maintain
connection with *oneself*, as well as always only with "the other." Yet precisely this is the central need underlying the problems presented by the
women in the clinical examples.

In a sense, then, despite their feminist orientation and attention to
women and their development, the Stone Center researchers' theoretical
writings read as if their real intended audience were male, as if it were in
fact the male-dominated psychological establishment they are addressing and criticizing. In attempting to reclaim and promote "women's"
psychological values and strengths for a culture that has all too little
compassion and empathy, they seem to be focusing much more on what
men need to learn from women than on psychological perspectives that
might best serve the actual entrapped women themselves. Celebrating
"women's relationality" will not help readers who are oblivious to their
own needs while already exclusively fixated on others.

In fact, in a trenchant critique, Marcia Westcott suggests that
the Stone Center researchers' naïve-seeming reclaiming of "women's"
capacities is more ominously a validation of traditional roles, blind to
the devastating distortions of selfhood patriarchy inflicts on girls and
women. She writes,

> The problem occurs through their abstracting the mother-
> daughter relationship from the wider patriarchal contexts in
> which this bond is actually cultivated, and then idealizing the
> relationship as if it were free of patriarchal influence. . . . The

---

32. Surrey, "Self-in-Relation," 60.

consequence is a mystification of the patriarchal interests that
are served by women's empathetic and relational traits.[33]

Far from initiating girls into a lifetime of mutually-supportive and
empowering relationships, the mother-daughter patterns extolled by
Surrey and others represent a terrible violation of the mother's parenting role of her daughter, forcing the girl from a young age to sacrifice
her own needs in development and instead attend to her mother's emotional needs which of course are largely unmet by herself, her husband,
or society.

In her work on the mother-daughter relationship, Janet Surrey in
fact writes,

> Within the early mother-daughter relationship, the daughter
> is encouraged to learn to take the role of the mother (or, we
> could say, the "provider," the "listener," or "surround") as well as
> the daughter (the "receiver," the "speaker," or the "figure"), de-
> pending on the needs of the situation or the individual at any
> given time. We have called this the "oscillating mother-daughter
> introject."[34]

With Westcott, I agree that such statements, far from providing a
positive and empowering model of parenting in fact suggest terrible
damage to the child by forcing her from an early age into inappropriate "mothering" roles.[35] Needless to say, when such emotional abuse is
compounded by concomitant physical or sexual abuse of the girl by
either parent, very little if any space remains for the sort of attention
to the *child's* needs that is supposed to be the whole point of parenting.
Westcott writes,

> if a girl learns through being sexualized that she is an object
> to be used for male pleasure or purposes, she learns that les-
> son again from the devaluation of her efforts to become a self-
> directed human being. Sexualization of a girl's body transforms
> her desire into desirability; devaluation of her agency shifts the
> fulfillment of *her* needs into a wish to be valued through *meet-*

33. Westcott, "On the New Psychology of Women," 10.

34. Surrey, "Self-in-Relation," 58.

35. Westcott's critique of this aspect of the Stone Center analysis is found on pp.
11ff.

ing the needs of others. These two forms of treating a girl as an object rather than a subject thus mirror one another.[36]

But even in "normal" families where narcissistic abuse is confined to the emotional realm, girls pay a steep price for their early lessons in the necessity for survival of attending to the needs of others rather than their own. Westcott asserts, in fact, that the "self-in-relation" praised by the Stone Center is in fact a disfiguring facade, a "false self" created by patriarchal family structures. Here she is making use of Karen Horney's distinction between authentic or "true" selfhood and idealized or "false" selfhood.[37] That is, Westcott

> interpret[s] the Stone Center's concept of the self-in-relation as a form of the compulsory feminine. . . . The relational, altruistic qualities that the daughter then exhibits do not inform the flowering of some true female self [as the Stone Center theorists assert], but express the acquiescence to a caring and self-abnegating femininity that the mother herself needs.[38]

Such altruistic and empathetic females do not threaten the status quo; their ongoing self-sacrifice ensures not only that males will be attended to (so that they can appear to be "independent" in the world[39]) but also that the girls' own overlooked emotional needs will perpetuate this pattern, when they grow up, into the next generation of daughters.

I find Westcott's critique of the Stone Center self-in-relation theory enlightening. These theorists' apparent blindness to the destructive origin and effects of the shape of female selfhood they are attempting to valorize undercuts its adequacy as a tool for resistance to such culturally enforced selflessness. Nevertheless, the self-in-relation model does function as a description of precisely how *in fact* many female selves

36. Westcott, "On the New Psychology of Women," 13 (emphasis added).

37. See Horney, *The Neurotic Personality of our Time*, 119–20; and *Neurosis and Human Growth*, 168. See also note 62 of chapter 3 for more on true and false self.

38. Westcott, "On the New Psychology of Women," 15.

39. See Stiver, "Work Inhibitions in Women." There she writes, "The successful man gets cared for, and the successful woman is considered to be someone who can take care of herself" (226). Ironically, of course, this prototypical "independent" man is in fact utterly dependent on the behind-the-scenes care of his wife, girlfriend, and/or assistants. His female counterpart, who is assumed to care for herself, is discouraged from doing so in reality since she is supposed to "be there for others." So, in many cases, *no one* is caring for her, including herself! To add insult to this, of course, she is depicted as "dependent" for being so other-focused and nurturing.

are groomed from early childhood for their care-taking role, with all the ambiguity about boundaries and thwarted capacities for clarity, anger, self-defense or separation that accompany this. In later studies on depression,[40] anger,[41] and power,[42] the Stone Center authors begin to explore the negative implications of the traditional female socialization they promote. As in the disjunction between theory and clinical praxis in the earlier essays, however, even these more nuanced considerations of the actual effects on women of life within patriarchy not only fail to call into question the adequacy of the self-formation assumed but in their very analysis continue to use these problematic self-in-relation categories.

Kaplan, for instance, develops at length the overlapping similarities between traditional female socialization and the characteristics of women in depression. She writes, "the frequency of depression in women suggests that depression may not be an 'illness' superimposed on an alien or indifferent personality structure, but rather may be a distortion—an exaggeration of the normative state of being female in Western society."[43] Yet despite this powerful statement she never seems to consider whether this might call for a re-casting of the researchers' theories of women's development to allow for focus on and expression of long-suppressed anger, selfhood/individuation, desire, and agency. One of the few places in the book where anyone addresses the problems with the relational model they are developing is Miller's essay on anger. There she writes, "The problem is that these very valuable [relational] strengths have not developed in a context of mutuality, and they have not been complemented by the full right and necessity to attend to one's own development as well."[44] But even this observation does not result in a call for a less exclusively other-focused trajectory for women's development.

Throughout the volume, the authors speak glowingly of the empowering, authentic, and pleasurable dimensions of such other-focused mutual relationality. In the next section, however, we will see in Gilligan's

40. Kaplan, "The 'Self-in-Relation.'"
41. Miller, "Construction of Anger in Women and Men."
42. Miller, "Women and Power."
43. Kaplan, "The 'Self-in-Relation,'" 207.
44. Miller, "Construction of Anger," 185.

work some of the real-life effects on girls of growing up in, and into, the bewildering other-oriented world of patriarchal femininity. Here, far from the idealized depictions of mutually empathic and fulfilled female selfhood, is a different view of what actually happens to girls facing enormous pressures pulling them away from clarity of selfhood and into submersion, i.e., "being-in-relationship."

Carol Gilligan and the Harvard Researchers

For the last twenty years, Carol Gilligan has been a leading researcher in feminist psychology as well. Her publication in 1982 of *In a Different Voice*[45] pointed out the androcentric bias of influential theories of developmental psychology of her day and is often cited alongside Miller's *Toward a New Psychology of Women*, and Nancy Chodorow's *The Reproduction of Mothering*,[46] as a key text in the arena of feminist-inspired psychological research that has burgeoned since the 1970's. With colleagues at Harvard and elsewhere, Gilligan has increasingly moved into empirical studies of girls and teenagers, looking carefully and compassionately at the psychological shifts, contortions, and distortions that become evident during female adolescence. Their studies have made possible a level of detailed analysis of the actual shape of girls' lives that belies the Stone Center's portrayals of idealized mother-daughter relationships blossoming into empowered mutual relationality among girls and women.

In *Meeting at the Crossroads: Women's Psychology and Girls' Development*,[47] Gilligan and her colleague Lyn Mikel Brown describe the results of one such study, a longitudinal project at a girls' school in Cleveland, in which a team of eight researchers conducted annual interviews for five years with girls across a range of ages. Working especially with the central metaphor of *voice*, the researchers trace subtle and striking shifts in the tone, resonance, and clarity of these girls' voices across these years. They write,

45. Gilligan, *In a Different Voice*.

46. Chodorow, *The Reproduction of Mothering*.

47. Brown and Gilligan, *Meeting at the Crossroads*. See also reviews by Gold, "Book Forum: Review of *Meeting at the Crossroads*"; and Charmaz, "Book Reviews: *Meeting at the Crossroads*."

> Voice is central to our way of working—our channel of connection, a pathway that brings the inner psychic world of feelings and thoughts out into the open air of relationship where it can be heard by oneself and by other people. . . . Voice, because it is embodied, connects rather than separates psyche and body; because voice is in language, it also joins psyche and culture. Voice is inherently relational . . . yet the sounds of one's voice change in resonance depending on the relational acoustics: whether one is heard or not heard, how one is responded to (by oneself and by other people).[48]

They pay attention in their extended interviews to the connections between the girls' experienced voice (including a clear "I"), in its presence or absence, and the extent of described and observed freedom and authenticity in relationships. At the same time, they trace the presence of competing "voices" in the girls' psychic worlds, as the received authoritarian voices especially of parents and teachers, and the standards and values of patriarchal culture itself, come to be internalized.

Over the course of these interviews, the Harvard team witnessed striking losses of voice among the girls. The clarity, honesty, and relational boldness of the seven- and eight-year-old girls they interviewed have become muffled by age eleven; and with older girls, whose interviews began at age twelve and proceeded until age sixteen, the confusion and distress of negotiating bewildering relational worlds becomes even more dramatic. Using images of a "wall" or "abyss," Brown and Gilligan posit, in fact, a profound "relational impasse" or "crisis" that pre-adolescent and older girls run up against, a crisis that severely undercuts their psychological health and capacity for free and powerful action in the world even as they are progressing normally or even precociously in other cognitive developmental skills. They write of the girls in their study,

> When their voices are muted or modulated, when their experience is denied, their reality questioned, their feelings explained away, girls describe a relational impasse—a sense of being unable to move forward in relation with others, a feeling of coming up against a wall. The fears and confusion, the ambivalence and uncertainty, which many girls in our study give voice to seem to us not simply the natural consequences of the move from child-

48. Brown and Gilligan, *Meeting at the Crossroads*, 20. Here they are drawing also on the work of Kristin Linklater, *Freeing the Natural Voice*.

hood into adolescence, as some might suggest, but also a sign of
a truly disturbing and perplexing experience: a feeling of having
to not know what one knows, of losing one's mind, of building a
shield, an experience of losing voice and relationship.[49]

Such widespread self-silencing, they note, occurred across cultural
and economic lines at the school they studied, although some girls of
color or of minority ethnic heritages seemed better equipped to notice and resist these pressures, perhaps because of culturally and/or
parentally taught resistance to other forms of prejudicial silencing. It
was among "the girls in our study who, because of color or class, live
in the margins. . . . [that] we found many of our staunchest resisters" to
these pressures.[50] This is not universally true: the two girls of Middle-
Eastern and of Indian heritage highlighted in their study reflect the
same painful encounter with imposed standards of perfection as most
of the Caucasian girls they cite. And, of course, other girls whose culture
or class places them on the margins of society can find these additional
pressures, and the anger they cumulatively generate, unbearable rather
than inspiring of either resistance or the effort to fit in.[51]

To illustrate some of the features of the adolescent relational impasse the Harvard team is hypothesizing, I will use the example of one
of the girls they interviewed, whose pseudonym in the book is "Liza."
Liza is one of nine students (three at each age level) whose interviews
are described in more depth in the study in order to focus on distinctive
dynamics in different girls, dynamics that are nonetheless considered
representative of patterns characteristic of many.[52] In Liza's case, notable
features include her developing anorexia and the abusive dynamics of
her relationship with her boyfriend. In both these arenas, and their signaling of radical dissociation from her body and perceptions, she might

---

49. Brown and Gilligan, *Meeting at the Crossroads,* 160–61.

50. Ibid., 226.

51. On these dynamics of race and class, cf. ibid., 69, 72–73, 225–27. For more explicit attention to these patterns as they interlink with gender formation, see Taylor et
al., *Between Voice and Silence.*

52. Her story is found on pp. 203–14. Liza was twelve at the time of the first interview and fourteen at the final one. Her story thus picks up at the point in chronological
development where some of the younger girls' stories leave off.

be seen as an extreme case of the debilitating psycho-social tendencies manifest among all the girls interviewed.[53]

A pervasive and central feature of Liza's distress is her inability to perceive or name what she knows. This "not knowing" is one of the dominant motifs the researchers trace throughout all the interviews. In contrast to the clear and free assertions of the youngest girls (ages 7 and 8), who simply state what they observe and perceive, by their pre-teen years the girls move into a markedly more hesitant, confused discourse punctuated repeatedly by the phrase "I don't know." This excerpt from a thirteen-year-old named "Judy" is typical: when asked by her interviewer why it feels impossible to consider talking with her family about their painful dynamics, she says,

> I don't know, because I don't—I don't know. I mean, I do know. I just like—I can't explain it. I don't know what, how to put it into words.
> *[Interviewer: "What does it feel like? Or what does it look like?"]*
> I don't know, it's just like if—I don't know, it's like, I don't know, I can't even begin to explain it, because I don't even know if I know what it is. So I can't really explain it. Because I don't know. I don't even know like in my brain or in my heart, what I am really feeling. I mean I don't know if it's pain or upsetness or sad—I don't know.[54]

In Liza's case, the researchers note that at age twelve her interview contained an astonishing *154* "I don't know"'s.[55] As Judy's example above indicates, this speech pattern also demonstrates pronounced hesitancy, agonized self-contradiction ("I don't know ... I mean, I do know ... But I don't know"), and a sort of doubled-over garbling of syntax that makes

53. "Liza" comes from a privileged background and is Caucasian. Another student, "Victoria," also a Caucasian, may be seen to represent a different form of painful coping with the pressures of her life, in her case by acting out and running with a "bad" crowd. Both these girls are attempting to survive impossible and crippling expectations in their lives, though by very different means: Victoria's "shield" of rage is a far cry from Liza's "cover girl" strategy. Yet both are seen by the researchers as especially vulnerable to abuse (150–51, 155–56, 158; 214–15). For Victoria's story see pp. 141–59.

54. Ibid., 135. "Judy" is a very sensitive girl who elsewhere in her interviews is straining to find language to describe the sort of "knowing" she has experienced slipping from her. Tellingly, her segment of the narratives is entitled, "Judy: Losing Her Mind" (123–40).

55. Ibid., note 12, chapter 5, 241.

straightforward utterance nearly impossible. In many cases, nearly the
only "I" that remains in their speech is this "I" who "doesn't know." More
and more, they speak of a generalized and abstract "you," who as the
researchers point out is the internalized voice of authority and social
norms that comes to dictate the girls' relationship patterns and even
their perceptions of their experience.[56] All these patterns show up over
and over in the girls' speech as they move toward and into adolescence,
bearing witness to the painful inner contortions to which they are experiencing themselves subjected in the world.

The following example from Liza's speech manifests several aspects
of this, both the garbled syntax and "not knowing" and the characteristic consuming concerns of the girls:

> You're either more careful about what you say or you are sort
> of faking it, you know. You are faking . . . I don't know. Like if
> you are, I don't know, if you're sort of like thrown together with
> someone you try to, like, adapt to like them, so I don't know. You
> just sort of have to, I don't know, sometimes, if you know you are
> not going to get along by being yourself.[57]

Note that, although this speech seems almost to make no sense at all, Liza
herself is a bright girl who has always excelled in school; her problem is
not insufficient command of basic English syntax. Rather, this is typical
of how these girls speak, with an excruciating self-consciousness that
renders them nearly unable to use language as a tool of self-expression
or agency. Liza's words also testify to the consuming urgency for these
girls of being liked, of liking everyone, of fitting in, of being perceived
as nice and agreeable. What matters in their world is in fact not self-
expression at all ("you are not going to get along by being yourself");
what matters is conforming oneself to the perceived expectations of
others ("you try to, like, adapt to like them"), or of social norms in general that dictate appropriate female behavior in stifling ways.[58]

These dynamics are enacted in equally toxic ways in Liza's dating
relationship. She has become involved with an emotionally abusive and
controlling boyfriend four years her senior, and she is unable to tell him

56. See, e.g., ibid., 166, 174, 177.

57. Ibid., 208.

58. These are not merely "Liza's" problems; such patterns are documented in detail throughout the book. See, for instance, the introductions to the older girls' stories
("Approaching the Wall," 89–107; and especially "Rivers into the Sea," 163–85).

of her discomfort with his jealousy and coercion. Instead, she decides that his controlling tendencies are signs of his "love" for her and reinterprets her version of reality to assert that her initial attempts to set boundaries to protect herself were immature and "irrational."[59] Liza is reluctant to ask him to back off,

> for fear of making him "really mad . . . He acts sort of like, 'You are going out with me and that's it,'" she explains, "and I don't know." She decides to "let it"—meaning her feelings—"go" for a while, "put [my wishes] out of my mind," she says, "contradict" herself, by which she means override her voice, change her priorities, and, because "I wasn't sure of his reactions, so I didn't tell him . . . He could have gotten mad, he could have gotten upset. I mean, I didn't know what would come, you know, I didn't know what would come of it."[60]

Here, "I don't know" and the desire to adapt oneself in order to be liked take on ominous overtones of self-sacrifice to avert the threat of violence, in order to maintain a romantic relationship that, while oppressive and potentially destructive, is apparently preferable to no relationship. The Harvard study provides a glimpse of how choosing relationship with others at the cost of faithfulness to oneself (which as they note is ubiquitous in the literature of women's psychology [61]) takes root in the psyches of pre-adolescent girls, with devastating consequences.

Corresponding to this sweeping movement from knowing to not knowing, Liza and the other girls also demonstrate therefore a movement from seeing, perceiving, and naming their experience to a position of *being* seen and evaluated. The locus of authority to name reality shifts from within themselves to an outside source of judgment, as that both comes to them in their friends', parents', teachers', or culture's evaluations of them, and as those external voices are progressively internalized into the girls' own psyches. In her study of women and depression, Dana Jack formulates this as a shift from the clear and authoritative "I" to a focus on the "Over-Eye" of ever-scrutinizing and relentlessly judging cultural norms: "The Over-Eye carries a decidedly patriarchal flavor, both in its collective viewpoint about what is 'good' and 'right'

59. Ibid., 213.
60. Ibid., 211.
61. Ibid., 176.

for a woman and in its willingness to condemn her feelings when they depart from expected 'shoulds.'"[62]

The Harvard researchers note this shift as well in Liza. By age thirteen, it has become rare in her increasingly complicated and rigidified existence to hear her speak using clear "I" language about an unstructured and spontaneous moment; and this moment doesn't last.

> As Liza overrides this "I" with the "eye" of the culture, and her girlfriends for the "true friend relationships of boys," she exchanges those rare experiences of spontaneity, times when she feels "impulsive," "so natural," and like her "true self," for a maturity which sounds forced, artificial, and fake. . . . Equating her relationship with her boyfriend to getting in a car with a drunk driver, Liza conveys what she cannot say directly—her fear that she is in a life-threatening situation.[63]

Liza cannot say this directly because she has lost most of her access to her own feelings and perceptions of reality, let alone the capacity to take these seriously as the basis for potentially disruptive speech and action. Instead, she bases her self-evaluations on her perceptions of others' impressions of her, and she is pleased with that perception and with others' startled reactions to her new blonde hair and extreme thinness at age fourteen.

> Liza's appearance (or disappearance) is striking. Becoming thinner and thinner has changed . . . her social life, especially her relationship with her boyfriend and her best friend. Through visual metaphors she positions her self and her relationships in space and time: "I am all around better looking," she says, speaking again of how she has changed over the year. "[Me and my boyfriend] drive around in [a sports car] together," she says, explaining why her best friend calls their relationship "perfect." "You know, we look good together, have a good relationship."[64]

Liza's description of what it means to "have a good relationship" means that she and her violent, controlling boyfriend, of whom she is afraid, "look good together." She is trying desperately to conform to the image of perfection promulgated by media, culture, and norms of popularity (and, with no less authority, by parents and teachers who praise the self-

62. Jack, *Silencing the Self*, 94.
63. Brown and Gilligan, *Meeting at the Crossroads*, 210.
64. Ibid., 212.

sacrificing and obedient girls and discipline the outspoken or "disruptive" ones).[65]

In a fascinating reflection on the stories of Liza and the other older girls, the Harvard team speculates on this movement "from flesh to image,"[66] i.e., from the loud, assertive, demanding, and unselfconsciously honest younger girls, whose voices are rooted in their embodied clarity of perception, to the increasingly breathless, voiceless speech of the adolescent girls whose inner entanglements seem to stem from the impossible burden of conformation to the image of "the perfect girl."[67] Yet for all her apparent power as an icon of identification, this perfect girl is also marginalized. She is unreal, dissociated from body and feelings and speech and rudeness and flesh, "for images, unlike bodies, do not know or speak";[68] she is merely the passive object of the omniscient and omnipotent external gaze. In striking language that demonstrates the imprisoning power of this position as "image," i.e., as merely an "object" of others' scrutiny, they describe Liza as "[h]eld in place by the gaze of others and now by her own self-observing ego."[69]

The researchers mention no girls who escape these pressures toward silence, duplicity, niceness, and bodily/psychic dissociation from emotion and experience. Even those who most successfully find ways to resist these damaging expectations expend enormous amounts of energy doing so and/or sacrifice status or relationships in order to hold on to their own integrity. Those girls develop the capacity for "political resistance," i.e., for staying in touch with and speaking the truth of their own experience even in the face of powerful and suffocating pressures

---

65. The researchers describe the impact on girls of observing these dynamics in themselves and others, of "seeing them[selves] favored by their teachers and praised by their parents when they dissociated or dissembled" (218; also, in the case of a young girl, 45–47), and eliciting anger and punishment when they attempted to bear witness to reality as they perceived it (186–87, 190–91).

66. Ibid., 168. Here Brown and Gilligan are making use of a paper by Deborah Tolman and Elizabeth Debold ("Made in Whose Image?") that explores this "move from embodiment to image" and its enormous psychological costs for girls.

67. "The Perfect Girl" is their heading for the story of "Neeti," an Indian girl (195–203); but they use this image of idealized perfection often in their descriptions of the impossible standards to which many of the girls interviewed aspired.

68. Brown and Gilligan, *Meeting at the Crossroads*, 168, citing Tolman and Debold.

69. Ibid., 212.

to the contrary.[70] For instance, Anna, a working-class student, at twelve and thirteen is following the familiar trajectory of her peers (multiplying "I don't know"'s, self-enforced silence, suppression of anger and other "unacceptable" feelings in order to fit in). But at age fourteen she has given up the attempt to conform and has become "outspoken," willing to express herself freely to teachers and classmates. By sixteen, from her position increasingly outside the social mainstream, she is able to detect and name inauthenticity as she perceives it and to accept the anger, caricature, and exclusion this provokes from others as the price she pays for her own clarity of vision and speech.[71]

But most of the girls surveyed fall somewhere between Anna, with her clear-eyed capacity for truth-telling, and Liza, whose aspiration to fulfillment of the ideal image forces her into extreme dissociation from her body and her deepest perceptions. To greater or lesser degrees, in varying configurations, all the girls bear psychic wounds from running up against this "wall," this encounter at early adolescence with the pressures of a patriarchal culture intent on forming them into selfless, compliant, "nice" women. The researchers write, in their summary of their findings,

> Honesty in relationships began to seem "stupid"—it was called "selfish" or "rude" or "mean." Consequently, a healthy resistance to losing voice and losing relationship, which seemed ordinary in eight-year-old girls and heroic by age eleven, tended to give way to various forms of psychological resistance, as not speaking turned into not knowing and as the process of dissociation was itself forgotten. . . . [They] enacted this disconnection through various forms of dissociation. . . . so that *some girls came to ignore or not know signs of emotional or physical abuse.* . . . Girls, we thought, were undergoing a kind of psychological foot-binding. . . . People, as many girls were told, did not want to hear what girls know.[72]

70. The researchers distinguish such "political resistance," which characterizes a healthy capacity for speech and action in correspondence with reality, from "psychological resistance" that is unhealthy. The latter term refers to the strategy by which many girls "resist" or deny the truth of their own experience, in favor of the culturally-promoted values being forced upon them. See page 30.

71. Brown and Gilligan, *Meeting at the Crossroads*, 185–94.

72. Ibid., 217–18. Emphasis added. The language of psychic "wounds" or "scars" is found on p. 219.

Thus these interviews point precisely to the link between patriarchy and women's characteristic psychological difficulties that the Stone Center research tends to obscure. They provide a window into the enormous psychic costs of female socialization and reveal "the relational lies that are at the center of patriarchal cultures: subtle untruths and various forms of violation and violence that cover over or lead to women's disappearance in both the public world of history and culture and the private world of intimacy and love."[73] Even more horrifyingly, they reveal ways this disappearance takes place fundamentally in the psychic world of girls' own inner reality itself. As these interviews demonstrate, the greatest devastation occurs when girls disappear *to themselves*.[74] This historical, social, and psychic "disappearance" of women takes on manifold forms: from the 60 million girls now "missing" worldwide due to sex-selective abortion, infanticide, and neglect,[75] and millions more women throughout history killed by fanatics or family members; to victims of eating disorders like Liza, in which healthy "fleshy" girls shrink away into shadows, wisps; to the cosmic level itself, devoid of femaleness in God the Father, Son, and Holy Spirit, not coincidentally ruling a male-dominated world and church, "His" Word resounding in a "male-voiced" culture.[76] On the links between such patriarchal culture and the voice of "morality," Brown and Gilligan write,

> Morality, or the voice that speaks of how one should or would like to act in relationships, became of interest to us . . . insofar as moral language carries the force of institutionalized social norms and cultural values into relationships and psychic life. Listening to girls' voices, we heard the degree to which morality, in a male-voiced culture and a male-governed society, justifies certain psychologically debilitating moves which girls and women are encouraged to make in relationships and creates

73. Ibid, 218.

74. "Women's psychological development within patriarchal societies and male-voiced cultures is inherently traumatic. The pressure on boys to dissociate themselves from women early in childhood is analogous to the pressure girls feel to take themselves out of relationship with themselves and with women as they reach adolescence," 216. Thus for both girls and boys dissociation from the female (i.e., oneself or the other) triggers crisis, often leading to depression.

75. See note 2 of this chapter.

76. On the image of a "male-voiced" culture, playing on the researchers' central metaphor of "voice," see especially 21, 29, 216, 218.

internal as well as external barriers to girls' ability to speak in relationships and move freely in the world.[77]

Thus the Harvard studies provide an important glimpse of how girls' socialization shapes and deforms them psychologically in ways that cause tremendous pain throughout their lives, and thereby initiates them into a world in which their reality as authentic human subjects is invisible or trivialized. But the work of Gilligan and her colleagues raises a more fundamental question, namely what developmental or intrapsychic factors may make girls susceptible to precisely this erasure of themselves from relational, social/political, and cosmic "reality." In asking this question, I take note of Pamela Cooper-White's important caution against thereby seeming to blame the victim for her own traumatic oppression, due to "flaws" in her psychological make-up.[78] Nevertheless, I believe that the Harvard team's work does not go far enough in laying bare the psychic roots of traumatic gender socialization, with all its lifelong ramifications. How are male/female conceptions of selfhood, power, violence, and agency first shaped in ways that might make "political resistance" difficult for girls? For insight on this question I turn to the feminist psychoanalytic work of Jessica Benjamin. Having begun this chapter with the Stone Center's writings on adult women, and moved "back" in time developmentally through the Harvard center's studies of school-age girls, we will continue with Benjamin into gender dynamics in infancy and early childhood that, she asserts, shape both girls and boys into self-perpetuating patterns of submission and domination both mirroring and reinforcing the broader patriarchal shape of society.

Jessica Benjamin

The psychoanalytic work of Jessica Benjamin provides an explanatory framework for understanding the mutually reinforcing phenomena of domination and submission as these take shape in individual psyches and as they are played out socially in a patriarchally-configured world. Far from being "located" merely in ultimately impersonal structures of evil, nor solely in the selfish will to power of oppressors, domination and submission root in widespread patterns of gender-linked social-

77. Brown and Gilligan, *Meeting at the Crossroads*, 21.
78. Cooper-White, *Cry of Tamar*, 118.

ization. Benjamin's framework is intended to blame neither abuser nor victim of abuse for their part in enacting these roles but to make clear on a developmental psychoanalytic and social-cultural level how these roles take such persistent shape in human life, as well as the tremendous cost of their ongoing perpetuation. She writes, "This book is an analysis of the interplay between love and domination. It conceives domination as a two-way process, a system involving the participation of those who submit to power as well as those who exercise it."[79] In fact, rather than contributing to a "victim-blaming" mentality (that women end up in abusive relationships because they are somehow defective or passive "victims" of others' violently-imposed subjugation), Benjamin's work sees those who suffer under domination as fully human and acquiescent participants in a complex, deadly psychological complementarity to which they see no alternative. The very persistence of shifting patterns of domination and submission throughout history makes all this seem somehow inexorable, the nature of things. We often see no alternative, Benjamin asserts, because "domination [is] a system that transforms all parts of the psyche"[80] and is passed down to each new generation of children from their earliest, preconscious introduction to the world and their place within it. Yet, she asserts, feminism now does provide just such an alternative, illuminating and criticizing the normativity of male authority that traditional psychoanalysis had accepted without question:

> [T]he contemporary consciousness of women's subjugation has profoundly challenged the acceptance of authority that permeates psychoanalytic thinking. Feminism has provided a fulcrum for raising the Freudian edifice, revealing its foundation to lie in the acceptance of authority and gender relations. Thus what appeared in Freudian thought as the psychological inevitability of domination can now be seen as the result of a complex process of psychic development and not as "bedrock."[81]

The fundamental psychological problem underlying ever-perpetuating systems of domination is one of inadequate differentiation on the part of both mother and father, forcing them to assume complementary

79. Benjamin, *Bonds of Love*, 5.
80. Ibid., 4.
81. Ibid., 7.

rather than mutually subjective stances toward one another and thus to enact these roles also with their children. The rampant use of "object" language in traditional psychoanalysis, for those relationships of which the bond to one's mother is paradigmatic, is telling in Benjamin's view.[82] It betrays the fundamental male-oriented perspective that all reality revolves around the (male) infant, the boy, the man, the father; and that women exist to serve the primary needs of these males, as themselves the selfless loved or hated "objects" of male gaze and desire, rather than as subjects of their own development, agency, and desire. Indeed, the very concept of "mother" seems a polar opposite from that of a "self"; the idea of mothers setting clear limits to their children's demands, simply for their own sake as human beings with lives of their own, seems "selfish," impossible to reconcile with the vision of the ideal mother, who is by definition selfless and who transcends such needs. Yet Benjamin argues that in fact the entrenched and guilt-inducing image of the selfless mother is harmful not only to the mother herself but also to the children who thus grow up with a primary caretaker who is no-self, selfless, rather than with an actual subject able to both receive and grant the mutual recognition central to the children's own healthy psychological development. Traditional theories are inadequate in their sole

> view of the mother as the baby's vehicle for growth, an object of the baby's needs. . . . She is external reality—but she is rarely regarded as another subject with a purpose apart from her existence for her child. . . . Yet the real mother is not simply an object for her child's demands; she is, in fact, another subject whose independent center must be outside her child if she is to grant him (*sic*) the recognition he seeks.[83]

Benjamin thus does see an alternative to patterns of domination and submission, and develops an intersubjective approach that sketches a different developmental route: one of "mutual recognition." The vision of mutual recognition suggests that from earliest infancy both parent and child participate in a relationship to which each contributes; in

82. See note 14 of this chapter.

83. Ibid., 23–24. Throughout her work, Benjamin alternates male and female pronouns in reference to the child in cases where no confusion with the mother ("she") is possible. Where she is speaking of both mother and child in any given sentence or section, she uses the male pronoun for the child.

which each becomes deeply attuned to the other's presence, feelings, and desires; and in which each experiences her- or himself as a subject able both to influence and to respond to the other.[84] When successful in any given interaction, this state of mutual recognition is experienced by both infant and parent as highly pleasurable, as they engage with one another by means of sounds, touch, gaze, and body language in complex forms of play and intimacy.[85] Even an infant's needs for withdrawal or lessened engagement can be a means for pleasure, if the parent responds neither with an insecure further imposition of his or her own intimacy needs, overwhelming the already overstimulated baby, nor with abrupt termination of time together, punishing the baby with abandonment. A parent who is able to remain with the child even as s/he turns away provides the baby with the reassuring experience of companionship even in the baby's need for solitude. This is the "holding space" (Winnicott) so important for the baby's development of a distinct sense of self, as s/he becomes able, in the presence of a trusted but non-intrusive other, to experience her or his own feelings as real and separate from those of others.[86] This interplay of engagement and companionable solitude, of becoming attuned to the other and simultaneously aware of oneself, describes what Benjamin means by mutual recognition, a form of development that of course changes in complexity over the course of the child's growth but that ideally retains this inherently intersubjective character, both parties able to experience their own authentic subjectivity in the presence of the other. It is a very different model from traditional psychoanalytic conceptions of the infant as "passive" and "helpless,"[87] unable to contribute to or help shape the relationship with the mother but entirely at her mercy. Here the mother-infant relationship is characterized primarily by the mother's meeting (or not meeting) insatiable needs; and the child's (especially the boy's) further development is marked by ever-increasing and unilateral separation from this all-providing yet shapeless and overwhelmingly powerful mother.

84. Some of the primary infancy research Benjamin cites includes D. Stern, *First Relationship*, and *Interpersonal World of the Infant*; Lewis and Rosenblum, eds., *Effect of the Infant on Its Caregiver*; and Goldberg, "Social Competence in Infancy."

85. On this section, see Benjamin, *Bonds of Love*, 27–29.

86. Cf. Winnicott, *Maturational Process and the Facilitating Environment*.

87. See Benjamin, 16–18, on Freud and others.

Healthy human development, according to Benjamin's theory, rests on the capacity of both individuals in a relationship to sustain over time an essential balance or tension: that between self-assertion and recognition of the other as a separate subject.

> Assertion and recognition constitute the poles of a delicate balance. This balance is integral to what is called "differentiation": the individual's development as a self that is aware of its distinctness from others. Yet this balance, and with it the differentiation of self and other, is difficult to sustain. In particular, the need for recognition gives rise to a paradox. . . . The self can only be known by his (*sic*) acts—and only if his acts have meaning for the other do they have meaning for him. Yet each time he acts he negates the other, which is to say that if the other is affected then he is no longer *identical* with what he was before. To preserve his [own] identity, the other resists instead of recognizing the self's acts ("Nothing you do or say can affect me, I am who I am").[88]

This paradox can be formulated also in this way, that "at the very moment of realizing our own independence, we are dependent upon another to recognize it."[89] Following Hegel's analysis of the development of master-slave relationships, Benjamin asserts that "domination and submission result from a breakdown of the necessary tension between self-assertion and mutual recognition that allows self and other to meet as sovereign equals."[90] When this breakdown of tension occurs, as it inevitably does, then what had been a relationship of two fully human subjects (taking into account the enormous differentials in power, need, and responsibility between parent and child) devolves into a bond in which one party alone is permitted to be a "subject," marked by over-emphasized self-assertion, while the other party becomes an "object," minimizing self-assertion and over-emphasizing recognition of the other.

The dissolution of the healthy balance between self and other can go either way. Some children are treated in such a way that the child's insistent demands for recognition, as self-assertion begins to flower in early toddlerhood, are met with the unconditional and unwavering

88. Ibid., 12, 32.
89. Ibid., 33.
90. Ibid., 12.

attentiveness of the "perfect mother," the perfect "mirror," who asserts no boundaries of her own selfhood and distinctness in response.[91] This parental stance does the child no favors, however, for it deprives the child of a real boundary and a fully and pleasurably subjective other to whom to relate. Instead, it reinforces the child's grandiose but terrifying fantasies of his or her own omnipotence, or self-assertion moving out of control. The debilitating illusion that accompanies this experience is then that the other, on whom one depends for life, does not truly exist.

> The child who feels that others are extensions of himself must constantly fear the emptiness and loss of connection that result from his fearful power. Only he exists; the other is effaced, has nothing real to give him. The painful result of success in the battle for omnipotence is that to win is to win nothing: the result is negation, emptiness, isolation.[92]

What strikes me here is the clear resonance of these images with the experience of the empty, isolated, "omnipotent" self described by Bonhoeffer in both autobiographical and formal writings, as we saw in chapter two. In fact, many of Benjamin's descriptions of this personality and the experience it engenders read like citations from Bonhoeffer himself: the empty isolation the person experiences, the "bubble" of the self, the illusion of one's own mastery of reality, etc.[93] This provides further corroboration of the thesis that Bonhoeffer himself wrote from

91. Benjamin's criticizes the "mirror" terminology of self-psychology: "The mother cannot (and should not) be a mirror; she must not merely reflect back what the child asserts; she must embody something of the not-me; she must be an independent other who responds in her different way" (24). Also, see Gilligan, "Remapping the Moral Domain," for a further feminist critique of "mirroring" language.

92. Ibid., 35.

93. This sort of language occurs throughout Benjamin's book in reference to the dominating or aggressive form of selfhood traditionally formed in boys. Cf. Benjamin, 67–68, 69–71, 83, 163, 190–91. Here are characteristic phrases and images with resonance to Bonhoeffer's descriptions of the human person: the experience of "the self encapsulated in a closed system—the omnipotent mind" (67), "unable to make 'live' contact with outside reality" (68) from within "the bubble of the self" (195). The "omnipotent self [is] imprisoned in his mind, reflecting on the world from behind a wall of glass" (190). The deepest wish of such a person is "to get outside the self into a shared reality" (73), "to break the encasement of the isolated self" (83). This sort of dominating self is marked by "grandiosity and self-absorption . . . flying off into space [with] . . . no limits, no otherness. The world now seems empty of all human life, there is no one to connect with, 'the world is all me'" (70–71). Later in the book, she notes that the "damage . . . [inflicted] on the male psyche . . . [is] disguised as mastery and invulnerability" (161).

within the experience of what both Benjamin (here) and Green (earlier) call "dominating" selfhood.[94] Yet that this form of selfhood, far from being universal, exists only as one-half of a complementary dynamic enmeshed with "the other [who] is effaced" means that Bonhoeffer's experience, while real and powerful, is different from those at the other end of this spectrum.

For in contrast, some mothers or early-childhood caregivers allow the balance between self-assertion and recognition to break down in the other direction. For fear of spoiling the child, these mothers ensure that the child knows very well his or her clear limits and the penalties for violating them. In this scenario, the child is expected to grant full and obedient recognition to the mother's wishes but is granted extremely limited capacities for his or her own self-assertion in testing these boundaries. The child learns that self-assertion is met with punishment and gravely jeopardizes the all-important relationship on which survival depends. In this case, then, the fantasy of omnipotence reinforced by the breakdown of healthy self-other tension is not that of the self, who is effaced, but of the mother and the unbending moral universe she represents. In the face of the mother's lack of recognition, the child's experience is that the self does not truly exist. Again in this case the rich pleasure of real encounter is lost as the child learns that the longed-for recognition comes not through the assertion of one's actual desires, feelings, or needs but through obedience and conformity to the other's wishes: the other is the only "subject" allowed in this relationship. The child will

> continue to see the mother as all-powerful and himself as helpless. In this case, the apparent acceptance of dependency masks the effort to retain control by remaining connected to the mother ("I am good and powerful because I am exactly like my good and powerful mother wishes me to be"). This child does not believe he will ever gain recognition for his own independent self, and so he denies that self.[95]

94. Note that I intend by this attribution to Bonhoeffer of "dominating" selfhood not to speculate about the dynamics of his relationship with his early caregivers (a nurse, governess, and his mother). Rather I simply wish to point out the uncanny similarity between Benjamin's and Bonhoeffer's descriptions of the experience of such a self and to suggest that this itself suggests his location there.

95. Ibid., 53. On p. 36, she writes of this scenario, "the parent remains omnipotent in her [i.e., the child's] mind."

As different as these two scenarios are in terms of their effect on the growing child, they share a basic commonality in dissolving the balance between self and other in favor of one or the other party. "In both cases the sense of omnipotence survives, projected onto the other or assumed by the self; in neither case can we say that the other [or the self] is recognized."[96] In Benjamin's view, then, these fundamental breakdowns in favor of other or self, as they take shape in early childhood and are reinforced throughout life, set the stage for the child's formation in the stance of submission or domination. But these are not the only factors at work, for this alone would not explain the gendered structure of these patterns.

At this point in the argument, two other factors come into play in addition to the sweepingly maternal nature of parenting in infancy and very early childhood described thus far: the role of fathers and of the broader culture. As Benjamin describes the "rapprochement" crisis of toddlerhood (age 18 months or so), it is essentially a drama of mother and child as the growing baby's needs for recognition and self-assertion are played out against the primary caretaker's limits; by and large, the primary caretaker is still typically the mother.[97] It is at just this point, however, that fathers begin to play a new role in their baby's development. While the mother's role tends to be one of nurturing, holding, and ordinary intimate caretaking in all the minutiae of the child's physical and emotional needs, the father comes onto the scene as the more "exciting" parent, a diversion from the intensity and exhaustion of the primary relationship. He is more playful, more stimulating, throwing the child into the air, running around the house or yard. Also, significantly, he (still) tends to bear more of the thrilling scent of the outside world,

96. Ibid, 36.

97. Note that throughout her discussion Benjamin presupposes a traditional family structure. She does this not because she is unaware of contemporary family patterns, which often look very different. In fact she states at various points that it will be interesting when today's children have become parents to see how these psychological dynamics may have shifted as a result. But she is examining the traditional post-industrial nuclear family of working father and stay-at-home mother partly because, even with working mothers, these underlying dynamics still hold true, and partly because this is still the cultural norm so that its effects shape children raised in very different-appearing families. At the end of this section I will raise further questions about this, but for now let me simply note that her analysis is helpful also for the reason that this is the family pattern within which Bonhoeffer himself was raised, and which he endorsed all his life.

seemingly less bound to the maintenance and comforting but confining messiness of the home.

And the father plays an important role in providing an alternative emotional reality as well. His recognition of the child allows the child to identify with him positively as precisely such an exciting and worldly alternative, for both boys and girls, to the mother's care alone.

> The father's entry is a kind of *deus ex machina* that solves the insoluble conflict of rapprochement, the conflict between the desire to hold onto mother and the desire to fly away. . . . [T]he father has been experienced by both boys and girls as the original representative of excitement and otherness. Now, as the child begins to feel the wish and the excitement as his or her own *inner desire*, he or she looks for recognition from this exciting other. While the child doubtless seeks recognition from both parents at this time, the exciting father is the one the child wishes to be *like*.[98]

Thus the father's recognition of the child provides a separate focus for the child's identification, enabling a broader sense of the child's selfhood especially in the direction of desire, autonomy, and worldly agency. This is also the point (in toddlerhood) at which children's conceptions of gender (their own and others') begin to come into focus. Yet precisely this new complicating factor of gender in the child's experience and in the dynamics of paternal recognition can have debilitating effects on daughters in particular. This is not due to girls' inability to identify with their male parent and reap the emotional benefits of such identification, for at early ages both boys and girls appear able and eager to identify with persons of both genders; and for healthy psychological development they need to be able to do so, and to have their identification confirmed in turn. Conceptions of gender are still fluid and shifting, not yet rigid or exclusive.

Rather, the factors making healthy and empowering paternal recognition of girls so difficult appear to be a function of fathers' own relative lack of interest in their daughters.

> [F]athers often prefer their boy infants; and, as infants respond in turn to parental cues, boy infants tend to form an intense bond with their fathers. The father recognizes himself in his son, sees him as the ideal boy he would have been; so identifica-

---

98. Benjamin, *Bonds of Love*, 104–5.

tory love plays its part on the parent's side from the beginning. The father's own disidentification with his mother, and his continuing need to assert difference from women, make it difficult for him to recognize his daughter as he does his son. He is more likely to see her as a sweet adorable thing, a nascent sex object.[99]

On this point of many fathers' difficulty in identifying with their daughters, another psychoanalyst, Doris Bernstein, writes, "To the extent that the father's individuation rests on the biological base of difference from mother, to the extent that he mobilized or continues to mobilize the 'no, I am unlike' to maintain his autonomy, the more *unable* he is to permit or welcome his daughter's identification with him as he is his son's."[100]

This obvious or subtle rejection of a girl's attempts at identification with her father has harmful effects. Benjamin writes, "The thwarting of an early identificatory love with the exciting outside is damaging to any child's sense of agency, in particular to the sense of sexual agency. . . . Unfortunately, this solution has the cast of normalcy for women."[101] The girl suffers the loss of an exciting, stimulating other whose validating recognition affirms her own developing capacities for will, power, desire, and agency; this is devastating enough, for any child, as Benjamin notes. In addition, however, she learns that this painful absence of recognition, this invalidation of her desire and independence, is inexorably tied to her gender. For her there is no identificatory alternative to the mother, for whom, as we have seen, agency, power, and autonomous selfhood are noticeably downplayed. The child's anger at this non-recognition, finding no outlet but only a confusing gender-based explanation, becomes turned against herself and her inability to merit recognition from her father or to deserve more of a self than her mother is permitted. On this, Benjamin notes, "the mother's lack of subjectivity, as perceived by both male and female children, creates an internal propensity toward feminine masochism and male sadism."[102]

Thus the gender patterns revealed in the mother's selflessness and the father's lack of recognition shape girls in powerful ways, teaching

99. Ibid., 109. On fathers' preferences for sons, she cites Lamb, "Development of Parental Preferences," and Gunsberg's literature review on the subject in "Selected Critical Review of Psychological Investigations of the Early Father-Infant Relationship."

100. Bernstein, "Female Superego," 196. Emphasis in original.

101. Benjamin, *Bonds of Love*, 115–16.

102. Ibid., 81.

them that the locus of desire and agency cannot be found within themselves but must be sought through an other. The girl goes through life seeking from the internalized father image, and his substitutes, the access to power denied her at an early age. This explains, for Benjamin, the phenomenon explained by Freud with the term "penis envy," namely the girl's longing for the male prerogatives symbolized by the "missing" sexual organ. Rather than a wish to be male necessarily, let alone merely for its physical icon, she asserts that girls are longing instead for the father himself in his capacity to validate her own human selfhood and desire. In conjunction with the selfless mother, it is the "missing father" whose absence creates the often-reported void where women's own desire, will, and agency ought to be, access to which is possible only vicariously, through becoming the object of another's desire and will. The destructive effects on girls' psyches glimpsed by Freud's "penis envy" take place

> when the father himself is "missing"—that is, when he is absent, not involved, or offers seduction rather than identification. . . . I conclude that the little girl's "lack" is the gap left in her subjectivity by the missing father. . . . Thus, I believe, for women, the "missing father" is the key to their missing desire, and to its return in the form of masochism.[103]

As noted above, what drives this process is the breakdown of the tension between self-assertion and mutual recognition into complementary gender-coded alternatives whereby one gender, the "subject," asserts itself and embodies power and desire, while the other, the "object," confers unconditional recognition, and finds access to power and desire through that of the other.

> Submission becomes the "pure" form of recognition, even as violation becomes the "pure" form of assertion. The assertion of one individual . . . is transformed into domination; the other's . . . recognition becomes submission. Thus the basic tension of forces *within* the individual becomes a dynamic *between* individuals.[104]

Having very little validation of her own will or autonomous desire, the traditionally socialized girl and woman is permitted to taste these goods

103. Ibid., 110, 107.
104. Ibid., 62.

only through her obedient validation of them in another. She gains hold of agency and desire through "accepting the other's will and desire as [her] own; from there it is just a step to surrender to the other's will."[105]

The question persists about the extent to which fluid and even disruptive changes in traditional family structures in the past half-century undermine the entrenched gender patterns described throughout Benjamin's work. The model of the nuclear family in which the father is the sole bread-winner (the "exciting father" who returns home each evening from being out in the world), while the selfless, stay-at-home mother tends the children, is verified today in only a minuscule percentage of all families. What, then, about "non-traditional" families in which those roles are reversed (with a working mother and "Mr. Mom" father); or families in which both parents work, or children raised by single parents, or grandparents? What about blended families with complicated step- and in-law relationships? Or what about gay or lesbian parents, in whose families both the "exciting" and the "calming" parent/s are of the same gender? What difference do class, race, and cultural patterns make in terms of these gender dynamics? Or, finally, what about families whose dynamics and dysfunctions differ in various ways from the "traditional" norm, such as in terms of maternal domination, or parents (such as, we might presume, Benjamin herself who dedicates this book to her husband and young son) who have struggled to come to terms with their own upbringing and are attempting to raise their children, both boys and girls, in ways less susceptible to these norms?

Benjamin does address some of these questions, being careful for instance to note that changing patterns of work and family configuration will surely ameliorate some of the most destructive gender socialization, within particular and more flexible families as well as within the culture as a whole. She also, importantly, highlights the potential in such families for liberating dynamics such as those practiced by self-embracing mothers and child-embracing fathers who undercut the culture's one-sided dualisms and promote *all*-embracing models of psychological wholeness and mutuality for children of both genders.

Yet she reminds us that such individual and family-based efforts can only go so far to counteract the overwhelming gender stereotypes still being broadcast loudly and clearly in the media and in the

105. Ibid., 122. See also 78ff.

broader structures of society. She cautions against over-optimistic or over-individualized views that ignore the necessity of cultural critique and transformation.[106] For her, psychology is a tool both for intimately personal or relational exploration *and* for far-reaching social analysis, as in her chapter on "Gender and Domination" she probes the roots of even the most impersonal or "neutral" social structures in precisely these deeply patriarchal patterns of psychic development.[107] This extension of her analysis into broader cultural structures and debates is a real strength of her book, showing the entrenchment and perpetuation of these patterns not merely in individual psyches and families but in society itself. Yet I wonder whether her awareness of the insidious force of these structures, resisting even the best parents' attempts to raise their children differently, itself overlooks the extent to which those parents' efforts, multiplied across the culture even in only gradually more flexible children, themselves represent a (if not the) key strategy toward undermining just those seemingly impervious cultural structures. Nevertheless, Benjamin rightly reminds us of the enormity of the task facing those who desire to live in a society less crippled by patterns of domination and submission. Not merely individual mothers and fathers, those convenient scapegoats, but the innumerable and subconscious messages of the human society in which we live conspire to teach and reinforce these patterns in all of us, and to insist that the only alternative to degrading submission is its complementary opposite, namely to become an oppressor oneself. In contrast, Benjamin's presentation of a truly intersubjective alternative on the intrapsychic, interpersonal, and cultural levels provides concrete and life-giving hope for a different way forward. This means good news for both women and men, and their children.

Thus we have seen the overall contours of Benjamin's hypothesis about the psychic formation of patterns of domination and submission, and how these take shape in highly characteristic gendered forms. The following quotation provides a summary of this position, as well as a central interpretive thesis:

> The complement to the male refusal to recognize the other is the woman's own acceptance of her lack of subjectivity, her

106. See ibid., footnote, 105; and comments on 123.
107. Ibid., 183–218.

willingness to offer recognition without expecting it in return. (The classic maternal ideal of motherhood—a paragon of self-abnegation—is only a beautification of this lack). The female difficulty in differentiation can be described almost as the mirror image of the male's: *not the denial of the other, but the denial of the self.*[108]

It is this "self-denial" that is therefore the central problem of female development in Benjamin's view, not an ideal to be sought. In the next section, we shall see how such entrenched tendencies toward the most fundamental self-denial are indeed highly problematic in relationships. Far from bringing women pleasure (as Freud suggested in his studies of masochism), Benjamin notes that "intense pain causes the rupture of the self, a profound experience of fragmentation and chaos."[109]

This section of the chapter has attempted to demonstrate how traditional gender socialization functions to pattern both boys and girls in ways that explicitly or subtly normalize abuse. Seeking neither to blame nor to excuse those who enact these patterns in actual relationships of unequal power, desire, and will, Benjamin's analysis sheds light on the psychological and cultural pervasiveness of domination and submission. This illuminates, for instance, the difficulty girls exhibit (in the ongoing work of Gilligan et al.) in resisting precisely these ongoing pressures on the relational-social level. In the next section, I will use the work of Judith Herman to show briefly how these underlying patterns are violently reinforced, and women's selfhood further degraded, by the devastations of enacted abuse.

What Happens to Women in Abuse?

Judith Herman is a psychiatrist who has worked extensively with survivors of trauma and abuse, from veterans of combat or prolonged captivity and torture, to survivors of incest, rape, and domestic violence. Her ground-breaking study, *Trauma and Recovery: The Aftermath of Violence—from Domestic Abuse to Political Terror,* first appeared in 1992 and has been a formative text in the emerging discipline of trauma studies. Herman gives a history of the successive waves of perception and

108. Ibid., 78. Emphasis added.

109. Ibid., 61. Freud, "Economic Problem of Masochism (1924)," SE 19:155–72. Benjamin cites also Bersani, *Baudelaire and Freud*, at this point.

denial in psychiatric treatment of survivors of violence, beginning at the outset of the field in Janet's and Freud's work with "hysterical" women and continuing through the century's war-triggered studies of "shell shock," "combat fatigue," and post-traumatic stress disorder. Her chapters intentionally demonstrate the parallels between arenas of experience erroneously thought to be gender-based: chapters 2 and 3, "Terror" and "Disconnection," chart the shattering effects of traumatic violence in survivors of both combat and rape, while chapter 4, "Captivity," draws similar links between the experiences of those who endure torture and imprisonment for political reasons, including Holocaust survivors, and those whose captivity is at the hands of a domestic tyrant. These chapters are cumulative: those whose experience is examined in chapter 4 suffer recurring terror and disconnection in situations of traumatic violence (like those in chapters 2 and 3), yet with the additional element of captivity that renders their initially horrifying experience gradually invisible. It becomes normalized into "reality," the reality proclaimed and enforced by their captors, a degrading reality destructive of human life. And for those whose abuse begins in childhood (chapter 5), this "reality" is all they know. It is the physical, emotional, and spiritual world in which they must struggle to construct meaning, to make sense of themselves, others, and the pain in which they live.

Herman's work is meticulous in its detailed tracing of the psychological effects of trauma and overwhelming in the resulting unsparing portrait of human devastation.[110] If Benjamin has charted the genesis of these patterns in the psychic formation of stances of domination and submission, enacted on personal, social, and national/political levels by means of violence, then Herman's work delineates the effects of these patterns on all those forced into the position of submission. In that sense, she provides an important correlate to Benjamin by demonstrating that the effects of forced submission to another's violently imposed dominance cut across gender lines. Men who have survived horror in combat report the same debilitating symptoms as rape survivors; and the guidelines developed by groups like Amnesty International for

110. For other works on the effects of violence in abuse, see Walker, *Battered Woman Syndrome*; Neuger, "Narratives of Harm"; Cascardi and O'Leary, "Depressive Symptomatology, Self-Esteem, and Self-Blame in Battered Women"; Hoff, *Battered Women as Survivors*; Jacobs, *Victimized Daughters*.

political prisoners read like survival manuals for victims of domestic abuse.

Herman's work thus makes evident the soul-rupturing violence at the heart of all forced or conditioned submission, including (by extension) that which begins in the cradle in "normal" gender development for girls. She demonstrates that, far from being somehow biologically intrinsic to hysterical females, the ensuing traits and symptoms are in fact *human* phenomena, means of psychological survival in situations of subtle, blatant, or overwhelming trauma. Thus Herman's book documents Benjamin's assertion that the stance of submission is not "normal" for women (or anyone), let alone pleasurable.[111] It is a mark of internalized violence whose "intense pain causes the rupture of the self, a profound experience of fragmentation and chaos."[112] Herman writes,

> People subjected to prolonged, repeated trauma develop an insidious, progressive form of post-traumatic stress disorder that invades and erodes the personality. While the victim of a single acute trauma may feel after the event that she (*sic*) is "not herself," the victim of chronic [abuse] may feel herself to be changed irrevocably, or she may lose the sense that she has any self at all.[113]

This mirrors Benjamin's statement that the "female difficulty in differentiation ... [is] not the denial of the other, but the denial of the self,"[114] and again reveals the "insidious, progressive" violence at the heart of female socialization itself. On a certain level, then (as the Harvard research team also asserts), the psychological experience of women in abuse is different only in degree, or in the extremity of its manifestation, from that of "ordinary" women socialized to be perfectly agreeable, attractive, and available for those to whom they belong. The experience of trauma by definition overwhelms a person's capacity for self-defense, escape, or response: it "dissolves" the self.[115] Enacted socially, then, it produces a widespread "soluble" selfhood.

111. See note 113. See also Horney, "The Problem of Feminine Masochism," 214–33.

112. Benjamin, *Bonds of Love*, 61.

113. Herman, *Trauma and Recovery*, 86.

114. Benjamin, *Bonds of Love*, 78.

115. Herman, *Trauma and Recovery*, 35. Here she cites the original work of Janet, *L'Automatisme Psychologique*, 457, as well as van der Kolk and van der Hart, "Pierre Janet and the Breakdown of Adaptation in Psychological Trauma."

In any case, the effects of abuse (encompassing physical, emotional, and verbal assault as well as dynamics of manipulation and control) are enormous, as Herman documents. Persons subjected to chronic torture manifest symptoms of deep psychological damage, compounded greatly of course in cases where abuse had begun in childhood. Those whose homes are places of coercive torment and violation develop exhausting forms of hypervigilance, constantly scanning the environment and the abuser for signals of imminent outburst, and expending enormous energy warding off these explosions, placating the abuser, walking on eggshells, anticipating every whim.[116]

> The worst fear of any traumatized person is that the moment of horror will recur, and this fear is realized in victims of chronic abuse. Not surprisingly, the repetition of trauma amplifies all the hyperarousal symptoms of post-traumatic stress disorder. Chronically traumatized people are continually hypervigilant, anxious, and agitated. . . . [They] no longer have any baseline state of physical calm or comfort.[117]

Another psychiatrist working with women in abuse writes, "Any symbolic or actual sign of potential danger resulted in increased activity, agitation, pacing, screaming, or crying. The women remained vigilant, unable to relax or sleep. Nightmares were universal, with undisguised themes of violence and danger."[118] The abuser's demands and moods shape every waking moment, and his rages make sleep impossible due to endless tirades or coercive sexual demands and because of the night-

116. Herman describes the phenomenon of hyperarousal on pp. 35–36 as a primary after-effect of trauma; throughout the book she continues to refer to such extreme and debilitating vigilance in situations of ongoing trauma, such as domestic violence. For instance, the victim of abuse "has learned that every action will be watched, that most actions will be thwarted, and that she will pay dearly for failure. To the extent that the perpetrator has succeeded in enforcing his demand for total submission, she will perceive any exercise of her own initiative as insubordination. Before undertaking any action, she will scan the environment, expecting retaliation" (91). See also pp. 98–99 on the development of such hypervigilance in children subjected to abuse. Throughout her analysis, Herman tends to use feminine pronouns for victims of abuse and masculine for abusers.

117. Herman, *Trauma and Recovery*, 86.

118. Hilberman, "'Wife-Beater's Wife' Reconsidered," 1341. Cited in Herman, *Trauma and Recovery*, 86. See also Herman, *Trauma and Recovery*, 36, 37–39, 62, 78, 119, on the phenomenon of nightmares and sleep disturbances in post-traumatic stress survivors.

mares filled with terror that shatter sleep. All this makes increasingly impossible the devotion of time, energy, or resources to one's own care or development, even to the preservation of one's health and bodily integrity.

The abuser's voice comes to fill the victim's whole reality, crowding out any needs or feelings or perceptions of her own; these get beaten out of her if ever she dares to defy him:[119]

> Although violence is a universal method of terror, the perpetrator may use violence infrequently, as a last resort. It is not necessary to use violence often to keep the victim in a constant state of fear. The threat of death or serious harm [to her or to children or pets] is much more frequent than the actual resort to violence.... Fear is also increased by inconsistent and unpredictable outbursts of [verbal or physical] violence, and by capricious enforcement of petty rules. The ultimate effect of these techniques is to convince the victim that the perpetrator is omnipotent, that resistance is futile, and that her life depends upon winning his indulgence through absolute compliance.[120]

His demands, rages, insults, jealousy, surveillance, lies, and threats undermine her sense of reality, isolate her, and are backed up with violence should she cross him even in tiny ways or threaten to leave. Her autonomy and human capacity for initiative and freedom are pervasively degraded from the chaos of living for years or decades in a hell of unpredictable tyranny.[121] Enforced isolation from friends, family, and support networks, and destruction of her symbolic connections to them, also contribute to the destruction of her separate subjectivity and personhood. "Inevitably, in the absence of any other point of view, the victim will come to see the world through the eyes of the perpetrator."[122] Taking on the captor's "reality" as one's own can include internalizing his voice in self-hatred and -blame for all that is wrong in one's life, participating in one's own sexual degradation, overlooking children's

119. See Herman's description of psychological domination, *Trauma and Recovery,* 76–83.

120. Ibid., 77.

121. This increasing destruction of the self is described in Herman's analysis of the ultimate result of torture in captivity, namely "total surrender" into non-personhood. See *Trauma and Recovery,* 83–86. Later she writes, "Unable to find any way to avert the abuse, they learn to adopt a position of complete surrender" (98–99).

122. Ibid., 81.

terror or inflicting abuse on them oneself, etc.[123] Such abuse can result in the captive's being "bent to the will of [the] enemy," the "shame and defeat" of realizing "that [the] captor has usurped [one's] inner life" as well in making the victim feel unworthy of release because of her felt complicity with the abuse itself.[124] This happens not because of some culpable weakness on the part of the abusee but as part of one's survival itself, along with the practice of full-fledged dissociation:

> When the victim has been reduced to a goal of simple survival, psychological constriction becomes an essential form of adaptation. . . . People in captivity become adept practitioners of the arts of altered consciousness. Through the practice of dissociation, voluntary thought suppression, minimization, and sometimes outright denial, they learn to alter an unbearable reality.[125]

All of this completes the "surrender" of self that leaves a person in a state of self-loathing, feeling unworthy of help or care, unworthy in fact of any escape from this hell. Each time a person chooses to stay in a situation of abuse (often for good reasons), each time one turns a blind eye to violence against oneself or a dependent as abuse escalates, these self-attacking feelings of complicity in the abuse itself are magnified. Thus even the most noble reasons people choose to remain in abusive situations (fidelity and loyalty, hope in the sincerity of repeated repentance, belief in the transforming power of love), i.e., their own most precious human values, end up functioning in distorted ways against them, as tools in the hands of the abuser. At this point they experience literally *nothing* of themselves as truly good. And the more degraded the sense of self becomes, the more incapable a person feels of survival on her own: the prison bars of this captivity are as real and effective as any made of iron.

Presented here in broad strokes, this is a devastating cycle that leads to death: death of the psyche, death of the self or soul, and very

---

123. Ibid., 83.

124. Here she is referring to the experience Elie Wiesel describes of his own captivity and torture in a Nazi concentration camp; ibid., 84. I have altered the pronouns from the male form, whose antecedent was Wiesel, to reflect both male and female experience to correspond to the rest of this section. Herman's point, again, in weaving together these experiences as she does is that the reactions people experience in situations of extremity are human and not gendered ones.

125. Ibid., 87.

often death of the body as thousands of women are murdered every year at the hands of an intimate other.[126] To conclude this section, I will highlight three specific psychological effects of submission to traumatic violence as elucidated by Herman and others. These are the formation of a fragmented and other-focused identity, problems with boundaries, and self-attacking forms of emotional regulation. Of these, the first is the primary underlying problem; the latter two disorders can be seen to flow from the first.

First, then, victims of abuse, especially children but also adults, develop an increasingly fragmented identity. Even in individuals who to all appearances function well in the world, the experience of abuse is internalized, as noted above, into a degraded sense of self deeply at odds with this ideal self-presentation.[127] Herman describes this in reference to children growing up in abusive homes:

> The child entrapped in this kind of horror develops the belief that she is somehow responsible for the crimes of her abusers. Simply by virtue of her existence on earth, she believes that she has driven the most powerful people in her world to do terrible things. Surely, then, her nature must be thoroughly evil. The language of the self becomes a language of abomination. . . . By developing a contaminated, stigmatized identity, the child victim takes the evil of the abuser into herself and thereby preserves her primary attachment to her parents. Because the inner sense of badness preserves a relationship, it is not readily given up even after abuse has stopped; rather, it becomes a stable part of the child's personality structure. . . . [They] take upon themselves the shame and guilt of their abusers. . . . This malignant sense of inner badness is often camouflaged by the abused child's persistent attempts to be good. In the effort to placate her abusers, the child victim often becomes a superb performer. She attempts to do whatever is required of her.[128]

Persons in abuse, being progressively stripped of their own personhood, become increasingly dependent on the perceived valuations of others.

---

126. Cooper-White, *Cry of Tamar*, 102.

127. Herman writes, "The formation of a malignant negative identity is generally disguised by the socially conforming 'false self'. . . . None of her achievements in the world redound to her credit, however, for she usually perceives her performing self as inauthentic and false" (*Trauma and Recovery*, 110, 105).

128. Ibid., 105.

Having lost touch with (or, in the case of children, having never been allowed to develop) their own subjectivity and separate reality, they are unable to integrate the reactions and judgments they receive from others, and focus increasingly outside the "bad" self in the desperate attempt to ferret out and cater to others' perceptions, especially those of the abuser.

There develops then a "disordered and fragmented identity deriving from accommodations to the judgments of others."[129] Over time, this may extend into major psychiatric illnesses such as depression, borderline personality disorder, or multiple personality disorder: it literally drives people into insanity.[130] Although these effects are greatest, of course, in those whose abuse began in childhood, nevertheless Herman and others demonstrate that the "crazy-making" patterns of abuse have the potential to create these disordered fragmentations of self in all but the most extraordinarily healthy and self-assured adults as well.[131] Yet because often victims' "false selves" appear well-functioning or generously self-sacrificing in the world, this internal fragmentation and self-loathing may be invisible to others.

Second, victims of abuse whose sense of self is fragmented, whose focus is outside themselves in their reading of and conformation to others' perceptions, have great difficulty paying attention to their own boundaries, let alone protecting those against assault. The ability to defend oneself is a primary capacity of a healthy body and spirit yet

129. Rieker and Carmen (formerly Hilberman), "The Victim-to-Patient Process," 360.

130. See Herman's discussion of these diagnostic categories in chapter 6 ("A New Diagnosis"), along with her recommendations for an encompassing diagnoses of "Complex Post-Traumatic Stress Disorder," 115–29.

131. See, e.g., Herman, 57–61; Cooper-White, 110ff., esp. 118; and Martin, "Whose Soul Is It Anyway? Domestic Tyranny and the Suffocated Soul," 69–96, esp. 83–87. Note that Bonhoeffer's ability to sustain a life of prayer, ministry, and theological reflection in the situation of a Nazi prison and concentration camp marks him as a likely candidate among that "small minority of exceptional people" whose innate resistance to abuse derives from their "high sociability, thoughtful and active coping style, and strong perception of their ability to control their destiny" (Herman, *Trauma and Recovery*, 58). The description of such extraordinary persons (from a study of Vietnam veterans) on p. 59 reads like a report on Bonhoeffer himself, such resistance in him presumably deriving from the ego strength cultivated by his family along with the capacities for intimacy and trust developed in his Christian formation. But Herman notes that, "With severe enough traumatic exposure, no person is immune" (*Trauma and Recovery*, 57).

it is one that in abuse victims has been attacked relentlessly. Physical problems, often quite serious and exacerbated by the incapacity to care for oneself, mirror the ways verbal and emotional abuse destroys the person's capacity for self-defense. Needless to say, this leads to real danger of continued abuse:

> Many survivors have such profound deficiencies in self-protection that they can barely imagine themselves in a position of agency or choice. The idea of saying no to the emotional demands of a parent, spouse, lover, or authority figure may be practically inconceivable. Thus, it is not uncommon to find . . . survivors who continue to minister to the wishes and needs of those who once abused them and who continue to permit major intrusions without boundaries or limits.[132]

Effective self-defense relies on healthy boundaries and, even more fundamentally, on the capacity to distinguish oneself from another, to recognize boundaries at all. This is precisely what becomes problematic in abusive, highly enmeshed relationships.

Third, the victim of abuse has to contend with enormous levels of unexpressed (and often unrecognized, forbidden) rage. This rage, whose direct expression at the abuser feels impossible, in fact could jeopardize survival itself, goes underground.[133] Turned against oneself, it vents its highly charged energy in self-hatred and recriminations, as noted above, and it also shapes and limits the ways persons feel able to care for themselves. Dissociated from reality, from their own physical, emotional, and spiritual needs, abuse victims often find solace and learn to regulate their "bad" and uncontrollable-seeming emotions by enacting their own self-injury. In its most direct form, bodily self-mutilation allows sufferers a form of release from overwhelming emo-

132. Herman, *Trauma and Recovery*, 112. Add to this mix preachers talking about Christian self-sacrifice, and the capacity for self-defense becomes all the more difficult to develop.

133. See Herman, *Trauma and Recovery*, 94–95. Jean Baker Miller notes (*WGC* 187) in reference to women more broadly, "women have lived in the situation of being subordinate, a situation that continually generates anger; simultaneously women have been told that to be angry is destructive to their psychological being and sense of [feminine] identity." The situation of anger continually generated *and* constantly suppressed leads quite simply to madness. This situation is especially true in contexts of abuse, where both the generation and the suppression of anger occur by means of actual and internalized violence.

tional distress by drawing them into physical pain instead, which feels more manageable and provides a "real" wound, a real locus for pain otherwise inchoate, vast, and inarticulable. Other sufferers somatize their pain in other ways, in sleep disturbances, illnesses, headaches, eating disorders, drug or alcohol addictions, sexual impulsivity, or other forms of risky, even life-threatening, behavior.[134] This is thus another manifestation of boundary problems and basic self-other disturbances: the victim has trouble feeling and directing rage toward the abuser, and care or attention toward herself. She participates in his "reality," in which care and attention are to be directed toward him, and rage toward herself. These behaviors allow for the discharge of pent-up emotion and anger that could otherwise threaten the maintenance of the relationship. For one whose very survival is or feels caught up in this relationship, therefore, such behaviors not only announce bodily the very shape of the pain itself but permit one's ongoing participation in it. In this sense, they are adaptive responses: cries for help that simultaneously allow the person to survive in an unbearable and seemingly inescapable situation.

Psychological Formation of Women in Abuse

[O]ne of *the* most destructive psychological phenomena . . . is the suffering of an experience, but then not having the "permission" to truly suffer it—that is, not being able to go genuinely through the experience, know it, name it, and react with the emotions that it evokes. . . . The trouble comes when powerful people surrounding you say that you cannot react that way and, more importantly, that *you do not have* the emotions and the perceptions that you, in fact, have. . . . Not only do you suffer deprivation or attack per se, but you suffer the experience of complex emotions and the simultaneous "disconfirmation" of them—often followed by punishment for any attempt to express the feelings directly. Such experiences make it almost impossible even to know what you are experiencing. This is terrible and confusing for adults. It is even more so for children.[135]

134. Herman, *Trauma and Recovery*, 108–10.

135. Miller, *The Construction of Anger in Women and Men*, 192–93. Emphasis Miller's.

Denying the reality of my experience—that was the most harmful. . . . Good therapists were those who really validated my experience.[136]

In the final section of this chapter, I will look briefly at healing alternatives to the violently imposed gender-coded psychological patterns that make possible and sustain abuse. This section will begin with a summary of Benjamin's psychoanalytic framework for understanding how such healing happens and will continue with more specific strategies from other authors (primarily Judith Herman) by which women in abusive relationships may experience the possibility of liberation from these patterns and new growth as human beings. This liberation and growth necessarily take place within the context of a relationship that both implicitly and explicitly challenges the psychological hegemony of the abusive worldview and provides for new constructions of reality. Such a "healing relationship"[137] can take many forms; for these psychologists writing of abuse and recovery it is most often conceived in terms of the relationship between therapist or analyst and client.

I will highlight three interrelated aspects from Benjamin's work of how this relationship heals: her development of the motifs of open space, inner space, and the good teacher. All of these are realities that ideally form a central part of the experience of young children. If they are lacking in the child's experience, however, they can be reproduced in the later therapeutic relationship. In fact, this relationship is intentionally structured to provide them.[138] The first of these, the experience of "open space,"[139] or "transitional space,"[140] takes place when a parent is able to remain present with an infant without demanding attention or interaction in return. Freed by the presence of a trusted other and secure in the arms of love, the child experiences this as formative time

---

136. "Tani," subject of a 1986 interview cited by Herman, *Trauma and Recovery*, 128.

137. See Herman's chapter by that name, 133–54.

138. This of course assumes that the therapist or analyst is competently protecting this holding space for the client. In cases where this central professional responsibility is violated, enormous damage can ensue. See, e.g., Rutter, *Sex in the Forbidden Zone*; and American Psychological Association, *Ethical Principles of Psychologists*.

139. Sander, "Polarity, Paradox, and the Organizing Process in Development," 322.

140. Winnicott, "Capacity to Be Alone," 34.

to explore and be present in her or his own perceptions as real. It is namely

> what Winnicott called "being alone in the presence of the other," that is, in the safety that a nonintrusive other provides. . . . In these moments of relaxation . . . when there is no need to react to external stimuli, an impulse can arise from within and feel real. Here begins the sense of authorship, the conviction that one's act originates *inside* and reflects one's own intention. Here, too, begins the capacity for full receptivity and attention to what is outside, the freedom to be interested in the object independent of the pressure of need or anxiety. In this sense, the earliest transitional experience forms a continuum with the most developed [later] capacities for contemplation and creativity, for discovering the outside as an object existing in its own right.[141]

This experience, so crucial to the formation of a sense of one's own separate reality, is precisely what is lacking for those whose development is marked by abuse. Those who are never or inadequately provided with "open space" as young children never learn to experience themselves as fully real but are instead necessarily focused entirely on the other. They learn to create a false self that will win the approval of the other, a self oriented to the other's wishes or demands rather than emerging from within the security of non-intrusive presence. This false self is "what makes a person feel unreal to himself (*sic*), with the deadness and despair that accompany the sense of unreality."[142] Those whose false selves are overly compliant, i.e., those who have been conditioned into the posture of submission, have had their desire for just such undemanding and self-focused mutual presence met with

> retaliation, in the form of either punishment or withdrawal. . . . The masochist despairs of ever holding the attention or winning the recognition of the other, of being securely held in the other's mind. . . . [This] self is "false" because, lacking this space, [overly compliant children have] not been able to realize the desire and agency that come from within. [They have] not experienced

141. Benjamin, *Bonds of Love*, 42. The Winnicott quotation comes from the page cited in the preceding note. Benjamin's italics.

142. Ibid., 37, drawing on Winnicott, "Ego Distortion in Terms of True and False Self."

[their] impulses and acts as [their] own, arising without direction from outside. This experience is what [they long] for.[143]

The experience of abuse in adulthood recapitulates this childhood deprivation, creating again the situation of being forced for survival into a "love" entirely focused on the other's needs and demands, and inhabiting a "self" unreal in its ever-shifting adaptive fluidity. This incessant recapitulation can be broken only, Benjamin asserts, by the experience at some point along the way of precisely that "open space" that will at last allow for the sort of authentic self-discovery in the liberating presence of a trusted other that is alone transformative. Here is the extended enactment of that primal relationship never fully experienced in childhood: a relationship of "mutual gaze," in which the client can slowly relax into the sort of "holding" that allows for focus on oneself instead of always on the other, and thereby also makes possible "being transformed."[144] Benjamin cites a favorite line of poetry that evokes the nature of this holding space: "'On the seashore of endless worlds children play.' The image suggests a place that forms a boundary and yet opens up into unbounded possibility; it evokes a particular kind of holding, a feeling of safety without confinement."[145]

Thus the experience of "open space" or "holding space" in the presence of a trusted other allows the child's or adult's gaze to encompass herself and to attend to the feelings, perceptions, and desires that emerge as clues to the reality of this newly embraced self. Needless to say, this is a revolutionary shift in attention as the person learns to know herself directly rather than only as confirmed or distorted in the eyes of others. For those who move into this experience only as adults, it can be disorienting and even terrifying, evoking lifelong fears of "selfishness" (and concomitant punishment, attack, or abandonment) for the crime

143. Benjamin, *Bonds of Love*, 72.

144. These terms ("mutual gaze," "holding," and "being transformed") describe three primary modes of relationship, according to Benjamin. She writes that the baby's experience of "nursing, as a primary metaphor of infancy, encompasses all three kinds of relationship to the other that . . . appear in psychoanalytic thinking: being transformed by another (as in tension relief), complementarity (as in being held), and mental sharing (as in mutual gaze)." Benjamin, footnote on p. 46, drawing on Stern, "The Early Development of Schemas of Self." Also see footnote, p. 127; and note 75, pp. 276–77.

145. Benjamin, *Bonds of Love*, 127. The line, by Tagore, is cited frequently by Winnicott; see, e.g., "The Location of Cultural Experience," in *Playing and Reality*.

of shifting one's gaze away from the other and onto oneself.[146] Yet in the context of psychotherapy or analysis, the client gradually learns to trust that such nascent self-awareness will not be punished, that the other is still there and still listening, that the open space is safe space for self-exploration and the deepening encounter with reality.

In time, then, this makes possible a further shift in perception, namely from the open space being located only "between" oneself and a trusted listener, to its gradual location "inside" oneself as well. This marks a vital new capacity:

> the ability to hold oneself, to bear one's feelings without losing or fragmenting oneself—an ability crucial to introspection and self-discovery. This "inside" is the internal version of the safe transitional space (open space) that allows us to feel that our impulses come from within and so are authentically our own. . . . The ability to hold oneself gives to every act its authority, its purposefulness in regard to the other, its authenticity for the self.[147]

Here at last is the internal aspect of the "room of one's own" so central to women's growth. Here the one doing the holding is oneself; and the space emerging, interior. Benjamin goes on, "The significance of the spatial metaphor for a woman is likely to be in just this discovery of her *own, inner* desire, without fear of impingement, intrusion, or violation. . . . [W]oman's desire to be known and to find her own inner space . . . [is often] expressed as the wish for an open space into which the interior self may emerge, like Venus from the sea."[148] In dreams or fanta-

146. On this terror that often accompanies the psychic move away from the abuser's world, see Herman on "traumatic transference," 136–40.

147. Benjamin, *Bonds of Love*, 128. Other authors who have developed this motif include Erik Erikson, "Womanhood and the Inner Space," and, more recently and from a feminist perspective, Bassin, "Woman's Images of Inner Space," 200.

148. Benjamin, *Bonds of Love*, 128–29 (her italics). She goes on to suggest that this embrace of one's own interior space may be the female-biological analogue to (or, more accurately, healing from) the "penis envy" that keeps one's focus on goods obtainable only externally and vicariously (Benjamin, *Bonds of Love*, 127–32). Further, she suggests that this capacity for exploring one's own interiority is similarly cut off in boys in their early severance from maternal identification (in fact this, she hypothesizes, is the "cutting off" graphically articulated in castration anxieties; see 163ff.). Thus boys grow up forever dependent on finding another female to provide that "holding" for them, albeit at the cost of her own. Just as women come to discover their own desire within them, releasing them from the need of another's "penis," so men as they heal can take

sies, women who have suffered psychological captivity speak of longing for the freedom of new spaces opening and new adventures unfolding, both within themselves and, gradually, in their lives and relationships as this interior spaciousness expands.

The final dimension I am highlighting of Benjamin's delineation of the healing relationship is her framing of this relationship in terms of the "good teacher." This dimension focuses particularly on the flow of power and authority within the relationship, both acknowledging that a power imbalance does exist and attempting to let this structural authority be used in empowering and reparative ways rather than reinforcing ingrained submission to authority figures. The "good teacher" terminology comes from a client of Benjamin's named Elaine, who asserts that

> [t]he good teacher is one who provides you with structure *and* allows you the freedom to immerse yourself in your own imagination, to explore, even make mistakes, until you can finally express your own vision. . . . [W]hen you have got it right, the teacher recognizes that rightness with you.[149]

This is a way of naming the "holding" relationship that gives it a bit more content than the original "open space" image. Here, the good teacher is focused particularly on providing the structure and safety that will allow the student's imaginative creativity to flourish, and in time to find expression in a vision that feels "right" to both teacher and student.

This sort of playful creativity requires an environment of trust and freedom in which mistakes are not punished. Benjamin writes, "Elaine's image of desirable authority is not the (oedipal) authority of judgment, with its possibility of condemnation. The controlled abandon that is associated with creative expression is only possible in an atmosphere that has been purified of judgment."[150] Although the therapist, like the good teacher, can of course be male or female, Benjamin is showing how this figure subverts the internalized authority of condemnation (whose voice, in a patriarchal culture, is male). In doing so, she is attempting to link the experience of the "good teacher" with that of the exciting father of young toddlerhood, the father whose validating identification,

---

responsibility for their internal archaeology, freeing wives or girlfriends for their own lives.

149. Ibid., 120.

150. Ibid.

so important for the developing self-differentiation of both boys and girls, is often absent for daughters. The love of this early father, made newly possible in the good teacher,

> differs from the later love of the oedipal authority figure. The latter figure demands prohibition, conscience, and self-control, whereas the preoedipal ideal fits in with the rapprochement phase in which the father is seen as powerful but playful, more a figure of liberation than of discipline.[151]

Thus, if the "holding space" provided primally by either male or female therapists is a re-enactment of the traditional maternal role, the same therapist in the role of the "good teacher" can also provide the sort of validating and liberating context, "where play and self-exploration are possible,"[152] that characterizes the traditional role of the early-childhood father.

All these dynamics contribute to a healing relationship in which, often for the first time, the victim of abuse can experience herself as the focus of non-judgmental—indeed, warmly accepting—attention: the recognition by which alone, Benjamin asserts, human beings are able to grow psychologically. This space is one in which boundaries are clear and inviolable, in which the truth is increasingly fully told, in which the client's experience can slowly be named, remembered, spoken, felt, touched, seen, and heard—in which, that is, it can actually be *experienced*. This gradual reconnection with the truth of one's experience, however agonizing to the client or upsetting to the therapist at times, is profoundly healing: it sets a person free from suffocating layers of repression, denial, silence, and alienation, and releases that energy both for real grief and anger, and eventually for the work of moving on.

Judith Herman names three stages of this process of recovery within the context of this healing relationship and of the client's life as a whole. These stages, which she develops in successive chapters of her book, yet which (she cautions) take place in varying ways for different individuals, are safety, remembrance and mourning, and reconnection. The first of these, safety, is a *sine qua non* for the later steps of healing. It can include things as fundamental as escape from a rapist or emergency medical care following assault (as well as the safety of the therapeutic

151. Ibid., 275, note 67.
152. Ibid., 121.

setting itself) but eventually also needs to encompass the safety of the client's entire environment. Herman writes,

> Issues of bodily integrity include attention to basic health needs, regulation of bodily functions such as sleep, eating, and exercise, management of post-traumatic symptoms, and control of self-destructive behaviors. Environmental issues include the establishment of a safe living situation, financial security, mobility, and a plan for self-protection that encompasses the full range of the patient's daily life. Because no one can establish a safe environment alone, the task of developing an adequate safety plan always includes a component of social support.[153]

Needless to say, the establishment of safety in each of these areas is a monumental task, and the move from a context of ongoing and life-threatening abuse to one of optimally realized safety can take a great deal of time. Certainly much remembrance and mourning, as well as reconnection, can and does take place even as this process of establishing ever-greater safety is progressing. Nevertheless it is still true that the work of recovery in these later stages is crucially tied to, and made possible by, the degree of safety experienced along the way; and none of it can begin before basic degrees of physical and psychological safety are ensured. Like the healing relationship itself this is a necessary form of "holding" expanding to embrace ever greater aspects of one's life, there making possible new integrative work at each new stage.

The work of remembrance and mourning is at the heart of recovery from trauma and abuse. Here, Herman writes, "the survivor tells the story of the trauma. She tells it completely, in depth and in detail. This work of reconstruction actually transforms the traumatic memory, so that it can be integrated into the survivor's life story."[154] This narrative process is not a one-time event. The survivor, beginning with the frozen, fragmentary, or fully repressed memories typical of trauma victims, only gradually begins to be able to put words on shattering and surreal-seeming events. Memories return only slowly. And only after many fragmentary or contradictory re-tellings, therapist and client slowly piecing together more and more of the puzzle, does even the narrative outline itself begin to appear. Even then, it is only after gradu-

---

153. Herman, *Trauma and Recovery*, 160.

154. Ibid., 175. On this process, see also the excellent work within the theological context of Keshgegian, *Redeeming Memories*.

ally becoming able to bear the weight of the excruciating emotions "held" in these narratives and their attendant memories that a person can slowly begin to tell the full story, can let its emotion flood forth and be experienced in real time. Such a process is agonizing, and Herman notes that it is the journey into the heart of one's own grief that inspires the greatest fear.

> The descent into mourning is at once the most necessary and the most dreaded task of this stage of recovery. Patients often fear that the task is insurmountable, that once they allow themselves to start grieving, they will never stop. . . . To the extent that the patient is unable to grieve, she is cut off from a part of herself and robbed of an important part of her healing. Reclaiming the ability to feel the full range of emotions, including grief, must be understood as an act of resistance rather than submission to the perpetrator's intent [i.e., I won't let him make me cry]. Only through mourning everything that she has lost can the patient discover her indestructible inner life.[155]

This too does not happen quickly or in a straightforward manner. Survivors may feel irreparably damaged by the abuse, incapable of love, unworthy of healing. They tell their story over and over, in increasingly horrifying completeness, and each time fear they will be ripped apart by the grief, the rage, the desolation of it all. It seems unbearable; it *is* unbearable; one feels it will never end. Yet, Herman writes, "[a]fter many repetitions, the moment comes when the telling of the trauma story no longer arouses quite such intense feeling. It has become part of the survivor's experience, but only one part. The story is a memory like other memories, and it begins to fade as other memories do."[156] Of course, throughout this process, the patience, genuine compassion, and emotional clarity of the therapist are indispensable. This holding space gives the client a touchstone of non-abusive reality within which all these unbearable memories can gradually be borne, their crippling devastation gradually released.

As this process moves to a close, the story of trauma having slowly been transformed from an unspeakable horror into an aspect of one's larger experience, the person experiences her self similarly transformed. "The reward of mourning is realized as the survivor sheds

155. Herman, *Trauma and Recovery*, 188.
156. Ibid., 195.

her evil, stigmatized identity and dares to hope for new relationships in which she no longer has anything to hide."[157] This then makes possible the eventual transformation of one's broader relational life. In the stage of recovery Herman calls "reconnection," a survivor emerges from the relentless and necessarily inward-focused remembrance and grief to begin to construct a new life in the world. This includes of course new ways of being with herself and with others (including the capacity for active self-defense, or "learning to fight"[158]), new relationships, new vocation (in the broadest sense, including "finding a survivor mission"[159]), and new ways of making meaning of life.

> Having come to terms with the traumatic past, the survivor faces the task of creating a future. She has mourned the old self that the trauma destroyed; now she must develop a new self. Her relationships have been tested and forever changed by the trauma; now she must develop new relationships. The old beliefs that gave meaning to her life have been challenged; now she must find anew a sustaining faith. These are the tasks of the third stage of recovery. In accomplishing this work, the survivor reclaims her world.[160]

Here we see drawn together many of the themes highlighted by other authors as well. At this point, the survivor becomes able to insist on her own subjectivity in the face of others' demands. She becomes able to stop, at last, "denying herself" (Benjamin), such self-denial merely allowing the machinery of domination and submission to grind on unabated and be perpetuated to the next generation. Here, as well, the survivor truly begins to speak in her own voice (Gilligan et al.), to live in a world in which the truth can increasingly be spoken and heard, without retaliation or silencing. And here the survivor is able to live and make a home within her own experience, as well as being able to recognize and appreciate others' (Stone Center).

Finally, this is the point at which women recovering from abuse can find common cause with men recovering from their own distorted selfhood. Girls and women are not the only ones whose authentic experience is suppressed in a culture of violence, whose true selves are

157. Ibid., 194.
158. See ibid., 197–202.
159. See ibid., 207–11.
160. Ibid., 196.

hidden or lost under socially-sanctioned masks. The denial of reality is widespread and can best be countered by conversations among those of different experiences, whose varying perspectives allow for more encompassing shared truth-telling. In the hope of fostering such a conversation, I turn in the next chapter to a dialogue between Bonhoeffer and these feminists on the subject of the self. And, because ultimately the exploration of one's experience at its deepest level is a matter of spirituality, it is appropriate that the more specific focus of this next chapter is the spiritual formation of the self, in particular the Christian spiritual formation of women who suffer abuse. Here, the insights of Bonhoeffer, the faithful Christian man, will be tested against (and, in turn, complement) the perspectives of these secularly-oriented feminist psychologists. How can one speak of the healthy and life-giving Christian formation of women in abuse? That is the question to which this chapter will turn.

5

Conversation Between Bonhoeffer and Feminist Psychology

Introduction

IN THE LAST THREE CHAPTERS I HAVE DELINEATED BROAD CONTOURS of both Bonhoeffer's and selected contemporary feminist psychologists' understandings of the (gendered) self and its trajectory toward health and freedom. The present chapter will attempt to bring together into one conversation Bonhoeffer's Christian spiritual formation described in chapters two and three and the psychological processes of healing and maturation outlined in chapter four. That is, in this chapter I propose to construct and mediate a dialogue between Bonhoeffer and these feminists on the subject of a psychologically healthy spiritual formation of soluble selves, specifically women in abuse.

As noted in chapter one, such a specification in no way limits the relevance of this inquiry to victims or survivors of abuse. But women in abuse represent an extreme instance of the "soluble" selfhood that characterizes many women to some degree as well as those men who have similarly internalized familial or social rejection into the self-silencing, self-attacking submission characteristic of soluble selves. Thus I hope this chapter's constructed conversation will prove germane to central aspects of the experience of a wide audience indeed. In this way, we see revealed the recurring biblical motif of the paradoxical and surprising centrality of precisely those persons regarded (by their oppressors, by society, and even by themselves) as marginal, failed, invisible, or worthless. That the experience of battered women could shed powerful new light on the teachings of Dietrich Bonhoeffer in ways that prove illuminating for many beyond themselves seems initially quite improbable. Yet, were he alive today, Bonhoeffer might be among the first to acknowledge the Christian mystery at work here: that attention to these bruised and bleeding bodies and spirits, despised and rejected by the powerful, both radically contextualizes (or even subverts) the best wisdom of the wise and in fact reveals the very heart of God for the world.[1]

Before turning to an overview of this chapter a few words are in order on the relation between the spiritual formation outlined for Bonhoeffer in chapters two and three and the processes of psychological development described in chapter four. That is, how do psychological and spiritual formation correspond and differ? Or, for my purposes, how can voices from the "secular" realm of feminist psychology be appropriately included in this chapter's conversation about Christian spiritual formation?

Of course the engagement between psychology and religion is a subject of no little scholarly interest, including texts engaging Christian spirituality specifically in dialogue with psychology.[2] Though I cannot address here every aspect of this initially wary but increasingly appreciative interaction, I will make some broad assertions with regard to my

---

1. Certainly it is no coincidence that Bonhoeffer's love and grasp of this mystery deepens precisely as he himself moves into the place of the marginalized, the captive, the tortured—as he too learns the revelatory power of the "view from below" ("After Ten Years," LPP 17). Perhaps sensing his own imminent bodily relegation to this position, but certainly growing in his sense of its central hermeneutical significance for Christians, Bonhoeffer wrote in this essay, shortly before his imprisonment, "We have to learn that personal suffering is a more effective key, a more [fruitful] principle for exploring the world in thought and action, than personal good fortune" (cf. DBW 8: 38).

2. For studies of the engagement between psychology and religion broadly, see the material gathered in Jonte-Pace and Parsons, eds., *Religion and Psychology*; Jacobs and Capps, eds., *Religion, Society, and Psychoanalysis*; and such textbook-scope surveys as Hood., et al., *The Psychology of Religion*. For specifically Christian engagement, see, e.g., Browning, *Religious Thought and the Modern Psychologies*; Jones, *Religion and Psychology in Transition*; Roberts and Talbot, eds., *Limning the Psyche*. For work in Christian spirituality in relation to psychology, see J. Conn, *Spirituality and Personal Maturity*; W. Conn, *The Desiring Self*; and Hardy, "A Winnicottian Redescription of Christian Spiritual Direction Relationships." Less common though notable are texts by psychologists or psychoanalysts interested in resources from Christian spiritual formation. An example of such work related to my concerns here is Watson, "Toward Union in Love: The Contemplative Spiritual Tradition and Contemporary Psychoanalytic Theory in the Formation of Persons." See also the materials gathered in Walsh, ed., *Spiritual Resources in Family Therapy*; and Riley, *The Psychology of Religious Experience*.

use of psychological material in a conversation and chapter on spiritual formation. The over-arching assertion guiding this chapter is that both psychology and spirituality in their descriptive, theoretical, and practical expressions aim at the fullest well-being of the human person by means of increasing mental/emotional or spiritual (respectively) correspondence with reality.[3] While both fields concur in affirming and, ideally, fostering physical health as the foundation and expression of a fully somatic well-being; and while both fields tend to appreciate and take account of the other's characteristic focus, nevertheless the fields differ in their primary attention to the mental/emotional or spiritual dimensions of human being. Yet because both psychology and Christian spirituality, broadly understood, tend to view these dimensions of human life (physical, mental, emotional, and spiritual) as inseparable and indeed powerfully mutually influential,[4] they can collaborate in fostering well-being across the complexity of human functioning. The fields also share a parallel vision of the *means* of movement toward greater health: namely the subject's increasing participation in reality, whether defined as the shared human reality of therapist and client broadening to include all of a client's relationships, or as the ultimate reality of the triune God experienced in prayer, human relationships, church, and world.

To move into the language of the previous three chapters, I assert that, for a Christian subject, the "true self" arrived at by good-enough parenting and/or successful therapy or analysis can be seen as one's authentic created humanity simultaneously participating in, and being formed by, Jesus Christ. And, conversely, any adequate spiritual formation depends on, is inseparable from, and fosters concomitant psychological maturity. Thus the feminist psychologists whose thinking is explored in chapter four provide indispensable tools for naming the cognitive and emotional dynamics that suffocate soluble selves, includ-

3. "Correspondence with reality" is of course Bonhoeffer's language, which he develops in distinctive ways (see pp. 83–92 in chapter 3). I find it helpful and appropriate for use more broadly here as well.

4. A burgeoning literature explores the interrelationships between spiritual, mental, and physical health. For a bibliography of scholarly articles in this area, see the Duke Center for Spirituality, Theology, and Health website: http://www.dukespiritualityand health.org/publications/latest.html. A congregationally-based ministry that operates at this intersection of many arenas of human health is parish nursing. On this see Solari-Twadell, ed., *Parish Nursing*; and Westberg and McNamara, *Parish Nurse*.

ing many Christian women, and describe resources that allow these women to experience the healing work of Jesus Christ in their lives on those levels. Their spiritual formation as a whole both requires and (ideally) contributes to these crucial psychological dynamics of healing. Using Bonhoeffer's three-fold framework of spiritual formation,[5] I assert that the experience of conformation with, first, the Incarnate One includes the psychological dimensions of movement into the healing relationship and self-acceptance as the person one truly is. Second, the experience of conformation with the Crucified One includes the psychological dimensions of truth-telling about oneself and one's life (facing sin, brokenness, and woundedness); the stripping of illusions and mourning one's losses, including important fantasies and/or God-, self-, and other-images; and increasingly disclosive self-offering before God and others. Finally, the experience of conformation with the Risen One includes the psychological dimensions of the birth of the true self, healing of old wounds, joy, and the creation of new connections in the real world.

Thus in this chapter I will place into conversation the previously-outlined visions of human formation offered by Bonhoeffer and selected contemporary feminist psychologists, doing so not only with an eye to their challenges to one another's perceived blind spots but also with appreciation for their respective contributions to the development of a psychologically healthy Christian spirituality for soluble selves. In this constructed conversation I will present four different relative stances toward one another's insights that emerge from my reading of these authors, ranging from outright feminist critique of Bonhoeffer to Bonhoeffer's challenges to them. Of course, this conversation is my own invention. I do not know how the Bonhoeffer of 1935, 1945, or (were he still alive today) 2008 would respond to this feminist material nor how these contemporary psychologists might react to a reading of his theology. Therefore what appears here is my attempt to mediate through my reading of each perspective some salient and often striking, even provocative, points of respectful mutual concord, discord, and deepening insight.

The chapter proceeds as follows. First I outline the primary foci where the feminist psychologists I have read must criticize Bonhoeffer:

5. See chapter 3, pp. 92–100.

in his support of patriarchy and in conceptualizing the self-other relationship in terms that universalize the experience of his own gendered social location. Second, I explore Bonhoeffer's thought regarding the person and work of Jesus Christ, both aspects of which are potentially ambiguous in their impact and require careful examination as to their helpfulness for soluble selves. In particular, I look at the figure of Jesus for Bonhoeffer as a male authority, as well as his interlinked notions of *Stellvertretung* and responsibility. Third, I outline four key contributions Bonhoeffer makes to the healthy Christian formation of soluble selves and of abused women in particular. This section explores Bonhoeffer's insights in the areas of healing relationship, self-awareness, self-defense, and self-investment, developing these as "Bonhoeffer-ean" foundations for further growth in these areas. And finally I suggest an important way Bonhoeffer's vision in turn challenges contemporary secular psychology, namely toward the healing power of experienced transcendence and openness to self-surrender within the intimacy of a well-discerned vocation.

Critique of Bonhoeffer

Patriarchy

The first area I see feminist psychology criticizing Bonhoeffer is in his lifelong, nearly unquestioning support of patriarchal social and familial structures. As we saw in chapter two, Bonhoeffer grew up in a patriarchal family and appeared to have had every intention of creating a similar pattern with Maria von Wedemeyer, his fiancée. Again as noted earlier, this does not mean Bonhoeffer intended harm to women or consciously disrespected them. His mother and sisters, to whom he was close, were strong women, creative and devoted to the flourishing of culture and human well-being; and in Maria he chose a woman of formidable intellect who, after the war, eventually became a professor of computer science at MIT. Yet despite sharing the genes that led all the Bonhoeffer sons to take up careers in law, physics, and theology, none of the Bonhoeffer daughters received a degree and only one, Christine, attended university at all. One might wonder whether Maria herself, had she married into this family, would have been discouraged however subtly from pursuing her own interests. Bonhoeffer's choice of a much younger wife (17 to his 37 at the time of their engagement), his desire that she "conform" to him in literary and other matters, and his traditional wedding sermon to Eberhard and Renate Bethge upholding the man's headship in the family and representation of the family to and in the world suggest that, at the very least, Maria might have had a difficult time pursuing desires and interests of her own if they conflicted with Dietrich's sense of her proper role in family and world.[6]

The more significant point, however, is that to Bonhoeffer's mind the systems of patriarchy are quite unproblematic. For him this is the normal order of things, the way God intends human beings to live for their own flourishing and blessing.[7] Thus patriarchy, and women's subordination in general, do not represent shocking violations of women's full created personhood but a beneficial division of labor along gender lines. What is abnormal, to his mind, is women rejecting their traditional role in the family to pursue lives and careers of their own.[8] It never apparently occurs to him that living in a position of forced subordination could *cause* psychological or spiritual problems for women, let alone that God might want something different for them. Certainly he shows no awareness of any correspondence between patterns of subordination and of violation or abuse. Elisabeth Young-Bruehl, a psychiatrist, writes in relation to Freud what appears to be quite true of Bonhoeffer as well: "Women were considered not so much dominated as naturally subordinate."[9] That is, their suffering at this state of affairs would have been completely invisible, the "natural" state of things. Certainly the

6. This is in no way to assert that she was somehow better off because his death precluded their marriage, which both deeply desired, nor to rule out the possibility that being married to precisely this highly intelligent and strong-willed woman might have led Dietrich to see, in relation to Maria, the inadequacy of his patriarchal views.

7. As we saw in chapter two, for Bonhoeffer, patriarchy precedes the fall and is a good part of creation; in fact, for him what resulted from the fall was not patriarchy (in his terms, patriarchalism) itself, but only "patriarchalism understood as punishment" (SC 97). Of course this is insult added to injury: it is not women's subordination that is the sin but their chafing at patriarchy, i.e., their seeing it as a punishment!

8. For instance, an unmarried aunt, Charlotte Leubuscher, who had become a professor of economics at the Technical University in Berlin, a remarkable achievement, was viewed by the Bonhoeffer children more as a laughable oddity than in any way a role model. Renate Bethge writes, "the children made fun of her. . . . this woman could not serve as an example for the girls, nor did she especially impress the boys" ("Bonhoeffer and the Role of Women," 39).

9. Young-Bruehl, review of Jessica Benjamin, *Like Subjects, Love Objects*, 636.

idea that patriarchy manifests and perpetuates sin and suffering, blinding both men and women to crucial aspects of their own humanity and of God's deepest desires for their lives and for the world, would have been foreign to his thinking.

This blindness to the evil of patriarchy is on one level merely a regrettable oversight on the part of a person otherwise brilliant in his social and theological analysis and far ahead of his time in perceiving the spiritual poison of racism, anti-Semitism, nationalism, and pious quietism. No one can be expected to see and address every possible issue, especially something like women's oppression still (even in 1945) far from public consciousness. On another level, however, patriarchy in Bonhoeffer does not represent merely another "issue"; it undermines his entire analysis of the self and its spiritual formation. As noted in chapter two, Bonhoeffer recognizes the problems of dominance and the dominating ego, and he constructs a vision of ethical personhood and spiritual formation geared for the dominating, or separative, self. Yet because he does not see *patriarchal* domination as a problem but as God's will for himself, families, and society, he is unable to link his analysis to the actual social-psychic roots of the patterns he deplores. To implement his writings on ethical personhood and self-surrender as he seems to have intended means that separative selves would allow themselves to be "claimed" by one another's "demands" (as in the Finkenwalde community of peers) and soluble selves would do the same in relation to separative (wives submitting to husbands); but he has no intention that separative selves take seriously the claims of the soluble, at least not in any way that might threaten the ordering of gendered and class-based social relations. Maria is to "conform" to him, not he to her; the very idea of the contrary is ludicrous. Yet by refusing to imagine such a thing he dismisses the only way his theology of ethical personhood could prove truly redemptive: if it allowed the "dominant" to be confronted by the reality of the "submissive"—shattering both false selves (as dominant *and* submissive) by this reality's divine alterity—and to make change in response that could derail oppression.

Similarly, because he fails to see the corresponding patterns of submission as a problem but views them as the natural state of affairs for women (and all those in subservient social positions), he considers their ego problems to be the same as his own. This lack of recognition of differences in formation means that when his prescriptions on ethical personhood and self-surrender are read and enacted by soluble selves, they *reinforce* social and ecclesial conditioning toward submission and perpetuate the very pattern of domination and submission from which Bonhoeffer's vision desires and purports to liberate people.

His writings taken on their own terms thus fail to liberate either separative or soluble selves. To summarize, Bonhoeffer's support of patriarchy and social hierarchy 1) keeps him from considering that men (or women in positions of dominance) might ever truly "surrender" to the claims of women (or men in positions of submission), since in his mind that would lead to social chaos; 2) keeps him from seeing, let alone insisting on, the necessity of different patterns of growth and formation for those on the underside; and 3) keeps him thus from perceiving soluble selves as authentic human subjects on their own terms with demands and desires comparable to his own. In all these ways as they reinforce one another, Bonhoeffer's support of systems of domination keeps his proposals from actually addressing the alienation from which he longs for release. To insist on self-surrender that maintains mutual non-recognition of the already non-recognized only reinforces evil, doing so all the more insidiously for being "Christian."

To be fair to Bonhoeffer, let us note that on another level his thinking serves as an internal critique of this problem. His insistence on particularity and concreteness in all theological thought and spiritual discernment, along with his suspicion of any universalizing principles, is a powerful tool for deconstructing his own support of patriarchy, and his accounts of personhood and formation, as *themselves* particular and having everything to do with his gendered social location. This frees readers and interpreters from naïve application of his thinking and gives permission (from Bonhoeffer himself) for the consciously discerned appropriation, rejection, or modification of his thinking for new contexts. Those in positions of dominance may find his proposals liberating, especially as they are able to link them with a feminist or social class analysis addressing the underlying roots of these problems. And Bonhoeffer's rejection of a Nazi "orders of creation" theology in regard to matters of race criticizes his own understanding of patriarchy as grounded in just such a problematic "order of creation."

Finally, Bonhoeffer's journey to the underside as his life progressed gives inklings that he was becoming more aware of precisely this problem of the ultimate irreconcilability of any of his cherished systems of *oben* and *unten*, domination and submission, patriarchy and hierarchy, with the Christian worship of and conformation to an incarnate and crucified Lord. He was perceiving that "there's some contradiction here"; he was learning to see and live "from below" and to discover the extraordinary power and clarity of insight there.[10] Might he have emerged from prison desiring, for his own sake as well as that of others, to move beyond systems of privilege that had imprisoned him far from the underside where Jesus Christ dwells? We'll never know. But I find it helpful to attend to those aspects of Bonhoeffer's thinking and spirituality that move in this direction even if he did not live long enough to go at it himself.

Self and Other

The second area of feminist critique of Bonhoeffer I am suggesting is the relation between self and other. Various scholars have commented on this striking other-orientation in Bonhoeffer, finding it a salutary Christian alternative to self-indulgent pieties of American consumerism and privilege, and locating him within a developing tradition of philosophical alterity manifest also in such thinkers as Adorno and Levinas[11] and in liberation theology.[12] As we have seen, from the begin-

10. The line, "there's some contradiction here" comes from a character in his fiction in prison musing on precisely this irreconcilability (*Fiction from Tegel Prison*, DBWE 7: 108). The language of seeing "from below" comes from "After Ten Years," LPP 17 (DBW 8: 38).

11. See, e.g., Marsh, *Reclaiming Dietrich Bonhoeffer*; Floyd, *Theology and the Dialectics of Otherness*; Hale, "Dietrich Bonhoeffer and the Question of the Other"; Reuter, "Afterword" to DBWE 2 (*Act and Being*); Peters, "Der andere ist unendlich wichtig"; Bongmba, "Priority of the Other"; and Ford, *Self and Salvation*, which draws together themes of self and other from Levinas, Jüngel, and Ricoeur; see especially Ford's chapter "Polyphonic Living: Dietrich Bonhoeffer," 241–65. An interesting subject to explore, not possible here, would be the shifts in usage between the (predominantly male) postmodern and/or Christian language of the newly "de-centered" self; feminist and other attempts to reclaim notions of "self-centering" for those who have traditionally struggled with all too fragmented selves; and Bonhoeffer's own notion of "Christ the Center" developed most fully in his Christology lectures (DBW 12, 279–348). An overview of some of these motifs especially in feminist writings, making prominent use of the image of the "center," is Huffaker, *Creative Dwelling*.

12. On Bonhoeffer's importance for subsequently emerging liberation theology, see Gutierrez, "Theology from the Underside of History," 169–221; Chapman, "Bonhoeffer and Liberation Theology"; and de Santa Ana, "Influence of Bonhoeffer on the Theology of Liberation."

ning of his writings Bonhoeffer overwhelmingly identifies the "other" (divine or human) as the locus of transcendence, drawing a person's attention away from the "totally claimless," sterile, and isolated self to find authentic life and reality in surrender to the "absolute demands" of the other.[13] From the philosophical categories of *Sanctorum Communio* through the powerfully enacted surrender to Christ in *Discipleship* and to the human other in confession and service in community (*Life Together*), he continued to develop this motif of the priority of the other for Christian maturity. And at the end of his life, even as he was beginning to notice problems with "unconditional surrender" of self to other, nevertheless the dominant tone of his writings still reflects the sheer joy and freedom he experiences in self-surrender, a process simultaneously sacrificial and redemptive. That is, in one's own becoming a "person for others," one participates in the very being and mystery of Jesus Christ himself, the consummate "person for others." Thus for him

> a transformation of all human life is given in the fact that "Jesus is there only for others." His "being there for others" is the experience of transcendence. It is only this "being there for others," maintained until death, that is the ground of his omnipotence, omniscience, and omnipresence. Faith is participation in this being of Jesus (incarnation, cross, and resurrection). Our relation to God is not a "religious" relationship to the highest, most powerful, and best Being imaginable—that is not authentic transcendence—but our relation to God is a new life in "existence for others," through participation in the being of Jesus.[14]

This statement from August 1944 could stand as a summary of his lifelong reflection on and practice of the transcendence of the other and the transparency to Jesus Christ thereby disclosed. We find similarly moving reflections in these late writings on the relative place of the self as well, showing again how for Bonhoeffer this focus away from the self

13. SC 54. See chapter 2, pp. 32–43. In language typical of the studies of Bonhoeffer and alterity, Hale writes, "Bonhoeffer . . . embraces the recognition that both divine and human otherness . . . genuinely transcend the subject, the 'I'" (Hale, 4). Also, recall Green's summary of Bonhoeffer's notions of transcendence in the Editor's Introduction to *Sanctorum Communio*: "The other transcends the self in ethical encounter—indeed, the human You is a form and analogy of the divine You in precisely this present otherness. This personal-ethical model of transcendence . . . is found throughout Bonhoeffer's theology" (5–6).

14. LPP 381 (DBW 8: 558).

and toward the needs of others draws him into the heart of the paschal mystery itself:

> It is not the religious act that makes the Christian, but participation in the sufferings of God in the secular life. That is *metanoia*: not in the first place thinking about one's own needs, problems, sins, and fears, but allowing oneself to be caught up into the way of Jesus Christ, into the messianic event (Isa 53). . . . living unreservedly in life's duties, problems, successes and failures, experiences and perplexities. In so doing we throw ourselves completely into the arms of God, taking seriously, not our own sufferings, but those of God in the world—watching with Christ in Gethsemane. That, I think, is faith; that is *metanoia*; and that is how one becomes a human being and a Christian (cf. Jer 45!).[15]

Clearly this is the way of life for him; and to turn away from it in self-protective repudiation of the other would mean a denial of Jesus Christ himself and thus of one's own authentic existence. For him, to the end, the shape of sin ultimately remained the same: the selfish denial of the transcendent claims of the other.

Yet as difficult as it may seem to dispute the truth and beauty of these assertions, the feminist perspectives explored in chapter four make clear that such faith statements emerge not from some universally-valid human reality but from a specific psycho-social stance: that of the separative self, the traditionally-socialized male. Gilligan's studies, for instance, reveal powerfully how girls' problems tend to have more to do with a silencing of themselves, and over-orientation to others' judgments, than with the ignoring of others Bonhoeffer feared in himself. Or, as we have seen already in this quotation from Jessica Benjamin,

> The complement to the male refusal to recognize the other is the woman's own acceptance of her lack of subjectivity, her willingness to offer recognition without expecting it in return. . . . The female difficulty in differentiation can be described almost as the mirror image of the male's: *not the denial of the other, but the denial of the self.*[16]

15. LPP 361–62 (July 18, 1944, in DBW 8: 535–36) and 370 (July 21, 1944, in DBW 8: 542).

16. Benjamin, *Bonds of Love*, 78. Emphasis added.

Thus while many Christian women throughout the past half-century have found resonance with Bonhoeffer's prison writings, being drawn into participation in the very being of Jesus through attention to the sufferings of God in others, nevertheless even these lovely writings assume a stance all too familiar to women in abuse. For them, "being there for others"—or at least for the abuser—manifestly fails to redeem. It is not a window opening into the experience of transcendence. Instead, this focus on others and their needs, desires, and demands to the exclusion of oneself is the shape of an excruciating life, indeed the pattern of sin.[17] What for Bonhoeffer was the liberating experience of surrender, joy, and solidarity with others is, for these women, a grinding day-to-day suffocation.

Bonhoeffer's prison writings are much more nuanced and gracefull than his early writings about unrestricted surrender to the absolute demands of the other. Yet even these later sentiments about turning away from our own needs toward those of God in others mean one thing to Bonhoeffer; they mean something quite different to a victim of abuse, for this is the pattern of evil itself in her life. Bonhoeffer's lifelong illusion, from which he aches to be freed, is that of the self's omnipotence and others' unreality. For the victim of abuse, however, it is that the self is "nullipotent," unreal, effaced: the abuser is omnipotent. Not taking one's own sufferings seriously is the hallmark of daily life. It is what makes continued submission possible, but it is in no way a path to freedom and life in Jesus Christ—quite the opposite. Thus what feels liberating and life-giving to Bonhoeffer merely seals the prison doors for his abused sisters in Christ. For them, what is revolutionary, breath-taking, truly illuminative of reality would be a spirituality that in equally compelling terms invites them to "be there for themselves" and asserts that such unimaginable presence to *themselves* is their means of participation in the One who is there for them. Similarly, what opens those prison doors for Christian women in abuse is the obverse of Bonhoeffer's: namely to learn at last, perhaps for the first time, to take with ultimate seriousness

17. For a recent overview of contemporary Christian feminist thinking on the subject of sin, especially as to its characteristically female manifestations, see Lowe, "Woman Oriented Hamartiologies"; Gill-Austern, "Love Understood as Self-Sacrifice and Self-Denial"; and Gebara, *Out of the Depths*. Other studies exploring notions of sin from the perspective of those on the "underside" include Park, *From Hurt to Healing*; and Park and Nelson, eds., *Other Side of Sin*. See also McFayden, *Bound to Sin*.

the sufferings of God in their *own* flesh and hearts, and to tune out the overwhelming clamoring needs and demands of the abuser.

In chapter two I suggested that Bonhoeffer, writing from the perspective of the separative self, knew the lonely emptiness and rages of the dominating ego manifested in extreme form in abusers. I am suggesting that this is the voice that needs to be "turned down" for *both* abusers and victims: for abusers or others in positions of dominance in learning to look away from their own egos and attend to others (here Bonhoeffer can be helpful to them) and for victims in learning similarly to look away from the abuser's demands, to see and attend to *themselves*. In both cases, all attention is initially focused on the abuser's face and voice; in both cases, both parties learn to turn away from this and attend for the first time also to the victim, the woman as primordial "other,"[18] and find God there. The question underlying this shift is, therefore, What happens when the "other," the "non-self," is *oneself?* This is precisely the inversion of the relative positions of self and other I found so revelatory in learning to read Bonhoeffer against the grain (see chapter one). When soluble selves read Bonhoeffer, I suggest, they do not find their position reflected in that of the "self" he assumes, but in the "other." If this is correct, then in reading Bonhoeffer they must substitute "self" for "other," and "other" for "self," in order to make the redemptive move analogous to his: in their case from focus on the abuser/other to focus on oneself.

For those taught their entire lives that their goodness and survival depend on their focus on others and service of them, this shift in attention toward the self can feel terrifying and impossible, if not completely un-Christian. How important for victims of trauma and abuse, then, is the development of a powerfully *Christian* alternative to spiritualities of self-renunciation, toward mature discernment of the sufferings and life of God courting our attention in any given context, even and especially if those sufferings are one's own and not only those of others! For many women in abuse, "watching with Christ in Gethsemane" might turn out to have a great deal indeed to do with learning *not* to turn toward others but in fact, contra Bonhoeffer, to begin to take seriously their own sufferings, perhaps for the first time. I am suggesting that, for them,

---

18. De Beauvoir, *The Second Sex*.

precisely that "is faith; that is *metanoia*; and that is how one becomes a human being and a Christian."[19]

All this suggests that the survivor of verbal, emotional, and/or physical abuse has needs counter to those of Bonhoeffer's yet, while long invisible to pastors and theologians, no less valid: to turn away from focus on the other and toward the self. Bonhoeffer needs to turn down the volume of the *self* in order to hear the other; the victim of abuse needs to turn down the volume of the *abuser* in order to attend to herself. Bonhoeffer needs to submit his overbearing self to others' differing reality; an abuse victim needs to defy others' consuming reality in order to claim space for her own.[20] There is a whole universe within her, the uniquely created humanity God brought to life, that has been relentlessly attacked, often since childhood, and never had space to develop. To a greater or lesser extent, her very self has been suffocated.[21] Such selflessness is not holy and not to be naïvely praised; it is a mark of chronic terror and suffering, and cries out for courageous naming, remedy, and healing, for the abundance of life Jesus Christ intends for every person, every self.

Having surveyed two areas where feminist psychology challenges Bonhoeffer and finds limitations in the adequacy of his proposals for the health and well-being of women in abuse, I turn to consider two aspects of Bonhoeffer's christological thought that invite conversation from a feminist perspective. Unlike his views on patriarchy and his strongly gendered understanding of the self-other relationship, these topics are not so much impediments to Bonhoeffer's helpfulness for soluble selves as matters for more nuanced discussion. That is, while both these christological areas can be interpreted in ways harmful for abused women (by Bonhoeffer or his interpreters), each also contains liberating potential worth exploring. This section's questioning on behalf of soluble selves may in fact allow the liberating potential of these

19. LPP 370 (DBW 8: 542).

20. To use the language of *Sanctorum Communio*, the abuser needs to grow in the direction of the "openness" of the self toward others, while the abuse victim needs to learn to recognize and protect her own "closedness." Cf. SC 65–80.

21. Martin, "Whose Soul Is It Anyway?" Dana Jack, whose work on the "Over-Eye" of male culture we saw in chapter 4, uses the image of the "silencing" of the self in her book on women and depression. Finally, Janet Jacobs explores the "endangered" self with particular attention to women suffering violence: "Endangered Female Self."

motifs to come to light in ways otherwise inaccessible. Here I examine both the person and the work of Christ for Bonhoeffer, the latter as he sees it unfolding in *Stellvertretung* and responsibility. Because this christological material is so central to his spirituality as a whole, it is important to consider it carefully here in order to make life-giving use of it in the following section.

Areas of Mutual Interrogation: Christology

The Person of Jesus

As we have seen in chapter three, Bonhoeffer's spirituality is christo-centric, making prominent appeal to the person of Jesus Christ for the revelation of reality and the ongoing redemption of one's own life and all that is. This christocentrism is broad for Bonhoeffer, intended not to imprison ultimate truth within the Christian sphere but to open Christians to truth and reality wherever they encounter it. In the public arena, in the sufferings of the world's neediest, in partnership with non-Christians working for justice and compassion, even in one's own flesh and loves: there is Jesus Christ. Bonhoeffer's Christ is encompassing of all reality. . . . but he is still a male authority.

One of the earliest issues Christian feminism addressed, articulated by Rosemary Radford Ruether and others, questioned the adequacy for women of this masculine redeemer: "Can a male savior save women?"[22] While the discussion in this section does not hinge around Ruether's concerns for Jesus' full incarnation and women's resulting biological fitness for ordination (which in the contemporary mainline Protestant context and even in Bonhoeffer's Germany had ceased to be serious

22. Ruether, *Sexism and God-Talk*, 116–38. Writing within an ecclesial context that exalted Jesus' maleness as the primary impediment to women's capacity for embodying him in ordained ministry, Ruether argued that such a theology fixated on Jesus' biological maleness logically excludes women not only from priestly orders but also from salvation itself. If what is not assumed is not redeemed, as St. Athanasius insisted with regard to Jesus' full humanity, then a savior whose maleness is his distinguishing characteristic has clearly not assumed (and thus redeemed) female humanity. In this case, Ruether asserts, a male savior cannot save women. If however the humanity Jesus assumed in the incarnation is taken to encompass all human beings in all their diversity, then there is no biological reason why a woman (any more than a non-Palestinian-Jewish man) cannot sacramentally image Christ.

concerns for discussion[23]), nevertheless her question is an important one for my purposes as well. This section will address whether the male Jesus, in particular Bonhoeffer's Jesus, is a liberating figure for women in abuse and in what ways this is so (or not).

As chapter four demonstrated, women who have lived with abuse have had their lives, bodies, and spirits twisted by enforced submission to a male who claimed god-like power over them, whose commands demanded ready and willing obedience at risk of severe punishment, whose face and voice and whims insisted on unwavering attention. Similarly, Bonhoeffer's Christ in *Discipleship* (especially in Clifford Green's reading) has comparable features.[24] As the living Word of God, with full divine authority, this Christ commands both a spatial and a temporal immediacy of obedience to his call. In responding, a person is explicitly not to argue with or rationalize away unpleasant-seeming directives but simply to submit to them. When Jesus commands, the disciple is to devote the same unceasing and self-forgetful attention to his face and voice as the victim of abuse grants the abuser. Is this really a healthy model of Christian redemption? Does it not simply repeat the same dynamics all over again, keeping these women perennially enslaved to one male authority or another, only this time with "divine" sanction?

These are unsettling questions with which to approach Jesus as experienced and interpreted by Bonhoeffer. Of course Christian feminists will always have to come to terms with the fact that the one they confess as God incarnate was enfleshed as a biological male. In Jesus God became fully human, and humanity invariably includes gender, here male gender. That this concrete historical reality does not imply any masculine exclusivity in terms of either the full incarnational assumption of humanity or the revealed gender of the "true God" here enfleshed are points I take for granted.[25] Nor do I question Jesus' centrality in Christian spirituality or wish to sideline him discreetly as being too

23. See the essays collected in the volume, *'Darum wagt es, Schwestern . . .'*

24. See, e.g., Green, *Sociality*, 173. Green asserts that Bonhoeffer's statements about Christ "have a spirit which is nothing less than violent and which recurs throughout the book."

25. See the discussion in Johnson, *She Who Is*, 150–69 ("Jesus-Sophia"), for historical and theological discussion of these matters within the Christian tradition, as well as her proposals for a Sophia christology fully revealed in Jesus' own maleness.

male for use by women. Attempts to downplay the full particularity of the incarnation, whether in the name of openness to other religions, the most commendable feminist principles, or even Nazi anti-Semitism, strip Christian faith of both its concreteness, the inevitably scandalous carnality of an enfleshed God, and the profoundly intimate relational impulse at its core. Without the full humanity of Jesus, in whose very flesh we encounter and are drawn into the mystery of the Triune God, there would be little authentically Christian left. For the Christian women living with abuse whose experience this study attempts to explore, then, Jesus as he is preached, taught, worshiped, embodied, and questioned is at the center of faith. The question relevant here is not *whether* to deal with Jesus as male but *how* he functions in any given spirituality, whether in oppressive or liberating ways.

Therefore, in relation to Bonhoeffer's spirituality and portrayal of Jesus, I would make the following points, both critical and affirming. First, it is true that in *Discipleship* and others of his writings Bonhoeffer describes Jesus requiring submissive behavior (like total self-surrender or humble obedience) that for those on the underside represents nothing new. From what we know of Bonhoeffer's personality, however, such behavior was indeed new for him, whereas the "commanding Christ" of *Discipleship* has clear resemblances to the assumed authority Bonhoeffer himself displayed in life. This suggests to me that the Christ he longed for took the form (at least in part) of primary aspects of his own psyche, liberating previously submerged parts of himself for expression of new dimensions of human being: here, for his desire for surrender and obedience to a trustworthy and authoritative Other.

If soluble selves, however, particularly women in abuse, heal and recover most powerfully not by being told what to do by yet another authority, however well-advised or trustworthy, but by being given the freedom and encouragement to develop their own agency and initiative,[26] then this Christ seems an inadequate, if not harmful, companion for them. What these women need might be a compassionate Jesus, infinitely patient, in whose arms they find the safety they need to let go and rest, in whose care they experience never-ending streams of mercy and solidarity in grief, in whose wounds their own are healed, by whose

26. Herman, *Trauma and Recovery*, 133–36.

encouragement they can eventually rise up and move, transformed, into new life. Rather than the commanding Christ of Bonhoeffer's longing, perhaps they most need a "holding space," the comforting and protective arms of Jesus the Mother.[27] Just as I am suggesting Jesus came to Bonhoeffer in the image of Bonhoeffer's own strengths in order to invite him into new, frightening, or under-developed dimensions of himself, perhaps so too Jesus comes to abused women in their own strength as well: as mother, as "holding space," providing their own primary gift *back to them* in order to invite healing comparable to Dietrich's and the surfacing of submerged dimensions of their humanity. At a deeper level, then, perhaps Bonhoeffer's Christ functions most truly not as some paradigm of all readers' encounter with the Incarnate One but as a model of how Jesus comes to disciples in precisely the form they most need.

And fundamentally this very approach is essential to how Bonhoeffer sees Jesus functioning for people. One of his lifelong interests is the church's discernment and reclaiming of Jesus for very new situations. "God," he felt, was a misleading construct liable to be skewed according to the dominant presuppositions of any given individual or era.[28] Especially in his prison letters, he ponders the discrepancy between what Christian and other forms of religiosity have asserted about "God," an almighty, otherworldly *deus ex machina* who functions only at the boundaries of human life, and what is revealed of God in Jesus Christ. What matters and what is alone salvific, he believed throughout his life, is encounter with the Incarnate One who never ceases to surprise us, yet whose revealed concreteness in Word, sacrament, and community is an ongoing reality check against mere deification of the status quo or our own imaginings into "God." He writes,

27. For an exploration of ways Jesus actually has been imaged as mother in the Christian tradition, particularly in medieval mysticism, see Bynum, *Jesus as Mother*. On the healing role of the "holding space," see pp. 155–58 of chapter four.

28. The prison letters that deal with this theme include DBW 8: 402–8, 414–16, 476–82, 453–56, 503–4, 509–12, 515–16, 529–38, and 556–51. See also *Discipleship*, 59: "A Christianity in which there is only God the Father, but not Christ as a living Son, actually cancels discipleship." Finally, the *Ethics* develops this theme of Jesus as the ultimate criterion of God and reality. See *Ethics*, 47–75. Because of its central programmatic significance for Bonhoeffer's entire project, the new edition of the *Ethics* places this section at the outset of the volume.

> The key to everything is the "in him." All that we may rightly ex-
> pect from God, and ask [God] for, is to be found in Jesus Christ.
> The God of Jesus Christ has nothing to do with what God, as we
> imagine [God], could do and ought to do. If we are to learn what
> God promises, and . . . fulfills, we must persevere in quiet medi-
> tation on the life, sayings, deeds, sufferings, and death of Jesus.[29]

Thus for Bonhoeffer daily return to contemplative encounter with Jesus
Christ was the opening to the authentically transcendent God who
comes not in the forms we expect or imagine (i.e., for the abuse victim,
as just another abuser or judge, only omnipotent this time), but in surprising and liberating reality.

Yet ultimately this suggests that even for Bonhoeffer the image
of the "commanding Christ" is inadequate by itself. If this is all Jesus
Christ is for Bonhoeffer, then Jesus ends up looking more like just such
a projection of Bonhoeffer's own commanding ego than the authentically transcendent One. In fact I believe this to be true, on two levels.
First, it is true in that this is not all there is to Jesus for Bonhoeffer; I see
more to his Christ than merely the projection of his own authoritarian
ego. And it is precisely those qualities of Jesus *not* obviously inherent
within Bonhoeffer that I believe prove redemptive for him. Specifically,
my reading of *Discipleship*, unlike Green's, finds the motifs of trust and
intimacy with Jesus to be at least of equal importance to Bonhoeffer as
that of the commanding authority of Christ. This is not a relationship
marked by coercion, punishment, or arbitrary displays of power, nor by
dominance that squelches human freedom or insists on slave-like devotion. Bonhoeffer's Christ does display impressive authority, it is true; but
his power is bent on demolishing sin, all that destroys human life, not
human beings themselves. The power of Jesus bears divine authority
to break through the most entrenched and deadly forms of deceit and
imprisonment, realities only too familiar in 1937 Nazi Germany. But
its effect and goal are light-years removed from the terror an abuser
intends to effect in victims. The goal of Jesus' authority in human lives
for Bonhoeffer is no more or less than to make possible a free, loving,
and whole-hearted intimacy with him and those he loves. As we saw
in chapter three, there is no other content or agenda to discipleship for
Bonhoeffer than this *Bindung an Jesus*, an entrance (one might suggest)
into precisely that "holding space" essential to human flourishing on all

29. LPP 391 (DBW 8: 572–73).

levels. Jesus' authority for Bonhoeffer is a means whose end is marked by consummate trust and companionship. To mistake it for the central feature of Bonhoeffer's view of Jesus is to misread him, in my view.

On a second level, however, I consider Bonhoeffer's reflections on the inevitable projection that accompanies human God-images to be an appropriate caution with regard to his own views of Jesus as well. Perhaps it is because he recognizes this tendency to view Jesus in his own image that he insists throughout his life on the necessity of returning to the Word over and over in community, in order to come ever anew into contact with those stories and teachings, through others' eyes as well, that convey Christ in ever-shifting dimensions of fullness. For his own redemption, in fact, Bonhoeffer may need to hear of and be drawn to love the Jesus of abused women, a Jesus he might never imagine on his own, yet whose wounds reveal his own, whose tenderness gives him rest, whose protective arms stir his own maternal capacities toward himself and others and open his own "inner space" for self-awareness and healing (see pp. 158–59).

And, thus, by the same token, perhaps abused women can find dimensions of Jesus Christ in Bonhoeffer's vision similarly revelatory, precisely in its otherness. Bonhoeffer shows a Jesus who is not cowed by any human authority: the mighty outstretched arm of God who seeks out disciples and calls them by name, who bids them leave their nets, their places of taxation, even their families—all that would hinder their abundance of life in him. He calls them into freedom, breaks all imprisoning bonds with divine power, and claims people for a new life of trust and love. In fact, precisely in its liberating power, its exhilarating release to a life of abandon whose only purpose is love, Bonhoeffer's vision of Jesus might be seen for abused women as the psychic arrival at last of the rapprochement father, that lifeline of freedom and recognition whose absence for girls on the part of their early fathers can render them vulnerable to exploitative men later in life.[30] In this view, perhaps Jesus (especially a very "other" Jesus for abused women such as Bonhoeffer's), like a good therapist and as himself the Good Teacher, not only, as we have seen, creates the maternal holding space needed for self-awareness and self-love, but also provides that pre-oedipal paternal

30. See Benjamin, *Bonds of Love*, 107–14.

liberator whose experienced recognition Benjamin asserts is so important for the development of one's own agency, power, and desire.

Further, this Jesus not only provides the internalized validating
male presence crucial to women's escape from the pattern of submission to another's domination; he also *breaks the gender dynamics* sustaining these patterns. For this is a male who, rather than demanding
service and insisting on being fed, himself comes as servant and gives
his own body for food.[31] Caroline Walker Bynum writes of the Middle
Ages' association of the female, and especially the female body, with
food: "food was not merely a powerful symbol. It was also a particularly
obvious and accessible symbol to women, who were more immediately
involved than men in the preparation and distribution of food. Women's
bodies, in the acts of lactation and of giving birth, were analogous" to
food.[32] To a disturbing extent, our culture still associates the female with
body, food, being consumed; countless victims of eating disorders, for
instance, testify to this in vivid ways. Thus Jesus, this gender-subverting
redeemer, allows women to "eat" divine power through his flesh, nourishing *their* flesh, rather than always to be consumed, the ones "eaten"
by the demands of family, society, or self-hatred. This makes possible a
bodily link between Jesus and women, not anymore in the ways female
suffering passively echoes Jesus' in a violently misogynist world (the
meek she-lamb ever being led to the slaughter), nor only in his body's
life-giving "femaleness" (though certainly that), but even in his maleness. Counter to traditions of sexism the world over in which the female
cooks and serves and does not eat, is in fact the "eaten," while the male
reclines and consumes, is the "eater," here the Human One gives himself as food *for women*, to be handled, borne, blessed, and consumed by
them, and to nourish, empower, and transform them from within into
ever stronger and freer female selves and bodies.

Finally, Bonhoeffer's centering on Jesus may have an additional, unexpected benefit for women in abuse. That is, not only does
Bonhoeffer's Jesus himself embody liberating aspects, but the fact that
this spirituality focuses on Jesus rather than God (and in fact is suspicious of most ecclesial "God" images) opens space for new images of

31. Bonhoeffer does not develop a sacramental spirituality as explicitly as he does
his focus on Word, but he does cherish the Lord's Supper and in particular its physical-
ity in uniting our flesh with Jesus' own and that of one another. See LT 29, 117–18.

32. Bynum, *Holy Feast and Holy Fast*, 30.

the divine. A christocentric spirituality not closely bound to God the Father, like Bonhoeffer's, makes possible very different conceptions of the One Jesus embodies and reveals. Bonhoeffer himself does not move far in this direction, but one can build on his vision in ways that develop female face/s of God. Even Bonhoeffer, speaking in *Life Together* of God bearing human beings in the body of Jesus Christ, writes, "God bore them as a mother carries her child."[33]

Such personal and public naming of God as female is still considered shocking in many places, the degree of shock corresponding painfully to the extent to which women are unconsciously seen as not fully participating in the *imago dei,* thus the extent to which femaleness is not seen as an appropriate image of God. Just as women's authentic, separate, full humanity is often effaced in family, church, and society, so too is the female selfhood of God; the church's fear of God-images and metaphors that more richly mirror the diversity of all reality corresponds precisely to its fear of listening deeply to women's voices, needs, and experience. In both cases, the recovery and embrace of the female is seen as a threat to the structures of faith rather than an opening to divine and human *reality* that can only bless the church, its leaders, and its male and female members.[34]

The church may at times be afraid of reality in its emerging fullness, but within his own limits, as best he was able, Bonhoeffer was not. Bonhoeffer's conception of Jesus Christ *as* reality therefore opens new space for the Christian perception of reality in female dimensions. Far from representing an abandonment of the faith and its traditions, or somehow forcing people to relinquish the images of Father or Lord by which they have come to love God (in large part through the words of Jesus himself), this approach simply opens the door wider to allow the Spirit to go on revealing dimensions of reality we have not yet been able

33. LT 100. Of course, Bonhoeffer by and large implicitly assumes the primacy of God's fatherhood. See for instance his trinitarian-structured prayers for fellow prisoners, LPP 139 (DBW 8: 204–8). What is noticeable however is how relatively seldom he uses this image.

34. Of course, considerable work has been done within feminist Christian circles on the recovery of female God-imagery within Scripture and tradition, as well as the emergence of new imagery, placing all of this within an analysis of the symbolic, metaphorical, and reality-structuring significance of God-language more broadly. See, for instance, Ramshaw, *God Beyond Gender;* Johnson, *She Who Is;* McFague, *Models of God;* Mollenkott, *Divine Feminine;* and Bloomquist, "Let God Be God."

to bear, as Jesus promised. For those who suffer any sort of oppression, not only women, the discovery of their own image reflected in God is one of the most revolutionary dimensions of healing and empowerment faith can offer, just as stripping this *imago* of human forms to be suppressed (by means of purely male or, visually, purely Anglo God-images) is perhaps the most devastating form of spiritual violation. If in the example given above Jesus embodies for human beings of all stripes a maternal "holding space," then it is no great leap but in fact the same process by which Christian theology has always proceeded to assert that he is thereby revealing God as mother, or in fact God the Mother, a God who can be imaged and experienced fully as female, referred to and worshiped with female pronouns, a God who can connect in an immanent way with women's own femaleness just as men have always been able to experience with God's maleness. There is nothing scandalous about this. It is the ongoing process of revelation, necessarily trinitarian in structure and centered always in the incarnation of Jesus Christ, that has ensured faithfulness and fruitfulness through centuries of Christian reflection and prayer. And Bonhoeffer's simultaneous focusing on Jesus, and anti-idolatrous openness to the God Jesus reveals both personally and communally, provides explicit freedom for the emergence of reality as inclusive of the female in ways that can ultimately only bless and deepen Christian faith.

Can a male savior save women? I believe so, given a feminist reading of the significance of Jesus' gender as subverting rather than reinforcing patterns of male dominance, and of Jesus himself as truly revealing ultimate reality. And I believe that Bonhoeffer's vision of Jesus, while not sufficient by itself, provides surprising resources for the feminist encounter with Jesus. As "holding space" in reassuring and unfailing *Bindung*, as Good Teacher, as powerful and liberating rapprochement father, Bonhoeffer's Jesus creates space for abused women's psychological and spiritual healing, I suggest, even as his commanding style and insistence on self-renunciation reflects Bonhoeffer's own psychology in ways less directly applicable to them. But even there, Bonhoeffer's salvific encounter with a Jesus who met his deepest needs and called him into the forms of life he most needed can invite women in abuse (indeed, all readers) to the same. A reading that takes account of Bonhoeffer's biases, even as it appreciates his gifts to the church, will best make this possible.

Stellvertretung and Responsibility

If the previous section dealt with the person of Jesus Christ for Bonhoeffer, this section explores his conception of the implications of Christ's saving work. We saw in chapter two (pp. 53–55) Bonhoeffer's key doctrine of *Stellvertretung*, or "vicarious representative action." As outlined there, this term is intended to encompass both Christ's action on behalf of humanity and Christians' own faithful stance toward others in conformation with him. Like Jesus himself, Christians are drawn into a life whose overarching character is one of responsibility toward God, others, and the world.[35]

This *Stellvertretung* has three levels for Bonhoeffer. First, it refers to Jesus' role as the representative of God, enacting a vicarious reconciliation of humanity with God. He makes God present in his own flesh, even as he simultaneously makes present within God the new and redeemed humanity, the world's future. Jesus is thus the primal *Stellvertreter*, representing God to humanity and humanity to God, and to the extent Christians participate in his form, being con-formed to him, they too take on the role of *Stellvertreter* of others and of Christ in the world. Jesus is the One in and through whom we see God, others, and the world most clearly for Bonhoeffer; as fully God and fully human, he can represent each. Thus his being reveals how any given *Stellvertretung* both participates in the reality it represents and offers its face to others, transparent to Christ himself as the paradigmatic *Stellvertreter*.

Stellvertretung for Bonhoeffer asserts, second, that Christians stand in one another's place. This means, among other things, that any single Christian can be called upon to represent the church as a whole in faithful and courageous witness in society. In doing so, the Christian both participates in the church's reality as one of its members and also steps forward to represent it as an icon of Christ to others. For Bonhoeffer there is no sitting back on the sidelines, hoping someone else will move to speak or act; there can be no excuses of, "well, I didn't vote for Hitler, so it's not my fault," or "I'm not in a leadership position, so it's not my

---

35. See the section on vicarious representative action (*Ethics*, 257–60) in the portion of the *Ethics* devoted to "The Structure of the Responsible Life" (*Ethics*, 257–89). Following this section, he outlines "The Place of Responsibility," a reflection on vocation (*Ethics*, 289–97). The unfinished chapter was to have concluded with consideration of "Love and Responsibility." On these motifs, see Glenthøj, "Der unbegreiflich hohe Gedanke der Stellvertretung," and Mayer, "Beten und Tun des Gerechten."

responsibility." For him, responsibility ultimately describes the voca-tion of every Christian to act according to his or her station, and every Christian must see him- or herself as a fully adequate and important representative[36] of the church, the collective person of Jesus Christ.

This deep sense of the necessary congruence between personal faith, risk, and action has its roots in the Bonhoeffer family's suspicion of any hypocritical discord between word and deed, and its members' cherishing of such active personal integrity as a central element of their identity. In his case, this meant that if Jews were being deported to Auschwitz it was no other Christian's or citizen's responsibility more than his own to act in the most effective and well-discerned possible way to stop this, according to his own context and vocation.[37] And here, not coincidentally, he moved into a resistance in which this en-tire Bonhoeffer family participated and for which it suffered greatly. They saw their position of privilege (in terms of education, custody of German heritage, and social-political rank within the structures of power) not as a justification for evading risk, let alone a means of doing so, but as precisely the arena within which they were expected by God to devote themselves as fully as necessary to stopping the horror. While personal survival was obviously a priority in the conspirators' plans to construct a new, post-Nazi Germany, and Bonhoeffer himself enjoyed the tremendous gifts of human life and was in no hurry to depart from it, nevertheless the doctrine of *Stellvertretung* he developed did not al-

36. The earlier translation of the *Ethics* used the term "deputy" for *Stellvertreter*, and "deputyship" for *Stellvertretung*. While this translation has problems deriving from its law enforcement connotations, it captures Bonhoeffer's sense of personal responsibility on behalf of the whole. Just as a sheriff's deputy is not allowed to step back and pre-tend s/he doesn't notice a crime being committed, neither can any Christian, however "lowly." Each is *Stellvertreter* for all the rest, in acts of mercy and justice.

37. This insistence on congruence between faith and action allowed him very early in the Hitler era to critique the traditional Lutheran stance on the church's role vis-à-vis the state. The church, as *Stellvertreter Christi*, cannot sit idly by as the Nazis take over every dimension of society, while claiming irresponsibility for the "worldly" kingdom. Instead the church's role in situations of injustice is, first, to remind the state of its God-given mandates for justice, law, order, and compassion; second, to minister to all the victims of the state's wrong or evil actions (i.e., not only Christian victims); and, third, when necessary, actually to "jam a spoke in the wheel" of the state, that is, to engage in active political resistance. *Stellvertretung* means responsibility, for both individuals and the church as a whole, and no dimension of the created world lies outside the sphere of responsibility. Cf. "Die Kirche vor der Judenfrage," DBW 12:349–58, April 15, 1933.

low fears for survival ultimately to stand in the way of acting in responsibility for the coming generation.

For the third aspect of *Stellvertretung*, inextricable from the first and second, is that the Christian represents not only other Christians or citizens in faithful responsible action, but also Jesus Christ himself. Just as Jesus was the "person for others," so the Christian is to be a "person for others," and "the church is the church only when it exists for others."[38] Christians are to be Christ's representatives in similarly self-sacrificial devotion to others; this is not some sort of strategy for suffering but a central means of participation in the Beloved, in Jesus' own cruciform life in the world. In a context where by 1940 even the Confessing Church was struggling for survival rather than speaking out on behalf of the Jews and other Nazi victims, Bonhoeffer considered such ecclesial focus on self-preservation a sign of skewed vision, a failure to discern and participate in the form of Christ in the world. It is precisely this shape of Jesus' own life poured out for the world that underlies Christians' *Stellvertretung* and Bonhoeffer's risky move in solidarity with victims of Nazi evil into the conspiracy opposing Hitler. In his *Ethics* he writes,

> Jesus—the life, our life—the Son of God who became human, lived as our vicarious representative. . . . His entire living, acting, and suffering was vicarious representative action [Stellvertretung]. All that human beings were supposed to live, do, and suffer was fulfilled in him. In this real vicarious representative action, in which his human existence consists, he is the responsible human being par excellence. Since he is life, all of life through him is destined to be vicarious representative action.[39]

Thus he sees the primary significance of the outpouring of Jesus' life as being a model for our lives of similarly devoted love toward others and action on their behalf. This allows him to restate at the end of his life themes first sounded in *Sanctorum Communio*. For he goes on immediately to write, "Vicarious representative action and therefore responsibility is possible only in completely devoting one's own life to another person. Only those who are selfless live responsibly, which means that only selfless people truly *live*."[40]

38. LPP 382 (DBW 8: 560).

39. DBWE 6 (*Ethics*), 258–59.

40. Ibid., 259. Italics Bonhoeffer's.

Of course, all we have seen about the very different context of women in abuse indicates that this Christology alone is not adequate for them. Selflessness and surrender, the most Christ-like possible martyrdoms in conscious imitation of Jesus' own suffering for and with others, do not break this cycle of violence and are not redemptive. The new English translation of *Stellvertretung* may well use the term "*vicarious representative action*," but in regard to Christ's work very little emphasis falls here on its truly vicarious nature. Bonhoeffer's interest is in developing the implications for Christians of their own vocation to Christ-like action in the world. This is obviously in no way un-Christian, let alone unbiblical; yet by his great emphasis on Jesus as essentially "for others," making us "persons for others" as well, he tends to overlook Jesus as, crucially, "for me." The *promeity* of Lutheran christological spirituality is not absent from Bonhoeffer's thinking, but it takes a back seat.[41] Bonhoeffer seems to speak from a place already among the inner circle and is interested then in how he should relate, with Jesus, to others.

Again, this is to my mind an instance of Bonhoeffer's gendered tendency to locate himself and his presumed audience as "selves" rather than "others." For those who have been forced into the "other" location, however, the description of Jesus as the person for others reads differently. It means that he is fundamentally "for *me* as an 'other.'" When Bonhoeffer is read against the grain, when Jesus' focus on others turns out to include *oneself*, then the significance of this "other"-centeredness of Jesus is not first that it requires one's own ongoing other-focus like his. Rather, for those who are "others" it points out Jesus' great love of oneself, describing his embrace of one's actual alienated or suppressed self through every dimension of his life, death, and resurrection. Jesus' tremendous and unceasing devotion makes a person no longer merely "other" but a holy center able by grace to receive him and the outpoured life he offers.

For women in abuse, then, a liberating christological spirituality of *Stellvertretung* must include the truly vicarious aspect of Jesus' life and death. Prior to any statements about enacted responsibility toward

---

41. As noted earlier, this is in part a reaction against a piety that in its exclusive focus on personal salvation tended to ignore the public social arena. On Bonhoeffer's christology more generally see Abromeit, *Das Geheimnis Christi*; Pangritz, "'Who Is Jesus Christ for Us Today?'"; Aveling, "Dietrich Bonhoeffer's Christology"; and Phillips, *Christ for Us in the Theology of Dietrich Bonhoeffer*.

others, Jesus is simply gift, "for me," *pro me*. The full promeity of Jesus' attention enacts spiritually what the patient-focus of truly healing therapeutic relationships does psychologically; both create the attentive and unwavering focus of transformative "holding space." First and foremost, contra Bonhoeffer here, then, the life and death of Jesus are not merely a model to follow on behalf of others, keeping women (or anyone) continually crucified throughout the generations and focused on their oppressors' needs. Jesus' death is truly once-and-for-all, completely vicarious in its redemptive power. This death ends death and bursts forth into resurrection. These wounds heal wounds and do not inflict them. This One "for others" is, always, "for me," and the blood and water flowing from his body, his heart, are meant to birth and nourish, not to justify continuing hemorrhage. Marginalized and rejected, Jesus himself becomes "other" in solidarity with "others," in order to redeem each one for holy new *self*-centering, for conformation to one's own authentic being in him, for the sort of selfhood that alone is able to love in freedom and abundance.

This is far from the complete surrender of oneself that Bonhoeffer names as the heart of Christian *Stellvertretung*, the radical selflessness long associated with his courage and martyrdom and taught widely in his name. Yet, interestingly, in the very paragraph of the *Ethics* in which Bonhoeffer states that *Stellvertretung* consists of "the complete surrender of one's own life to the other [person]," he goes on to make a striking assertion. For the first time in his published writings, that is, he posits *two* ways the relation between self and other can go awry: "by absolutizing either my own self or the other person."[42] The first of these, of course, is the problem Bonhoeffer has deplored in himself for years and against which so many of his writings inveigh. But the second is new. For the first time, he is asserting the equal dangers that can result from absolutizing another person: the very problem that befalls soluble selves. He goes on to assert that in this case

> the welfare of the other person for whom I am responsible is made absolute while ignoring all other responsibilities. This leads to an arbitrariness in my action, which makes a mockery

42. DBWE 6 (*Ethics*), 259.

of my responsibility before God, who in Jesus Christ is the God
of all people.[43]

Thus Bonhoeffer is beginning to name the possibility that in fact
the "complete surrender to the other person" he otherwise unambiguously recommends may actually not be such a good idea in all circumstances. That is, he suggests that even "responsibility" can be taken too
far if a single commitment or relationship throws out of balance a person's obligations to the full scope of his or her responsibilities, including
(one might suggest) to one's own health, vocation, desires, conscience,
and worth. This echoes the Harvard researchers' findings that in fact
just such an imbalance characterizes the lives of adolescent girls, who
learn to overvalue relationships (especially the romantic relationship)
at the cost of connection to their own bodies, selves, and voices.[44] Such
an imbalance in favor of one overblown responsibility indicates, for
Bonhoeffer, the neglect of one's ultimate responsibility to God, who is
the God of oneself as well as of the other person. Over-responsibility
toward a particular person or situation, therefore, is a form of idolatry,
attempting to set up that person or situation as an absolute principle
(i.e., an abstraction) and denying the ever-shifting concreteness of well-
discerned vocation in every new situation. He goes on, therefore, to say
that whether a person absolutizes one's own ego or another person, "[t]
he origin, essence, and goal of responsible life is denied in both cases,
and responsibility has become a self-made, abstract idol."[45]

This is an important distinction to be heard among those for
whom "responsibility" does indeed become an idol, those whose devotion to partner or spouse above everything else blinds them to the costs
of such selflessness for themselves and others and distracts them from
the fearsome and liberating necessity of discerning God's actual call to
them and their true responsibilities. Bonhoeffer's ethics of responsibility can at times sound like simply an echo of the self-abnegating focus
on obligation to others that so often marks those living in situations of
abuse. These words, therefore, come as an important reminder that one's
ultimate responsibility, always, is to the living God, to whose call even

43. Ibid.

44. See pp. 122–32 of chapter 4. See also L. Stern, "Disavowing the Self in Female
Adolescence."

45. DBWE 6 (*Ethics*), 259.

the most central responsibilities must yield. And they make possible an embrace of responsibility that takes seriously *all* the interwoven obligations and relations of a human life, learning to weigh them against one another in an ongoing process of balance and discernment according to the ultimate responsibility of faithfulness to God.

I have hypothesized that it was Bonhoeffer's own movement out of safety and privilege that made possible his increasing awareness of the needs of the self toward the end of his life, along with the dangers of some of the more one-sided formulations of his earlier career. We see this in the passage above, where the responsible life of *Stellvertretung* comes into clearer focus later in his life within this new, broader awareness of abuses in favor of both self *and* other. Interestingly, a similarly tentative awareness appears at this point in regard to the vicarious nature of Jesus' suffering as well. In fact, Bonhoeffer's last circular letter before his arrest, an unfinished reflection to the scattered Finkenwalde community, perceives the difficulty of understanding *Stellvertretung* primarily as the Christ-shaped model for our own parallel action. He writes,

> we must guard ourselves against confusing ourselves with Christ. Christ endured all suffering and all human guilt himself in full measure—indeed, this was what made him Christ, that he and he alone bore it all. But Christ was able to suffer along with others because he was simultaneously able to redeem from suffering. Out of his love and power to redeem people came his power to suffer with them. We are not called to take upon ourselves the suffering of all the world; by ourselves we are fundamentally not able to suffer with others at all, because we are not able to redeem. . . . We are called only to gaze full of joy at the One who in reality suffered with us and became the Redeemer. Full of joy, we are enabled to believe that there was and is One to whom no human suffering or sin is foreign and who in deepest love accomplished our redemption. Only in such joy in Christ the Redeemer shall we be preserved from hardening ourselves where human suffering encounters us, and from becoming resigned under the experience of suffering. Only to the extent we believe in Christ, to the extent we . . . to Christ.[46]

---

46. *Conspiracy and Imprisonment* (DBWE 16), 378. The letter breaks off at this point. The term translated "suffer with" here is *mitleiden*, the verbal form of the German word for compassion, namely *Mitleid*. In this section Bonhoeffer creates a juxtaposition between "leiden" and "mitleiden" that is beautiful and crucial to his meaning. In trans-

A great myth that keeps people in abusive relationships is precisely that the suffering endured is somehow holy, even redemptive in its Christ-likeness. Bonhoeffer's reflections here are important in helping people release that misconception: only Jesus is God, not I. For those struggling to love an abuser, these words can be lifelines indeed, releasing them from the temptation to be the Messiah trying valiantly to redeem the beloved's agony by suffering it with or even somehow for him or her. Instead, Bonhoeffer gives permission to let Jesus alone be the one to go deep into the abuser's heart and pain, for he is the only one whose *mitleiden* (compassionate shared suffering) can ever, however slowly and mysteriously, prove redemptive. This frees the partner to let go, to release the impossible responsibility of the other's salvation, and to turn for salvation to this same com/passionate One. There the victim of abuse can meet at last the One who is truly present for *her* (or *him*); and there s/he can begin, in time, to discern the deeper contours of authentic responsibility to oneself, to others, and to God.

Helpful Themes of Bonhoeffer's for Women in Abuse

In the preceding sections of this chapter I have reviewed aspects of Bonhoeffer's thinking that are problematic or potentially ambiguous in their direct relevance for women in abuse. In these sections I have attempted both to highlight the difficulty of uncritical application of these elements of Bonhoeffer's thinking to soluble selves and to demonstrate ways his own work provides important self-critique or amplification. This next section continues this conversation between my readings of Bonhoeffer and of contemporary feminist psychologists regarding women in abuse. Here I move into the more unambiguously helpful aspects of Bonhoeffer's legacy in order to construct crucial "Bonhoeffer-ean" foundations for a liberating spirituality for soluble selves. These dimensions of Bonhoeffer's thinking are organized un-

---

lating this passage I originally tried "have compassion" for *mitleiden*. This both carries the implied connection to *Mitleid* as compassion and also has a nice, if subtle, linguistic tie to *Leiden* (suffering) via Jesus' Passion: so "passion/compassion" to translate "leiden/ mitleiden." But this translation does not encompass the other primary and more literal meaning of "mitleiden," namely "to suffer with." This carries Bonhoeffer's meaning better: that Christ is the only one who can truly suffer with others because he is the only one who can redeem them. Our compassion, he asserts, while essential, is not able to reach the level of shared suffering that alone is redemptive.

der headings describing necessary aspects of the health and growth of abuse victims: the healing relationship, self-awareness, self-defense, and self-investment. Just as the preceding sections included both critique of Bonhoeffer and a retrieval of ways his writings are helpful in the matters being examined, so here too each point includes two broad moments. I look first at contributions Bonhoeffer makes within each of the four areas and subsequently suggest ways these motifs point forward in directions Bonhoeffer himself did not (yet, or fully) recognize.

Healing Relationship

In chapter four we saw the importance of a safe and trustworthy relationship for the healing abuse victims need. Such "holding space" creates the transitional arena of trust and care that allows a vulnerable self to develop. For abused women, this provides the sheer novelty of a non-attacking other, a gaze that is profoundly loving rather than accusatory or punishing, a space for nascent self-awareness that evokes neither retaliation nor dismissal by the other. I find two major places in Bonhoeffer in which such holy or "holding" space takes shape: the relationship with Jesus Christ and the experience of friendship intimate enough to include confessional self-disclosure.

In chapter three we saw some of the ways Bonhoeffer experienced and described the relationship with Jesus as transforming for the disciple. I highlighted there the significance of the sensory metaphors Bonhoeffer uses to evoke this relationship, including gaze, voice, and touch. In all three cases, he employs these images in order to express the importance of remaining close to Jesus, in "touch" with him, within earshot, not distracted by sidelong glances. This takes place not out of compulsion or fear but out of trusting love; it is a devotion rooted in desire. We saw earlier in the present chapter as well how for those in abuse the person of Jesus can not only provide this healing space, a relationship marked by safety and love, but precisely in his maleness breaks internalized gender expectations and offers that deeply validating recognition whose absence can keep women vulnerable to abuse.

Thus the imagery of the voice and gaze of Jesus in prayer and in meditation on Scripture are important for Christian victims of abuse, for they are violently conditioned to watch the *abuser's* face for cues of imminent outbursts, to let the *abuser's* voice fill soul and body. In contrast, the gaze and voice of Jesus provide a healing and utterly trust-worthy alternative, with the power to break the helpless fixation on others' demands and create a new reality in which there is no attacking but only love. This holding space created in prayer draws the survivor out of the world controlled by the abuser's voice and hateful glare and into a world where Jesus' presence allows her to see herself and reality through new eyes.

Some theorists have questioned the usefulness for women of such "gaze" imagery, citing devastating ways the omniscient external and in-ternalized male gaze has been used to objectify women.[47] We saw this in the story of Liza in chapter four, who in adolescence found herself becoming a "cover girl," dangerously removed from her own body, voice, and perceptions of reality. Clearly, submission to the "Over-Eye"[48] of male-normed culture has devastating effects on girls and women, often mirroring their submission to male control in the relational arena and undermining their capacity to see and name their own reality. The visual realm too often seems to imprison women in categories created by others. For these reasons, Sallie McFague has suggested the impor-tance for women of "touch" metaphors rather than "gaze" or other visual metaphors. Unlike gaze, which can be all too distancing, touch requires immediacy of presence; it does not scan and categorize in a drive for remote control but claims access only to as much reality as lies directly at hand. Like the four blind men each with his piece of the elephant, it does not assert some ultimate power to name but simply describes its perceptions. And touch both allows for and necessitates a sort of skin-to-skin knowing that is intimate, vulnerable, and deeply pleasurable.[49]

Yet while these concerns are perceptive, they do not in my view reach the heart of the matter. As any abuse victim knows, touch or voice can be abused as violently as gaze; the problem is the attack itself that takes shape in various metaphorical and actual enactments of violation.

47. See, for instance, Mulvey whose 1975 film analysis "Visual Pleasure and Narrative Cinema" initiated this critique (reprinted as pp. 14–26 of *Visual and Other Pleasures*); also Rose, *Sexuality and the Field of Vision*; Silverman, *Acoustic Mirror*; and McFague, "The Arrogant Eye: Knowing Nature as Object," in *Super, Natural Christians*, 67–90. In her subsequent chapter (pp. 91–117), McFague contrasts this "arrogant eye" with the "loving eye" that corresponds to the sort of gaze language I am employing here: an explicitly intersubjective rather than objectifying vision.

48. Cf. Jack, *Silencing the Self*.

49. McFague, *Models of God*, 118–49.

Thus I agree that the hegemony of visual metaphors for "knowing" and "grasping" the real is problematic for the reasons Mulvey, McFague, and others cite, and that the recovery of other sensual images allows for critique of important aspects of patriarchal control and experience of new elements of reality, but I disagree that women should acquiesce to these understandings of vision as intrinsically "masculine," arrogant, or controlling. In fact, precisely because visuality and the power of gaze have so long been considered a male prerogative, I consider them all the more important for retrieval by women conditioned to see themselves as objects. As Elizabeth Grosz asserts,

> When they state baldly that "vision" is male, the look is masculine, or the visual is a phallocentric mode of perception, these feminists confuse a perceptual facility open to both sexes to use as they are able with sexually coded positions of desire within visual (or any other perceptual) functions as a means to an end. Vision is not, cannot be, masculine (nor the tactile or the auditory, feminine); rather, certain ways of using vision (for example, to objectify) may confirm and help produce patriarchal power relations.[50]

Thus the significance of gaze imagery in Bonhoeffer's evocation of the relationship with Jesus is, to my mind, more helpful than problematic. That is, it can be a liberating image by which Christian soluble selves both turn away from the power of the abuser's gaze and, more important, learn to exercise the power of their own seeing. Jesus' gaze creates a non-attacking world for the abuse victim that simultaneously invites the development of her own discerning, reality-shaping visuality. In a fascinating session on trauma and gender at the 2000 annual meeting of the American Academy of Religion, Serene Jones likewise developed this image of divine gaze as a holy or healing form of embrace for survivors of trauma. She highlights this in fact with the language of "beholding": from the cross, the place of God's own experience of shattering trauma, "God *be-holds* the survivor, who beholds God beholding her."[51] Thus we see gaze, "beholding," reclaimed from an oppressive weapon to itself a transformative "holding" in Jesus Christ. In visual, auditory, and tactile metaphors, as in the powerful divine friendship

---

50. Grosz, "Voyeurism/exhibitionism/the gaze," 449.

51. Jones, "Trauma Theory and Christian Theology."

these evoke, Bonhoeffer is sketching a "holding space" of irreplaceable, central importance for Christians.

The second instance of healing relationship I would note for Bonhoeffer is his experience of human friendship. We have seen already how transforming his relationship with Eberhard Bethge was, particularly in the practice of mutual confession, a revelation of embracing self-disclosure. Bonhoeffer was a charismatic figure who attracted people easily and who prior to Finkenwalde of course had friends; his relationships with Paul Lehmann and Franz Hildebrandt, for instance, were very important to him. But Eberhard was, it appears, his first real intimate on the level of no-holds-barred self-revelation, a man for whose gifts in emotional relations Bonhoeffer was grateful all his life. Renate Bethge, Eberhard's later spouse and Dietrich's niece, has written about the emotional environment of the Bonhoeffer family that shaped Dietrich:

> In [our] family it was a matter of course that one did not talk about everything, nor show all of one's feelings. Rather, one reacted moderately to joy and pain, more so than in other families. In [Bonhoeffer's prison novel] we read: "One did not talk about such personal matters but came to terms with them on one's own," and "she herself considered any show of inner processes to be reprehensible and exercised the utmost self-control." Of course, it was known then that we felt more than we were showing, and people reacted with small friendly hints to this, which means we learned to recognize even small signs of emotion, became sensitive to them and reacted defensively to uncontrolled acting out or talking about one's feelings.[52]

These deeply-ingrained Bonhoeffer family attitudes toward appropriate self-disclosure and the abhorrence of free expression of feelings meant that, despite his earlier friendships, the sort of truth-telling in which Dietrich engaged with Eberhard was unprecedented for him and produced similarly unprecedented levels of trust and healing from the demons that plagued him.

This in no way means that as a result of his friendship with Bethge Bonhoeffer became an advocate of indiscriminate self-disclosure as somehow cathartic; he even remained resistant all his life to the practice of therapy as a manifestation of what he considered a shameful

---

52. R. Bethge, "'Elite' and 'Silence' in Bonhoeffer's Person and Thought," 303.

human urge to tell all, an urge he thought should be met with stern self-control.[53] But it does indicate that in Bethge, and particularly in the practice of mutual confession that grounded their friendship, he found an instance of that "holding space" that is profoundly healing.

Thus Bonhoeffer's witness and occasional writings on this subject of friendship are resources for contemporary appropriation as well, bearing witness to the importance not only of professional listeners such as pastors, therapists, or spiritual directors, but of peer relationships committed to each person's whole well-being and encompassing of even the most self-disclosive truth-telling. Of course, women in contemporary U.S. society are widely seen as being better at developing friendships than men, so this might initially seem to be of more relevance for Bonhoeffer himself than for the typical American woman. But one of the hallmarks of abuse is its erosion of friendships, manifested both in the increasing isolation of the victim and in her own reluctance to name devastating realities. Thus Bonhoeffer's highlighting of the importance of radically honest peer relationships rings true for the experience of women in abuse as well; and once in the process of escape such women often find that peer circles with other survivors are essential to their recovery.[54] These are places of safe, revolutionary acceptance where the truth can be told and in which listeners know from their own experience the signs and the cost of self-deception. This frees them to insist for themselves and one another on an audacious honesty that changes lives and forges deep bonds, like the confession experienced by Dietrich and Eberhard.

The place I would like to push Bonhoeffer, precisely on the basis of his own transforming experience of holding space, is however in his dismissal of the therapeutic relationship. In his prison letters he rails against the practice of psychotherapy and therapeutically-influenced pastoral care as he knew it:

> Wherever there is health, strength, security, simplicity, [psycho-therapists] scent luscious fruit to gnaw at or to lay their per-

53. See, for example, DBW 8: 211, 228–29, and 324 for his conviction that secrecy and concealment are central to authentic truthfulness in Christian life and that the urge to talk about oneself and one's feelings should be met with great restraint, except in confession.

54. See the description of the powerful ministry occurring among groups of abuse survivors in Smith, "'We Are Where God Is,'" 210–19.

nicious eggs in. They set themselves to drive people to inward despair, and then the game is in their hands. . . . And whom does it touch? A small number of intellectuals, of degenerates, of people who regard themselves as the most important thing in the world, and who therefore like to busy themselves with themselves.[55]

The secrets known only to one's servants—to put it crudely— that is, the intimate arena (from prayer to one's sexuality)—have become the hunting grounds of the modern pastoral caregiver. In that sense they resemble (though with quite different intentions) the worst gutter journalists. . . . From the sociological point of view this is a revolution from below, a revolt of inferiority.[56]

Clifford Green has written a careful and insightful study of Bonhoeffer's attitudes toward psychology and psychotherapy, connecting them to his simultaneous critique of religion that similarly attempts, in his view, to ferret out people's deepest insecurities and needs in order then to "save" them.[57] Because of his strongly rooted convictions about the centrality of privacy and discretion in human life and relationships, Bonhoeffer considered attempts to probe beyond people's conscious and self-articulated awareness to be not merely inappropriate but inhuman:

Nothing is more ruinous for life together than to mistrust the spontaneity of others and suspect their motives. To psychologize and analyze people, as has become fashionable these days, is to destroy all trust, to expose everything decent to public defamation. It's the revolt of all that's vulgar against what's free and genuine. People don't exist to look into the abyss of each other's hearts—nor can they—but to encounter and accept each other just as they are—simple, natural, in courageous trust.[58]

Thus also the use in psychotherapy and psychoanalysis of the dynamics of transference or of dream interpretation as revelatory of aspects of a person's thinking invisible to him or her, or even frightening or abhorrent, strikes him as a violation of the person's conscious and

---

55. LPP 326 (DBW 8: 478).

56. LPP 344 (DBW 8: 509–10). Note the implicit upper-class vantage point Bonhoeffer assumes here. His line of argument continues through to page 512. See also DBW 8: 503–4.

57. Green, "Two Bonhoeffers on Psychoanalysis."

58. *Fiction from Tegel* (DBWE 7), 65–66.

spoken self-disclosure that has no knowledge of these hidden realities.[59]
In any case, his references in the prison letters to psychology and psychotherapy are universally negative, and that this corresponds more
deeply to a mistrust of the process of growth in introspection and self-
awareness can be seen in quotes like the following:

> In short, I know less than ever about myself, and I'm no lon-
> ger attaching any importance to it. I've had more than enough
> psychology, and I'm less and less inclined to analyze the state
> of my soul. . . . There is something more at stake than self-
> knowledge.[60]

For various reasons, then, Bonhoeffer was suspicious of the therapeutic enterprise as he knew it, even in its pastoral manifestations. As
far as I know, he was never introduced to the practice of spiritual direction, though depending on how it was practiced in the Anglican and
Roman Catholic monasteries he knew it may not have made a better
impression than therapy even if he had been. But in any case we find
little support in Bonhoeffer for the cultivation of professional healing
relationships for human or Christian growth and, instead, an active
suspicion and dismissal of them. Although perhaps understandable for
the reasons given, this is unfortunate. To my mind it represents most
fundamentally vestiges of the suspicion toward the self and its care we
have seen throughout Bonhoeffer' life. Yet precisely on the basis of the
importance he himself attaches to the central relationship with Jesus
Christ and to full self-revelation with human others in confession and
friendship, I would push him (were he able to respond) to re-think
his fear of the self-knowledge and divine intimacy that can come so
powerfully also through competent therapeutic and spiritual direction
relationships. To the extent his fear has to do with the power imbalance
in these relationships and the necessity of being exposed, vulnerable,
rather than himself always the professional or at least a peer, perhaps
growth in this direction could have represented a new step of courage

---

59. William Peck has suggested that some of Bonhoeffer's distaste for the practice
of psychotherapy may have come from the work of Nazi psychologists. See Green,
"Psychoanalysis," 75, note 49. And of course one wonders about the extent to which
Bonhoeffer's suspicion of psychologists reflects dynamics toward his father, who was
Germany's most prominent psychiatrist of the time. Green's article traces this question
with subtlety and insight.

60. LPP 162 (DBW 8: 235).

for him. Certainly for women emerging from abuse, the importance of safe and trustworthy therapeutic or spiritual professionals can hardly be overstated. These are the ones who in desperate times bring this divine and human friendship Bonhoeffer so cherished into tangible, powerful form, allowing for precisely that healing focus on the self about which, to the end of his life, he felt ambivalent. For the Christian, worship, prayer, friendship, and spiritual direction ideally come most fully to create that "holding space," holy ground, in which the unconditional love of God is tangibly and personally felt, allowing the pray-er to experience her own self and its movements and desires as well.

Self-Awareness

From the gift of healing relationship, as we learn from Winnicott, Benjamin, and Herman, flows in time an increasing capacity for self-awareness. The victim of abuse in any form has had her attention diverted from herself and her own needs and reality in order, for the sake of survival, to focus on the threatening yet apparently life-conferring other. The healing relationship interrupts the dynamics of domination and submission, providing a free zone in which attention can gradually be withdrawn from the dominating voice of the abuser and turned to those feelings, desires, and perceptions long violently suppressed in the victim and/or survivor. Thus self-awareness is both a fruit and a means of healing: as it develops, this new capacity for inclusion of the self within the world of perception begins to make more difficult the ongoing self-suppression on which abuse feeds.

We have seen many of the problematic ways Bonhoeffer, coming from a different place on the separative/soluble self spectrum, seems to be arguing for precisely that self-suppression fatal to abuse victims. Read on their own terms, without reference to the particular selfhood he inhabited, his sweeping assertions about self-surrender (and the necessary movement away from self-awareness toward service of the other) block healing and reinforce patterns of self-effacement among the already selfless. For instance, in *Life Together* he writes,

> Christians [are to] have a modest opinion of their own plans and intentions. They will know that it is good for their own will to be broken in their encounter with their neighbor. They will be ready to consider their neighbor's will more important and

urgent than their own. What does it matter if our own plans are thwarted? Is it not better to serve our neighbor than to get our own way?[61]

In fact, for victims of abuse it is *not* good for their own will to be broken in encounter with their neighbor, and the astonishing growing edge for them is to begin for the first time to consider their own will as important and urgent as that of the abuser (or even to perceive that they *have* a will of their own). For Bonhoeffer, again, becoming truly and deeply aware of the other's reality was the awesome novelty that felt redemptive to him; for the abuse victim, true and deep self-awareness is similarly awesome, similarly redemptive.[62]

Yet as we have also seen, Bonhoeffer has important things to say about claiming one's self in reality as well. Especially as he himself moves to the "underside" of Nazi history, he becomes able to see the self in new ways. Here I would especially emphasize two central aspects from his *Ethics* of his developing openness to self-awareness: conformation with the Incarnate One and the centrality of discernment. First, then, in the section of the *Ethics* entitled "Ethics as Formation," he draws a link between Jesus' incarnation as fully human and one's own:

> To be conformed with the one who became human means that we may be the human beings that we really are. Pretension, hypocrisy, compulsion, forcing oneself to be something different, better, more ideal than one is—all are abolished. God loves the real human being. God became a real human being.[63]

As I suggested in chapter three (pp. 93–94), here is an initial inkling of Bonhoeffer's discovery of a "true self," if you will, an authentic humanity different for him than the self one must flee. In the Incarnate One, Christians have permission to embrace their own created personhood. Thus somehow again proximity to the Incarnate One (in and through

61. LT 96.

62. In fact, of course, these overlap significantly: the "self" Bonhoeffer was trying to escape was not his true self, nor is the "other" abuse victims flee an authentic other; that requires true inter-subjectivity impossible for the enmeshed. In both cases, self and other are distorted, and what is being fled is in significant ways an illusion. Yet the respective movements away from those illusions are important: an abuse victim *needs* to flee that "other," and to do so by means of touching the self for reality, just as Bonhoeffer needed to flee his "self," by means of the other as real.

63. *Ethics* (DBWE 6), 94.

the Word, in others, in gaze, touch, and voice) creates a holding space within which true self-awareness can develop. Here, in Jesus' own ongoing conformation of disciples into his own image, they paradoxically grow ever more deeply into their own true selfhood as well and become able to see themselves, touch themselves, accept themselves as the real people they are, living fully in the real world. Just as he became fully human, so do they.

Second, the crucial significance of discernment for Bonhoeffer's theology and spirituality also opens new space for self-awareness. This is true implicitly, in that one cannot engage in a meaningful process of discernment without devoting extended and careful attention to movements in one's own heart, mind, spirit, and body, dimensions Bonhoeffer explicitly names as central to the process. But the new and necessary inclusion of the self within a spirituality of discernment is true for him also explicitly, in that this section of the *Ethics* on discerning ("probing," *prüfen*) the will of God also includes positive consideration of the concomitant "probing" of one's own self, and states that such self-examination ("self-probing," *selbst-prüfen*) is central to Christian faith:

> The reason why this exercise of self-examination is not superfluous, however, is the very fact that Jesus Christ really is and wants to be in *us,* and because this being-in-us of Jesus Christ does not simply occur mechanically, but again and again takes place and proves true precisely *in* this self-examination. . . . so Jesus Christ is completely in us in the very event of our examining ourselves ever anew in Christ.[64]

For Bonhoeffer, discernment of reality in Jesus Christ, that linchpin of his spirituality, thus necessarily comes to include the self. Self-awareness, again, is both a fruit and a means of healing.

These elements of Bonhoeffer's thinking point to hidden shifts in his understanding of the place of the self in his spirituality, as he begins to bring into speech the possibility of positive attention to oneself. Yet as we saw earlier regarding self-disclosure, here too Bonhoeffer does not move into outright advocacy of self-knowledge. Rather, he continues to mistake "self-reflection" for an obsession with the dominating ego (to be shunned at all costs) and to insist that significant self-awareness is

64. Ibid., 326. Italics Bonhoeffer's.

either impossible or irrelevant.[65] For instance, in his section reflecting positively on shame in the *Ethics*, he writes,

> It can therefore produce a sense of shame if a relationship that one has with another person is expressed in words, thereby revealing and exposing oneself to one's own eyes. The most profound and most personal joys and pains must also be kept from being revealed in words. In the same way, shame safeguards against any display of the relationship to God. Finally, human beings also preserve an ultimate concealment with respect to themselves, they protect their own secret from themselves, by refusing, for example to become consciously aware of everything that is germinating within them.[66]

I believe Bonhoeffer's dismissal of "self-reflection" derives from his lack of criteria to distinguish authentic from inauthentic selfhood. For him theologically, as we saw in chapter two, the self is overwhelmingly associated with sin; thus self-disclosure could only be linked to shame. Yet in confession and in his conspiracy experience and prayer he is learning, as if unbeknownst to himself, the importance of paying attention to oneself. This leads to mixed messages in his writings. In the *Ethics* for instance we read, "The knowledge of Jesus is translated entirely into doing, without any self-reflection whatsoever"[67] (self-reflection as bad), just four pages before the section on probing the will of God and the self, and his insistence on the centrality of such reflection (self-reflection as good). I sense Bonhoeffer struggling to reconcile the necessity of truthful self-awareness with his deeper fears about the trap of the false self and the shame of self-disclosure even to oneself. It is these lingering fears, unresolved at the time of his death, that give his assertions about self-awareness their characteristic ambivalence.

Ultimately however his real contribution in this area is his insistence, always, on the discernment of reality beyond or within all else that would lure us into illusion, however pious. What matters is not schemas of self and other and their relative positioning, because these will differ for different people at different times. What matters for him is the capacity to see self and other in the light of Jesus Christ who is reality

---

65. Recall his pride in his (asserted) lack of self-awareness in LPP 162.

66. *Ethics* (DBWE 6), 305. See also the subsequent reflections on shame, conscience, and hypocrisy that underlie his suspicion of "self-reflection," *Ethics*, 306–21.

67. Ibid., 318.

and to act in accordance with what is there discerned. For Bonhoeffer it was the capacity to see the other clearly that he felt persistently eluded him and needed attending to; for others it may, just as persistently, be oneself. Finally however, as Bonhoeffer was discovering, these capacities are inseparable; clarity of vision depends on the capacity to perceive *both* self and other according to reality.

Self-Defense

We saw in the previous section that self-awareness is central to ending the cycle of abuse. For the victim, the development of the capacity to perceive the self and one's own separate reality begins to make the ongoing self-suppression demanded by the abuser more and more difficult. Yet this is a dangerous process as well, since the survivor's efforts to move out of the emotional cycle of abuse often triggers anxiety in the abuser along with heightened violence to contain this threat to the balance of the relationship. This dynamic points to the crucial importance, as Herman indicates, of ensuring the safety of the victim first and foremost. Self-awareness can develop only in a place of safety, where the initially tentative withdrawal of attention from the abuser and toward the self will be met not with vicious attack but with patience, acceptance, and care. And just as important as this sense of safety within the healing relationship, self-awareness can develop only to an extent corresponding generally with the safety of one's life as a whole. Someone who returns home from therapy or spiritual direction to be harassed and punished will probably not be able to see or say or know as much of herself as someone in a safe shelter, let alone one whose abuser has healed or moved on and who lives securely in her own home and life.

Thus just as the healing relationship makes possible self-awareness, so self-awareness both enables and requires the capacity for self-defense. A central dimension of what one learns to recognize as such awareness grows is the very existence of one's own boundaries, long trampled, along with the desire and right to protect them. In this area one can learn a great deal indeed from Bonhoeffer. What appeared in the previous sections for instance to be a regrettable reluctance to open himself to others in self-disclosure is simply a manifestation of the fact that Bonhoeffer had extremely strong personal boundaries and was careful and intentional about what he revealed and to whom. Indeed, as a separative self the problem with which he struggled was of overly rigid boundaries he was tempted to protect with violence, manifested in the temper that plagued him all his life. I suggested in chapter two that he exhibited traits of an aggressor even as he was also experiencing liberation from that prison over the years. As he himself would be the first to assert, his is not a model of healthy selfhood to be uncritically emulated. Yet it does mean that from Bonhoeffer we can gain a respect for the place of boundaries along with the power of anger and self-assertion in faithful human relationships.

And in fact Bonhoeffer does develop an theology of human boundaries, making possible the self-defense abuse victims need. There are many forms of self-defense needed, from the capacity to say no on any level to various demands, to asserting one's voice and anger in making needed change, to ending relationships that are destructive of one's humanity. All these forms of self-defense rely on healthy boundaries. In abusive relationships, however, boundaries are over-permeable, enmeshed; this is where Bonhoeffer's emphasis on the centrality of clear boundaries for Christian communities is so helpful. Discernible through all his major writings, his insistence on the necessity of boundaries in all relationships, especially Christian ones, is a gift of protection for those whose attackers know no bounds. Jesus Christ *is* the boundary for Bonhoeffer between persons, so that I cannot relate to another except through Christ. As we saw earlier, for him there is no such thing as an "immediate" relationship, a relationship not mediated by Christ. Thus I cannot exploit or attack another except by coming face to face with the One who protects the selfhood of every other and who protects my selfhood from all would-be attackers as well. Far from being an exhilarating foray into greater intimacy, the illusion of un-mediated relationship—in romantic passion or Christian communal idealism—is in fact a violation of the necessary boundary between self and other.

For already in *Sanctorum Communio* Bonhoeffer distinguishes between *Gemeinschaft* and *Masse* precisely on the basis of the presence or absence of healthy boundaries between individuals; their absence makes community impossible.[68] The enmeshment of abuse as a marital form of *Masse* corresponds to the "psychic" or "emotional" relationships he deplores in *Life Together* and the illusion of "immediacy" he decon-

68. See pp. 37–39 in chapter 2, where these categories from *Sanctorum Communio* are developed.

structs in *Discipleship*. In all these cases he is describing relationships based on violence and illusion rather than on clear perception of the separate reality of selves. In his lectures on Genesis, in fact, he develops the importance of the boundary between persons with direct relevance for this study. In describing how sin incites persons to violate one another's created and holy boundaries, he writes,

> This means. . . . that the man claims his share of the woman's body or, more generally, that one person claims a right to the other, claims to be able to possess the other, and thereby denies and destroys the creaturely nature of the other person.[69]

And in his *Ethics* he lays out this understanding even more fundamentally grounded in the created physical personhood of each individual:

> The human body never becomes simply a thing that might fall under the unbounded power of another person, to be used only as a means to that person's ends. The living human body is always the human person himself or herself. Rape, exploitation, torture, and the arbitrary deprivation of physical freedom are all serious invasions of the right conferred on human beings at creation.[70]

Immediately following this quotation he draws implications for sexuality and marriage in distinction from rape, asserting that life-giving sexuality includes an element of healthy shame absent in rape and every other form of violation. Such healthy shame, for him, safeguards the other's freedom and one's own; and "[t]his freedom shelters the mystery of human bodiliness."[71]

All his life Bonhoeffer continues to speak of the necessary "boundedness" of healthy human relations, in every facet of body and spirit, and to see sin as the attempt at "unbounded" access to or coercion of another human being. Emotional fusion and the ensuing physical and emotional violation of the other destroy community (*Gemeinschaft*). Thus an abusive relationship has no right, Bonhoeffer would surely argue, to call itself a "marriage," no matter what vows may have been

69. Bonhoeffer, *Creation and Fall* (DBWE 3), 123.

70. Bonhoeffer, *Ethics* (DBWE 6), 214.

71. Ibid. Note again how a respect for shame, in healthy form, allowed Bonhoeffer to be such a staunch advocate for clear boundaries yet also impelled him to guard his privacy in ways that at times seemed to hinder self-disclosure.

taken, since marriage is a form of *Gemeinschaft* and is irreconcilable with any boundary-violating abuse of one another. In a true community, Jesus Christ stands between self and other; he both connects and protects both.

Second, this Jesus Christ who protects the vulnerable has the power to call a person out of an abusive situation, to strengthen her self-defense to the point of exiting an old life "without ambivalence or guilt."[72] Bonhoeffer's presentation in *Discipleship* of a God who invites a person into a complete break, a *Bruch*, with the old life, is good news indeed for those needing to get out of abuse.[73] It is a far cry from pastoral care of the abused that counsels them to suffer under attack as "just your cross to bear." In Bonhoeffer's world, both abused and abuser are called out of that old life for good and placed in a world where boundaries are clear, where each person's life runs up against the reality of Jesus Christ at every turn who alone leads them into life-giving relationships with others. Thus in his uncompromising insistence on radical obedience to Jesus Christ alone, including a decisive break with one's past, Bonhoeffer speaks a revolutionary word to those entangled in abusive relationships. Such ties need not bind a person—certainly not forever, and not even one moment longer now, at Jesus' call. Bonhoeffer's rigor in pushing for this *Bruch* is thus not merely Prussian sternness. It manifests the urgency of the call itself, from death to life. Don't linger in the tomb, feeling guilty for leaving, he might paraphrase Jesus saying to Lazarus (or to Shirley), but "*Come out! Now!*" And, then, "unbind her and let her go."

Finally, although many of Bonhoeffer's published writings suggest an acquiescent stance toward others, humbly surrendering to their interruptions, demands, and will, his career-long public resistance to Hitler indicates a much more complex reality. And his further step into the conspiracy shows a capacity to say No to evil that takes him beyond even what many Christians would endorse. Whether the tyrant is Adolf Hitler or the domestic abuser, Bonhoeffer's witness provides resources for active resistance, including an ethics of tyrannicide should life itself be at stake. His capacities for discernment give him a transcendent though always self-critical freedom for action in Jesus Christ, even action that violates entrenched notions of "good" and "evil." For him, as

72. Golden, "Relational Theories of White Women's Development," 235.

73. See chapter 3, pp. 76–78, on this.

we have seen, reliance on general norms (which in extraordinary situations prove useless) is no mark of morality. For it is deceit—in Genesis
3, the serpent—that tricks human beings into thinking they can *know*
good and evil rather than relying on the Word himself, Jesus Christ, the
voice of God spoken and discerned anew in each new situation. The
supposed "goodness" of marriage and "evil" of divorce, then, to return
to the example of an abusive marriage, may have nothing to do with
the will of God in a particular situation; and blind, "good" submission
to these categories may result in far worse evil. Thus Bonhoeffer's ethics
of discernment, the renunciation of good and evil judgments toward
oneself, others, or any given situation in favor of the well-probed will of
God, gives extraordinary freedom to all who suffer oppression. Never a
carte-blanche to sin, this reliance on discernment requires a person to
take seriously the concrete complexities of a situation in listening for
Jesus' voice, and then in freedom and trust to act, committing the entire
matter to the judgment of God alone.[74]

Because Bonhoeffer is so helpful in this area, providing both theological and lived testimony to the significance of boundaries and of
resistance to evil, I find little need to push him further, except in one
point. I find it important to complement his published call for the surrender of the aggressive self with a clearer sense of this corresponding
self-assertion that in reality was so central to his witness. For soluble
selves, particularly those in abuse, self-assertion needs to be promoted
as powerfully as Bonhoeffer pushes self-surrender, as a valid path of
Christian discipleship. Of course, just as Bonhoeffer discovered the
limits of self-surrender and through his life insisted on healthy boundaries, so too a spirituality of self-assertion would need to acknowledge
the necessity of growth into full-fledged Christian self-offering (see
pp. 216–22 below).

But in terms of the initial movement away from illusion and into
reality that for Bonhoeffer took place by means of self-surrender, I would
like to see comparable *Christian* theologies of self-assertion for abuse
victims. Benjamin has reminded us that in fact both self-assertion and
recognition of others are needed in healthy selves and relationships; for
those socialized into submission, assertion in and of itself is the path
of growth, risk, and freedom. Far from merely helping women "gain"

74. See "Stations on the Road to Freedom," a poem written the day after the failed
July 20, 1944, attempt on Hitler's life. LPP 370–71 (DBW 8: 570–72).

a self so they can then "lose" it, the former a secular remedial activity making possible the holy Christian one, I see both self-assertion and self-surrender as essential components of a mature Christian spirituality reflective of Jesus' own life and necessary for growth in conformation to him. How those are balanced in any given life depends on a complexity of factors impossible to outline in advance. But the possibility that self-assertion could be claimed to be as potentially holy and deeply Christian as self-surrender—this remains a step that Bonhoeffer himself could not have taken.

Self-Investment

Finally, the victim or survivor of abuse has great problems with self-investment, understood both as investment *in* the self in self-care and investment *of* the self in the world in free and creative ways. The term "self-investment" includes attention to both self and other in a way that traditional language about "self-offering" or "pouring out the self" doesn't. Investing *in* oneself and investing *of* oneself are inseparable; but for victims of abuse, the first is the creative growing edge, the risky new venture of faith, a trusting participation in the new creation God is calling forth. For persons whose selves are degraded or attacked, I am asserting, investment *in* the self is in fact a form of Christian discipleship as risky, radical, and faithful within their context as Bonhoeffer's courageous investment *of* himself is widely perceived as being.

In contrast to abuse victims, in his day-to-day life Bonhoeffer took completely for granted the fact that his self was invested in. This goes beyond things like his pleasure in good food, wine, clothing, music, and travel, and his generosity with himself and others in all these areas. But all his life, for instance, he had many servants of various kinds who took care of shopping, cooking, cleaning, laundry, and nursing him when he was sick, so that he was free to concentrate fully on whatever tasks of writing or teaching filled his days. For him it was an important step in the recognition of others simply to be willing to be interrupted in his work (as in the citation from *Life Together* above).[75] But the possibility of being expected to sacrifice hours of his own time, day in and day out,

---

75. This is especially significant for him given the sacrosanct nature of his father's work in his childhood home, where interruptions were treated with severe reprimand. Thus he is simultaneously sacrificing this sort of male prerogative for himself and perhaps trying to become the sort of person he wished his father had been.

for the routine chores of household maintenance, let alone child care, precisely so that his maid, sister, mother, or (eventually) wife could be freed for that many hours of *her* own time, would not have occurred to him. He simply assumed that his time was precious, that other people and the resources of his life existed to serve him, that his work and self were meant to be invested in by himself and others.[76] Of course his was not a decadent self-investment; its purpose was not merely pleasure in the good things of life and leisure but also, always, his further investment in others by his research, writing, teaching, and leadership. But he models a confidence in the manifest worthiness of his own care completely unimaginable to victims of abuse who have been taught that they do not exist except for others. To learn from him that a deeply Christian life can or even must include what would seem to them astonishing levels of self-investment is an important part of his legacy for soluble selves.

Another dimension of Bonhoeffer's helpfulness toward healthy self-investment for victims of abuse includes his development of an utterly this-worldly spirituality that takes seriously both the pleasures and the need for just relations within ordinary life. Even (or especially) in his Nazi prison cell, facing increasingly certain execution, he does not hold up heroic martyrdom as some Christian ideal to be emulated by downtrodden victims everywhere. Instead, he longs for home, for gardens and flowers and open sky, for trees and sunshine, abundant nourishing food, friends and family and music. And he insists in his theological writings in prison that what matters for the Christian is the enjoyment of these blessings of God (what he often terms a sort of "Old Testament" embrace of earthly life, as opposed to later Christian otherworldliness) and the freedom and justice that make possible all people's participation in such blessing. This approach provides resources for countering the pieties that exalt the wife, mother, or servant (or all three in one) whose self-sacrifice and refusal of any personal indulgence is seen as a noble Christian witness. If he felt no guilt about wanting un-

76. Renate Bethge recalls that her mother, Dietrich's oldest sister Ursula, was sent out at age 16 to care for the six children and alcoholic husband of a former servant during the servant's illness. Bethge writes, "Naturally, such a task would never have been expected from a son. . . . [O]ne was much more deliberate in dealing with their time. With them, always in the background was their later profession as their main task. They were to be able to prepare themselves for it without too many disturbances" (R. Bethge, "Role of Women," 38).

ambiguously out of the Nazi prison, perhaps he can encourage her as well to step out into the spaciousness of creation without fearing she is thereby renouncing her intended purpose on earth. Bonhoeffer explicitly names such embrace of earthly blessing as in fact God's desire for all people. Thus, for the long-battered woman putting down her mop to gaze out the window, or turn toward the door, this movement out of prison is no guilt-crippled violation of her Christian vocation but a means of its unfolding.

A dimension I suggest where Bonhoeffer could be amplified in this area is in regard to the Christian sacraments, whose importance he assumes but rarely develops.[77] A sacramental spirituality is deeply particular and concrete, as well as inherently communal. Thus it provides resources alongside Bonhoeffer's emphasis on the individually-discerned Word for Christian growth in self-investment. I see three aspects of this. First, the sacraments of baptism and Eucharist are personal: holy baptism is the occasion at which the new baby receives his or her name itself, where s/he is called by name and marked as Christ's own. And the sacrament of the altar has a similarly personal nature, especially in the Lutheran context where each element is given "for you." There can be no mistaking the Savior's intention that you, named and cherished in particular, be birthed, redeemed, fed, blessed, and loved. Yours is a self worth profound divine investment.

Second, the Christian sacraments are embodied: a person gets physically wet, touched, anointed, fed, slaked. In fact, for Christians (Lutheran, Anglican, Roman Catholic, Orthodox) who confess the real presence of Christ in the sacrament, one's very body participates in Jesus' own being, his body and blood. One's whole person, body and spirit, feeds on Christ and shares in his life; this powerfully physical communion is especially important to those who, for reasons of depression or shame, find it hard to take in emotionally the unconditional divine love proffered here and in the Word. And the bodily participation in Jesus' life not only draws into healing contact one's own wounds and crucifixion with his but reveals as holy and sacred even this wounded (and female) flesh. Thus a Eucharistic spirituality allows a person gradu-

---

77. Primary places where he deals with baptism and the Lord's Supper include *Sanctorum Communio* (DBWE 1), most centrally at 237–47; *Discipleship* 205–12 (baptism) and 228–29 and 232–36 (both sacraments); and *Life Together* 117–18 (Lord's Supper). See also DBW 15: 548–53, a theological reflection on the Eucharist.

ally to perceive even her own body as worthy of attention and care, like Jesus', in fact itself a locus for Jesus' self-revelation. Paying attention to one's body becomes a form of prayer, a means of attending to the One whose body and blood saturate the very cells of one's physical being. Experiencing and meeting one's physical needs for food, play, sleep, or love becomes a way of coming face to face with the One who feeds the hungry and offers rest to the weary, who in fact is at the heart of all the desires of one's being.

Third, a sacramental spirituality is transforming, making possible investment *in* selves needing healing, and *of* selves for others. One is baptized into Jesus' death not in order to remain entombed forever but so that one may participate as well in his resurrection. These intimate and deeply embodied forms of love reveal a God whose passionate interest in every last *you*, personally, is life in all its fullness. This God births and woos and invites and commands people out of prisons; here in every possible way tombs become wombs of life. Such transformation, as Bonhoeffer reminds us, is extremely costly, both for God and for human participants: grace costs one's entire life, uprooting identity, risking job, home, and relationships, gouging out eyes and cutting off hands. It leaves people as fragile as newborns, forced from their homes and bloody, yet poised at last for the adventure of a lifetime, of learning to draw one's first breath in new air, to be bathed by God and clothed and held at the breast. A baptismal and Eucharistic spirituality draws people into this divine mystery in Jesus Christ, moving with him over and over through his own paschal birthing and letting it gradually, or suddenly, transfigure not only their persons, their bodies, but their entire lives. A sacramental self-investment thus proves ultimately transforming of the world as well, as well-nourished selves allow love and passion to flow through their lives, leaving no one hungry or despairing.[78]

Participation in the divine investment in one's self is therefore not selfish at all, quite the contrary, for it makes possible an investment *of*

---

78. I make a similar point across the chapters of my book, *Truly Present: Practicing Prayer in the Liturgy*. A study of Christian prayer within a liturgical and sacramental context, the book includes treatment of 14 contemplative prayer practices: from baptismal remembrance (chapter 2) to Eucharist (chapter 8), this is a sacramental spirituality filled with the mercy of God. See in particular the prayer practice "Refraining from Self-Attack" outlined in conjunction with baptismal remembrance in chapter 2: the living, personal grace of God in Christian baptism exorcises all internalized voices of attack and makes possible an inner "home" of mercy through which love flows freely.

one's self that does not drain life but expands it. This, and not some heroic "selflessness," was what enabled Bonhoeffer's self-offering: well nourished all his life, he gave of himself out of freedom, desire, and love, an offering that far from leaving him depleted only deepened his gratitude for the gift of it all. To view Bonhoeffer's legacy through the eyes of abuse victims highlights the centrality of such consistent tangible reception of love for human thriving. For Christians, the sacraments provide the central means of nourishment in this divine care, a life whose *cantus firmus* is gratitude.

Bonhoeffer's Challenge to Secular Psychology: [Faith as] Self-Surrender

Along with the material excavated in an "against the grain" reading of Bonhoeffer in the first section, his christological contributions in the second section, and the more immediately applicable aspects of Bonhoeffer's thought in the third, this fourth dimension will provide a final instance of the encounter I am constructing between Bonhoeffer and contemporary feminist psychologists. I suggest here that in addition to self-awareness, self-defense, and self-investment, a final aspect of the Christian spiritual formation of women in abuse is a (carefully-conceived) self-surrender.[79] This final dimension represents an insight of Bonhoeffer's that goes beyond the recommendations of the psychologists I have been reading.

Of course I have been asserting throughout this analysis that Bonhoeffer' insistence on self-surrender is a central part of the problem of his theology for soluble selves. In no way do I intend here, therefore, to deny the destructive effects of interpretations of his work that, like Bonhoeffer, see un-nuanced self-surrender as a starting point in the Christian spiritual journey. Nor, in the other direction, would feminist psychologists deny the importance within a mature human life of self-offering on behalf of others, the sacrificial investment of oneself essential for the well-being of children, of committed relationships, and of society. Yet these self-investments in the world are seen by the psychologists I have read exclusively in terms of human relationships, the balance of

79. Thanks to Bradley Holt for raising this category for consideration at an early presentation of my work to the Nashville meeting of the American Academy of Religion, November 20, 2000. See also Coakley, *Powers and Submissions*.

speaking and listening, asserting and conceding, that structures healthy relations between free subjects. What Bonhoeffer provides is a model that includes the possibility of encounter in, with, and under these complex webs of human relationality with that transcendent reality who calls people by name and invites their response. It is in relation to this Holy One alone, who is one's own deepest reality as well as that of the world, that I find Bonhoeffer's language of self-surrender meaningful.

We have seen how central to Bonhoeffer's spirituality discernment is, providing resources for tracing his difficult and life-giving vocation in the midst of extremely oppressive times. But we have also seen that, perhaps because of his early formation as a separative self, Bonhoeffer at times wittingly or unwittingly conflates the human and the divine other. In *Sanctorum Communio* he repeatedly refers to the "other" (or "You") as apparently interchangeably human or divine, necessarily so since his point is to highlight the centrality of human sociality for theological reflection.[80] In *Life Together* he consistently equates the needs of others with "the visible sign of the cross raised in our lives to show us that God's way, and not our own, is what counts."[81] And in prison he writes that it is in the sufferings of others, and not our own, that we draw close to God's sufferings.[82] These examples could be multiplied by many others that reveal what for Bonhoeffer was both intuitively obvious and powerfully redemptive: that for the separative self God is revealed in transforming ways through the encounter with others' own separateness and claims. Only in the confrontation with the barrier of another's reality (the human thus bearing the divine alterity as well) can one truly be formed in one's own concrete personhood.

Yet in attempting to point out the necessity of human embodiment of divine encounter, he fails to insist with equal consistency on the necessary *distinction* as well between any given human other and the divine Other. For Bonhoeffer, as apparently a solidly separative self, this might not seem much of a danger; it is the encounter with alterity in general that proves redemptive for him in breaking the hold of the imprisoning self. Disentangling divine claims from human ones is not only comparatively unimportant for him but might seem to obscure

80. See chapter 2, pp. 32–43 and 55–59, for citations and further discussion on this point.

81. LT 99–100.

82. LPP 370 (DBW 8: 542).

his intended point that in fact the human You in its alterity really does embody the divine claim. In contrast, for soluble selves living with abuse, blurriness on this point is fatal; this distinction is of the utmost importance. Learning to distinguish the loud but not-at-all-absolute demands of the abuser from the claims of God is a *sine qua non* of life itself. Put differently, for the purposes of this section, such discernment is essential to any self-surrender that promises real freedom.

A curious passage from *Sanctorum Communio* highlights this tension in Bonhoeffer between recognition of the necessary limits of human love and an assertion of its divine unlimitedness. The passage is worth quoting in full, I believe, because it so neatly captures at the beginning of his career the ways this tension will be played out for years to come.

> *Christian love. . . .* has its limits where God has set them. Where we know that God has condemned we are not allowed to love. "Even if I could save the whole world in one day, if this were not God's will, I nevertheless shouldn't do it" (Luther). The hard saying in 1 John 5:16 goes even further, by warning us not to intercede where God *might* have condemned. . . . But we do not know where God condemns, and the command to love our neighbor, that is, to obey, is given without restrictions, and therefore love has no limits. *Love for our neighbor is our will to embrace God's will for the other person*; God's will for the other person is defined for us in the unrestricted command to surrender our self-centered will to our neighbor, which neither means to love the other instead of God, nor to love God in the other, but . . . to love the neighbor instead of ourselves.[83]

Here Bonhoeffer begins in a promising way, asserting the necessity for love to discern carefully the will of God and even stating outright that "love" which attempts to love indiscriminately, in fact to try to be the salvation of the world, is misguided and dangerous. This is helpful for abuse victims to hear, reminiscent of the statements later in his life about the will of God transcending human notions of good and evil and leading people in surprising ways, perhaps even ways that might appear unloving. But from here Bonhoeffer leaps unexpectedly into the very trap against which he had just been warning, namely to assert that love "has no limits," is completely "without restrictions." From this he

83. SC 170–71, emphasis Bonhoeffer's. The Luther citation is found at *WA* 17/2:53.

launches into precisely those problematic assertions about the relative places of self and other that comprise, I am arguing, the primary barrier of his work for soluble selves. These latter statements about God's "unrestricted command to surrender . . . to our neighbor . . . and to love the neighbor instead of the self" parallel the assertions I have critiqued as well in his later writings.

What, we might wonder, allows him to make such a surprising and problematic leap? The hinge on which this development swings is the short assertion that introduces his determination that love has no limits, namely (in relation to the limitation on our love drawn by God's own judgment): "But we do not know where God condemns." Thus it is discernment of God's reality that makes possible the limits to our love which foster healthy community life; and it is his perceived inability to discern this divine reality that opens the door to universal principles (the self unrestrictedly surrendering to the other) of the sort Bonhoeffer elsewhere consistently repudiates. Throughout his life Bonhoeffer is moving toward letting go of these absolute categories of self and other, and is doing so precisely as his capacity for complex discernment of the concrete call of God deepens, and as his experience of self and other shift in his move to the underside. This quote reminds us not only of the centrality of such discernment but of the problematic consequences when its practice is abdicated in favor of general principles.

Thus when I speak here of the importance of Bonhoeffer's invitation to self-surrender, I refer to a process centered in concrete discernment. Even for him, that is, the limitless self-surrender promoted in passages like this one is false, precisely because it is dissociated from discernment and made into a principle, an unworkable absolute moral norm.[84] Not only is whole-hearted Christian self-surrender inseparable from the well-discerned call of God, but it is *possible* only there; this is an insight abuse victims teach us all. Distinction between divine and human others is of such supreme importance for soluble selves because it is only in relation to God in Jesus Christ that "unrestricted self-surrender" is life-giving; indeed, this makes possible the essential restrictions on one's surrender to human others that are so desperately needed in that situation.

---

84. Bonhoeffer himself realizes this most fully in prison, where in the context of "selfless self-love" he also asserts that "[t]oo much altruism is oppressive and exacting; 'egoism' can be less selfish and less demanding" (LPP 287, DBW 8: 417–18).

The self-surrender I find helpful in Bonhoeffer, therefore, is not the sort he advocates above, nor a cowering before God as some new dictatorial authority, but rather the process of discernment itself. There a person opens into contact with God all the needs, feelings, contingencies, questions, and complexities of which s/he is aware in a given situation and pays attention to how these shift in the presence of Jesus Christ. Which anxieties fall away? Which desires deepen? Which path beckons? Is Jesus leading in some direction or inviting rest? For Bonhoeffer, "Jesus Christ now occupies the very same space in them that had previously been occupied by their own knowledge of good and evil."[85] He invites persons into this space freed of pre-existing categories or evaluations where a person can attend to Christ alone and can surrender one's whole being to the love and vocation revealed here. Because for Bonhoeffer Jesus Christ is reality, this self-surrender is on one level nothing other than acceding to reality itself. But because, in contrast to most contemporary psychology, this is reality imaged and encountered as Thou, then for him this is a reality with whom one can be in love, and into conformation, participation, and even union with whom a Christian is progressively drawn. If Jesus Christ is God's "Yes" to all that is, then the self-surrender that is faith (the living trust of one's whole being) is the Christian's own "Yes" to him as well. This "Yes" of trust in fact paradoxically also strengthens the person's capacity for self-assertion, providing unshakeable, "firm ground on which [to] stand."[86]

Thus Bonhoeffer's specifically Christian contribution beyond the psychologists I have read is his perception of the divine mystery at the heart of all these complex webs of human relationality and the invitation to grow in personal and even intimate relationship with this ultimate reality revealed in Jesus Christ. This invitation into the heart of divine love includes both self-embrace and self-surrender. But the self-surrender into which Bonhoeffer at his best invites Christians is that of faith itself: the trusting acceptance of one's authentic vocation of love. In a broken world, this vocation will surely include risk, suffering, and perhaps even martyrdom, as Bonhoeffer's own life reveals. But because this is a life of discerned call, it is borne by the presence of a You, the one calling. Thus for Bonhoeffer even the most wretched

85. *Ethics* (DBWE 6), 325.
86. LPP 391 (DBW 8: 573).

suffering experienced in the course of one's vocation simply draws a person more deeply into contact with this You whose shared suffering opens the heart of divine mercy and presence.

To use somewhat different imagery, my reading of Bonhoeffer's theology reveals that the encounter with one's limits and boundaries is not only neutral, or painful, but is always even more profoundly an experience of encounter with the Beloved, the Mediator (*Mittler*), Jesus Christ, regardless of whether the situation or person thereby also encountered is perceived as friend or enemy. Jesus Christ is the center (*Mitte*) of discernment in any concrete situation, providing the boundary against whatever a person must say no to (in self-assertion against evil) and within which one is invited to say yes (in self-surrender to the good). And the surrender to Christ makes possible a life of transcendent gratitude and freedom even in the midst of suffering. Far from somehow requiring a life of martyrdom or self-abnegation in the world, the surrender that is faith frees a person for grateful immersion in the goodness of life as well as courageous witness against any squelching of life. It makes possible, in fact, that polyphonic freedom of fully autonomous self-development that is in no way inhibited, but in fact rendered even more beautiful, by its relation to the *cantus firmus* in harmony with other voices.

This, I am asserting, is Bonhoeffer's uniquely Christian contribution to this chapter's dialogue on the subject of the spiritual formation of women in abuse: the life of faith that in, with, and under the complexities of human relationships experiences the divine You whose face and heart are love. Bonhoeffer was unquestionably a patriarch and was shaped in his sense of selfhood by an upbringing in gender roles that all his life explicitly and implicitly affected his conception of the problems, needs, and growth of the self in Christian maturity. Every aspect of his spirituality bears witness to this imprint by the norms of traditional masculine socialization and his struggle for liberation from its debilitating aspects. Thus Bonhoeffer's witness requires careful contextualization in order to prove helpful to people socialized differently.

Yet, as this chapter has also tried to show, such contextualization makes possible a reading of Bonhoeffer that is in fact liberating for soluble selves. In his emphasis on concreteness and particularity of discernment; in his insistence on the necessary balance between individual and community; in his freedom from categories of "good" and "evil" for a vocation that includes courageous self-defense as well as abundant self-investment, he provides ample and important Christian resources for those struggling to escape from abuse. And in his focus on Jesus Christ as an intimately and unswervingly redemptive figure for all who are caught in nets of deceit or sin, he breaks the power of both the abuser and of God-images in the abuser's image. Here is a Thou whose cherished alterity and reality simultaneously invite a person deep into the true self as equally participative in the real. Here is a God who shatters gender stereotypes and by Word, sacrament, and Christian friendships of radical self-disclosure invites women and men into a nourishing, transformative holding space of love. Here is One whose voice, gaze, and touch given *"for you"* make possible each person's discernment of the way into life, and give power and permission to claim it.

Here, therefore, are powerfully Christian resources *against* theologies of submission to abuse (even against Bonhoeffer's own at times). In the dialogue with selected contemporary feminist psychologists constructed here, we have therefore seen not only ways his thinking requires critique but also dimensions of what such a critically-nuanced spirituality might look like for soluble selves. In the final chapter, I turn to a brief consideration of implications of these insights of Bonhoeffer's for those who are engaged in ministry with abuse victims and survivors, as well as providing concluding remarks for the book as a whole.

6

Summary, Implications, and Conclusion

Summary

Bonhoeffer was clearly a commanding personality all his life. Despite his attempts in his writings and prayer to foster whole-hearted self-surrender to others, in fact he himself never remotely modeled the sort of passive meekness this might seem to endorse. From his university days, when he pulled out of voluntary military training exercises because he could not stand to submit to someone else's orders, to the end of his life, in which his experience of Nazi interrogation was the first time he had ever known forced submission, his nature was consistently that of the authority.[1] Had he taken completely to heart his own writings on the necessity of absolute surrender to the other he would never have been able to mobilize organized public ecclesial resistance to the Nazis in the face of tremendous antagonism; help found the Confessing Church; serve as a leader in international circles galvanizing ecumenical support; push through a structured, monastic rule of life for a Protestant seminary; or muster the creative energy necessary to audaciously rethink fundamental categories of theology, spirituality, and ethics in a time of desperate struggle.

We see, therefore, that Bonhoeffer's professed spirituality of radical personal surrender to the claims of the other is set within a life whose actual contours look very different. His experience of Jesus Christ was of one who liberates him from the sterile isolation of his commanding ego as its own god and allows him to taste the sweetness of divine and human intimacy for the first time in his life, indeed, even to humble

---

1. Green, *Sociality*, 177–78, esp. notes 201 and 202.

himself emotionally and spiritually in the deep honesty required in a life of confession, prayer, and discernment. This, not the force of his personality, was the only way to life for him. Yet it is clear that the depth of his spiritual vision and the power of his witness derive also from just this capacity for authoritative self-presentation in the world. To preach his theology of the transcendence of the Other to those whose posture is already one of self-abnegation does a grave disservice to his spiritual vision as a whole.

In this study we have seen some of the ways Bonhoeffer's conceptions of the self and its Christian spiritual formation function when applied to the lives of persons with very different experience and needs. In particular, I have traced some of the discrepancies in psycho-social location between Bonhoeffer and women who live in abusive relationships. Based on this analysis, I have asserted that significant elements of Bonhoeffer's spirituality (especially those colored by his understanding of the relation between self and other) require careful contextualization, and at times outright rebuttal, in order to provide a truly liberating vision for these women from the patterns of sin and captivity that suffocate them in the real world.

At its best, Bonhoeffer's spirituality is profoundly and concretely Christian: rich in prayer, friendship, and gratitude and courageously, incarnationally, engaged in the struggles and needs of the world. I have tried, therefore, by means of these chapters' contextualization, rebuttal, amplification, and retrieval, to trace the contours of a "Bonhoeffer-ean" spirituality similarly liberating, and equally Christian, for those whose redemption takes shape differently from his. This has included pointing out ways his vision was compromised by his support of patriarchy, not merely in terms of its obvious subordination of women in family, church, and world but more subtly and devastatingly in his resulting blindness to the different configurations of selfhood, sin, and growth emerging from the experience of having been made invisible even to oneself. Bonhoeffer is not the only one who has been oblivious to the widespread reality and experience of soluble selfhood: women in abuse similarly focus away from themselves and ignore their own reality, and pastors and theologians through the ages have reinforced this self-forgetfulness by encouraging "Christ-like" humility, submission, and selfless care of others even in situations of literally murderous abuse.

Yet as I have attempted to show, this entire theological framework in which women so often simply do not appear as real human beings in their own right, their human needs for justice, mercy, and redemption bracketed out of consideration, looks different when viewed from below. It looks different when those on the underside are no longer invisible but when their experience and needs at last help adjudicate the adequacy of any given spiritual teachings. Needless to say, this view from below has explosive potential for the structures of self, faith, and society; yet the dynamite it packs is not that of destruction but of the Gospel itself. Christians assert that the view from below provides a hermeneutical privilege in accurate discernment of reality, this privilege based on God's own particular attraction to places of darkness, weakness, suffering, and marginalization; this is the theology of the cross so central for Lutherans. And I am claiming it as well for those on the underside of selfhood, and more broadly for the despised or wounded aspects of the selves of all human beings.

I have made use of contemporary feminist psychology and psychoanalysis in order to explore at length the experience and needs of women in abuse, both for their own sake and as they are paradigmatic (in an extreme form) of the "soluble" dimensions of many people's lives and of all human beings at some level. I have done this so that these women's selfhood need no longer be invisible, dissolved, soluble, their voices silenced and suffocated, but so that they may come to speech as powerful critics of a theological status quo that is otherwise only too happy to go on reinforcing their submersion. Viewed through the eyes of these feminist theoreticians and the victims and survivors of abuse whose agonies they bring to light, some key aspects of Bonhoeffer's spirituality simply do not bring life (in Lutheran terms, they do not convey Christ) and must be qualified if not rejected outright. It is a scandal, in this day and age, to imagine that the social location and psychological conditioning of author and audience have no bearing on the relative adequacy of a given theology, and that one can therefore teach Bonhoeffer (or anyone) as if their insights were somehow universally valid, a proposition which as we have seen he himself would surely have rejected. We can no longer then go about naïvely proclaiming in print and from the pulpit in the name of Bonhoeffer, for instance, that Christians must submit to their enemies or that the way to spiritual growth is to let one's will be broken in the encounter with others. For many of our listeners, this is patently untrue; it gives "divine" sanction to the voice of evil itself. For a spirituality that claims correspondence with reality as its ultimate criterion for validity, such a critical disjunction between the theoretical and the real is anything but trivial, no matter how "unimportant" the reality in question may seem to those in power. Thus such ongoing un-nuanced appeals for submission as Bonhoeffer taught do not only violate his own fuller witness of self-assertion, voice, and agency; they are a tremendous violation of reality itself in their refusal to see and name the contours of evil in human lives different from his own yet equally precious to God.

In other dimensions however we have seen how powerfully Bonhoeffer can be of help to victims and survivors of abuse, precisely in giving them permission to name reality as it is and in asserting that action taken humbly and prayerfully in correspondence with this discerned reality is central to Christian discipleship, no matter how "un-Christian" such action may appear to others. Bonhoeffer invites Christians out of their stuck places and into an intimate and reality-transforming conformation with Jesus encountered in Word, sacraments, and deeply honest friendships, forms of intimacy that never violate the boundaries between self and other but find Jesus himself protecting these boundaries and making possible active self-defense as well as solidarity with others. Bonhoeffer provides an unarguably Christian model for lifelong, abundant self-care as a matter of course and for the power of voice to challenge injustice and push the church in new directions, even ones it finds unnecessary if not heretical (in his time, for instance, questioning anti-Semitism).

And he insists on similar searching honesty in confession regarding one's own broken places and self-deceptions, so that the call and mercy of God in Jesus Christ may transform a person's entire being, freeing a person for a life of well-discerned responsibility toward God, others, oneself, and the world. No one remains a victim long in Bonhoeffer's world: regardless of where a person may start out, the trajectory of movement for Bonhoeffer is always toward greater acuity of perception and integrity of action, of taking decisive responsibility for oneself and the world one inhabits. Although he was not conscious of the language of true and false self and its relation to the "self" he wrestled with, Bonhoeffer nevertheless reminds us of the dangers of the false self (however differently this may be configured for different persons, i.e., in terms of self-hatred rather than self-aggrandizement) and the prisons within which it confines people. Abused women can learn from him, *not* obviously about growing in self-sacrifice toward others, but indeed about the necessity of equally decisive rejection of their own false selves, those imprisoning projections and illusions that in this case reinforce the abuser's omnipotence and their own worthlessness. Ultimately Bonhoeffer's goal was the same as theirs: release by the power of Jesus Christ from bondage to the false self (including the gender-specific ways that is shaped psychologically in the structures of domination and submission) and the ongoing, life-encompassing formation in him of one's true self.

Implications for Ministry with Women in Abuse

The material gathered in these chapters and broadly summarized in the preceding section allows me to sketch briefly some implications of this analysis for the practice of Christian ministry with women in abuse. I intend this section to be relevant to the ministries of parish pastors, spiritual directors, pastoral counselors, and leaders of church shelters, groups, or programs for the abused, as well as for those who in friendship or solidarity, without a professional role, desire to be of assistance to them. These reflections are in no way however exhaustive. Not only could many more (and more specific) implications be drawn from the preceding chapters than I am able to do in this concluding section, but those that are mentioned here could also be developed much more fully in their own right.[2] This section is intended simply to point to these areas for further development, both as important considerations for ministers of all kinds but also, perhaps more importantly, as an indication of the sort of appropriation possible from this material.

The question guiding this section is, "Can Bonhoeffer's witness and spirituality actually help Christian abuse victims recognize, name, and resist the intimate enemy who terrorizes them?" If Shirley's experience with Bonhoeffer is typical, his track record and that of his interpreters may not be very good in this regard, precisely because they are oblivi-

2. For more information on ministry and spiritual direction with women in abuse, see, e.g., Smith, "Sacred Dimensions of Battered Women's Lives"; Adams and Fortune, eds., *Violence Against Women and Children*; Bussert, *Battered Women*; Cooper-White, *Cry of Tamar*; Pellauer et al., *Sexual Assault and Abuse*; Barrett, "Healing from Trauma."

ous to the gender dynamics that shape many women into submission. Thus they (along with many pastors, teachers, and writers of liturgical materials) seal the door on this prison for women by refusing to see or name it, becoming complicit in the dynamic of silencing itself by viewing only the abuser's problems as real or worthy of attention, only the patterns of domination or selfishness as "the" paradigmatic sins requiring everyone's confession. Despite the best intentions of their authors, therefore, un-nuanced presentations of Bonhoeffer that touch on the relation of self and other are as likely to reinforce oppression for many of their listeners as to liberate from it, leaving them (especially those still enmeshed even in subtle forms of abuse) blinded to reality and beaten down in their submission. My desire here is to sketch implications of Bonhoeffer's spirituality that have the opposite effect: to shed light on reality, to assist in the perceiving and telling of difficult and/ or liberating truth, and to empower voice, agency, and resistance to entrenched habits of submission. The areas I will examine include professional boundaries; the development of voice and accurate naming of reality; and more systemic analysis of gender, power, marriage.

Professional Boundaries

First, then, I would point out Bonhoeffer's insistence on clear boundaries within the Christian community. Especially for those who struggle in their homes and personal relationships with unclear and routinely violated boundaries, a primary gift of the church can be precisely this sort of "safe zone," an alternative reality. Here human beings can co-exist and interact without fear of attack; the mystery of each person is protected and revered by all, including in time herself; and religious professionals are consciously and intuitively attentive to their own boundaries and demonstrate unwavering respect of others'. Numerous studies have revealed the devastating effects of boundary violations committed by clergy and other spiritual leaders: that the sort of abuse that makes a hell out of one's home and a travesty of one's human worth should turn out to be the *modus operandi* even of God's trusted representative/s in one's life is a crime of shattering proportions.[3] Note that this is true

---

3. See, for instance, Fortune, *Love Does No Harm* and *Is Nothing Sacred?*; and the chapter entitled "Clergy Sexual Abuse" in Cooper-White, *Cry of Tamar*, 126–44. For an excellent overview of these matters, see Doehring, *Taking Care*.

not only of blatant sexual boundary violation but also, to varying degrees, of more subtle violations. In all cases, the problem consists in the professional's conscious or unconscious exploitation of the parishioner, directee, or client in ways that ultimately divert attention away from the parishioner's needs and toward the attempted fulfillment of those of the professional. Needless to say, this is not necessarily a matter of direct assault. Terrible boundary violations in fact can occur on the part of those who are too "caring," whose need to be needed entangles them in trying to meet every imagined demand on them as the ideal pastor. And paradoxically those who do keep clear boundaries can be accused of being "uncaring," refusing to participate in others' projections or to accede to inappropriate demands or desires.

But for Bonhoeffer this necessity of clear boundaries is of utmost importance for the health of the church. He does not worry about whether he is perceived as caring or uncaring; all that matters is the preservation between persons of that infinite holy space in which Jesus Christ dwells. In fact, he says, the closest possible relation between persons is not that of unmediated relation, which is a mutually destructive illusion, nor even of face-to-face presence (although of course he cherishes this), but actually that of intercession, for there a person approaches the One who is the very contact point to the friend or enemy I am praying for. He specifically warns against the cultivation of a personality cult around the leader that leads to disastrous diversion of focus away from Jesus Christ as the one leader and shepherd of the community, as well as to the "immediacy" that is in fact Bonhoeffer's own language for boundary violation. "The community of faith does not need brilliant personalities [or, one might add, super-pastors, best friends, or exhausted martyrs] but faithful servants of Jesus and of one another. It does not lack the former, but the latter."[4]

Thus it is the responsibility of the religious professional to care assiduously for his or her own boundaries, so that s/he can both model health for the congregation or directees and foster that safe space in which attention can move away from the authority figure and toward the parishioner or directee in relation to Jesus Christ. Anything that diverts a parishioner's attention onto the figure of the pastor or director him- or herself is a problem; and the only way for the pastor not to

4. LT 107.

become ensnared by this attention is by caring well for his or her own needs outside the professional setting. Any leaky boundaries or unattended needs can snag parishioners' projections and make possible just that idolization (or demonization) of the pastor that manifests a shift of focus away from the one Shepherd. To the extent pastors or spiritual directors allow this to happen, they are violating both their own office and the trust and safety of those in their charge.[5]

Here Bonhoeffer's modeling of very high levels of self-care is important. It is a crucial professional responsibility, no lazy self-indulgence, to care daily and well for the health and pleasure of one's body, to devote oneself to those relationships with friends and family that meet one's personal emotional needs for love, to make a commitment to ongoing personal self-awareness and professional supervision, and to invest deeply in one's own life of prayer, including regular spiritual direction and retreat. The maintenance of healthy professional boundaries also includes attention to such matters as clear and manageable job descriptions and accountability, regular and well-defended time off, avoidance of multiple relationships with parishioners or directees, and up-to-date professional reading and continuing education. These are not distractions from one's duty, nor necessary but lesser tasks. They are at the center of one's vocation, intrinsic to the call, of a piece with the ministry one is providing. They shape the person, that is, whose devotion to Jesus Christ is what fills and nourishes him or her, so that s/he arrives for professional responsibility rested, full, able to see others on their own terms, to give freely, to say yes or no from a place of clear discernment rather than unmet need, and to protect his or her own needs, thus not to exploit or be exploited (these two often inextricable).

Accurate Naming of Reality

A second arena of implications for ministry from Bonhoeffer's spirituality is in growth towards increasingly accurate naming of reality with victims or survivors of abuse. We have seen the destructive effects of spiritualities that attempt to fit the experience of one group of persons

5. In *Trauma and Recovery*, Judith Herman provides helpful and comprehensive reflection on these matters within the therapeutic world, especially in her sections entitled, "The Therapy Contract" and "The Therapist's Support System," 147–54. See Spiritual Directors International, *Guidelines for Ethical Conduct*, for parameters of professional responsibility in the practice of spiritual direction.

(here, abused women) into categories created by and for others (here, dominant men). In pastoral or spiritual direction work with victims of abuse, then, a crucial component of healing comes as these women learn in the healing relationship and by means of increasing self-awareness to name their real experience, including spiritual experience. For instance, Laureen Smith notes the importance for survivors with whom she has worked of discovering God not as an omnipotent being who turned a blind eye to their suffering but as that power that allowed them to survive horrific and life-threatening torture:

> "Imagine that I have been thrown to a very hard slate floor several times, kicked in the abdomen, the head and the chest, *and still remained alive.*" Battered women have survived, have remained alive. We seldom say that those who survive violence have experienced God, but battered women have. God is present with them in the suffering battered women endure and in their survival. . . . Claiming God's presence directly is an action filled with dignity and hope.[6]

Pastors and church leaders need to learn to listen carefully to the stories of those on the underside in order to discern with them exactly what happened, how events and memories have shaped them, and who God was and is along the way for them in real terms, not those imposed by others. The form or image of God they thereby discover may look surprising to themselves or listeners, but tracing its contours for oneself, the real ways they have really experienced God, is a powerfully liberating process. It is in fact the very discernment of reality so central to Bonhoeffer as well, and this reality named as victims become survivors and grow in the power of their voice can transform not only the survivors' own lives but also the vision of God they contribute to the community. In particular, the ready availability of spiritual direction, which is explicitly geared toward the exploration of people's experience of God, and allows this experience to deepen and take root in their lives, represents therefore a vital dimension of ministry with abused women.[7] Here is awesomely holy ground in which a person can turn at

6. Smith, "We Are Where God Is," 212, citing a letter of an anonymous battered woman, in *For Shelter and Beyond*, 6–7. Italics added to letter by Smith.

7. For information specifically on spiritual direction with women, see Liebert, "Coming Home to Themselves"; K. Fischer, *Women at the Well* and *Transforming Fire*; and Hall, "Gender Differences."

the deepest levels away from the abuser to behold the face of the Living One, the ultimate reality of one's life, the One whose voice and gaze and touch tenderly and powerfully draw a person out of death and into astonishing new life.

A second area of attention in ministry is the importance on the part of liturgical leaders of the use of confessions, hymns, sermons, prayers, and other worship resources that similarly reflect accurate naming of real spiritual experience, toward transforming reality: letting these women's stories shape how God is publicly named and worshiped. Too often, liturgical materials reflect the same taken-for-granted patriarchal bias that Sunday after Sunday, year after year of a person's life, grinds on promoting the virtues needed by those in positions of dominance, and blinding those on the underside of selfhood (who in fact are often the ones who fill the pews) to their very different needs, sins, and gifts. Confessions that name the wrong sin for a given person, or sermons that promote the wrong virtues, are not merely regrettable; they are a form of public spiritual abuse that actively subverts the attempts of both the person and the Holy Spirit to elicit accurate discernment of reality. This means, for instance, that confessions of sins against the self need to be offered with as much frequency and gravity as those against others, or that movements out of abusive relationships need to be encouraged and liturgically (even if privately) celebrated rather than privately discouraged and publicly ignored.

But it also means that, á la Bonhoeffer again, sermons and liturgies need to refrain as far as possible from attempting to achieve some impossible universal relevance. Rather, concreteness and specificity are key to naming how a given sin oppresses or God-experience redeems, in terms that do not attempt to claim applicability for all times and persons. It is also in this regard that Bonhoeffer's emphasis on the Word "for me" is so helpful, as Christ comes to persons in terms concretely relevant for their own life and experience. Preaching, therefore, that stays close to the particular shape of the divine encounter revealed in a specific Gospel story (or other Scriptural narrative), and relates it appropriately to concrete contemporary experience, will be able to become transparent to the living Word rather than abstracting from it into principles. This also means staying close to Jesus himself in preaching, since here even God becomes concrete, particular, then and now coming to people deep in the flesh in often shockingly tangible ways. Thus even listeners whose experience is very different from that described in the texts for the day will be able to perceive the redemptive power of a God whose movement is always personal, always concrete and shaped to the needs of the situation.

A final encouragement with regard to worship resources is to consider broadening the scope of communal prayer to include the prayer of lament. Brooks Schramm, a scholar of the Hebrew Scriptures, has noted how Lutherans' relative neglect of psalms of lament in favor of confession of sin skews communal piety into a narrow focus on personal sin and agency, and away from the Psalter's much greater emotional range.[8] Other Christian traditions show a similar bias against psalms or prayers of lament as well, often citing these psalms' uncensored venting of negative emotions (such as fear, rage, pain, and desires for revenge) as unsuitable for worship or, worse, unfit for Christian praying. Yet as Schramm makes clear—and numerous other scholars from Claus Westermann and Walter Brueggemann to Nancy Duff have demonstrated—in fact the psalms of lament are indispensable precisely in encouraging the emotional honesty in prayer this chapter is endorsing.[9]

They are equally valuable in giving expression to the complexity of human enmeshment in evil. Praying only confession, in the absence of broader forms of lament, frames the problems of the world implicitly in terms of "me and my sin" (*ours*, in communal confession) and thus privileges the voice of the one/s committing a given sin: in Psalm 51 we hear, as the traditional attribution tells us, the remorse of David, not the cry of Bathsheba. In contrast, providing space for prayers of lament gives voice to the experience of the "sinned-against"[10] and opens a broader space for prayer in relation to the multiple forms of evil people experience and within which they are enmeshed, beyond the narrow focus on personal culpability fostered in confession. As a number of worshiping communities in the U.S. found in the weeks following September 11,

8. Schramm, "Lament's Hope."

9. Schramm cites Westermann, *Lamentation*, and Brueggemann, "The Costly Loss of Lament," as well as Ricoeur, "Lamentation as Prayer." See also Duff, "Recovering Lamentation as a Practice in the Church."

10. See A. Park, *From Hurt to Healing*, and A. Park and Nelson, eds., *Other Side of Sin*. The language of confessing that "we are in captivity to sin and cannot free ourselves" (*Evangelical Lutheran Worship*—see the following note) can provide an opening also to this more complex and encompassing notion of participation in patterns of sin within which persons are enmeshed as both sinners and sinned-against.

2001, the invitation into lament can give voice to pain in prayer in ways that include culpability but also move into the terrain of grief, vulnerability, terror, rage, and trauma that abuse victims know first-hand.

And the human need for lament touches every person in the pew at one time or another, including children and teenagers, leaving them stranded or alienated from worship if the reality of raw emotion is never acknowledged liturgically. Worship materials providing resources for regular patterns of lament—in addition to the orders for confession or baptismal remembrance now common in many congregations—thus provide a means by which not only abuse victims but countless otherwise-neglected voices and human experiences can come to expression before God. The new worship book of the Evangelical Lutheran Church in America, *Evangelical Lutheran Worship* (ELW), includes orders for confession of sin and thanksgiving for baptism to precede the Eucharistic liturgy; its separately-published resource for occasional services (forthcoming 2008) will include rites of lament.[11] ELW also includes a section of hymns titled "Lament," with traditional and newly crafted texts and melodies expressing a powerful range of emotion for both personal and communal prayer of lament. These hymns too help give voice to experience often suppressed in worship; they thus model the "pray-ability" of agonizing levels of emotion and experience before God. To use such rites and hymns in public worship helps name and validate the experience of those on the underside—often invisible even to themselves—and contributes to the accurate and fearless naming of reality Bonhoeffer considered indispensable to the Christian life of individuals and communities.

Analysis of Gender, Power, and Human Relations

Finally, Bonhoeffer's witness encourages contemporary church leaders to be as thoughtful in our analysis of current power relations in light of the Gospel as he was for his time. In the case of those working with victims of abuse, this means being willing to undertake thoroughgoing consideration of the ways issues of power, gender, voice, and violence are played out in particular families, in the local congregation, in one's community, and in society more broadly. This also involves rethinking

11. See also Peterman, *Speaking to Silence,* for examples of a range of rituals intended for a variety of contexts, including but not limited to public worship.

traditional conceptions of marriage in which preservation of vowed relationships is given a higher priority than the quality of the relationship itself or the good of its participants. In the case where a survivor leaves the abuser, it is important to be clear about what exactly is ending the relationship (i.e., the violence, not her failure to love enough). Such a perspective likewise also upholds and explicitly validates those relationships that do model God's love *as* in fact the victim's real "family" to whom God invites joyful commitment. Congregations whose leaders are aware of the dynamics of abuse can help members to see separation from a violent situation as a step of holiness and God-given grace, not as a mark of failure. As noted above, rituals for separation and divorce can allow people to celebrate their faithfulness to God's call to new life, as well as to give voice to their grief and lament in prayer as their hopes for this marriage end. Further, such congregations can become leaders in public advocacy for battered women, children, elders, and men, and can move to support shelters, laws, judicial policies, and effective, life-giving treatment for abusers, all of which can assist in breaking the cycle of violence. And finally, leaders and communities who take seriously the stories, voices, and perspectives of soluble selves will grow in embodying and advocating for new models of sexual relations, child-rearing, and public and private gender roles that ultimately aim at the cessation of those embedded psychological patterns of gendered domination and submission that underlie and perpetuate abuse.

Conclusion and Significance

Looking at Bonhoeffer from the underside of selfhood confirms the best of his insights even as it opens new aspects of his significance invisible to those who share his biases. Learning to see, listen to, and be changed by the experience of those on the underside marked a powerful deepening in Bonhoeffer's own journey of faith; this study represents simply another step on this path, one that (I imagine) he himself might eventually have welcomed. Its framing within the academic field of Christian spirituality has allowed my work to open questions different from those previously undertaken in Bonhoeffer studies. Because this discipline is focused on human and Christian experience and—like Bonhoeffer himself—is fundamentally concerned with the particularity of human reality, it requires the scholar to take seriously questions of the social and historical location, psychological formation, and personal gifts and blind spots that shape a person's (here, Bonhoeffer's) experience. We have seen that it is precisely this attention to the particularities of Bonhoeffer's experience, including his gendered and privileged social location, that renders his writings intelligible within his context and of potential liberating relevance for those whose experience is different. Work in this discipline requires attention to the respective "locations" of subject/s, scholar, and audience, and suggests that examination of presuppositions underlying these locations allows a given spirituality to be explored in ways that continue to be fruitful, rather than succumbing to distortion in presentist or naïvely appropriative ways.

I have found the writings of selected feminist theorists in psychology and psychoanalysis helpful for my project in framing it as an exploration of (at least in part) psychologically explainable phenomena, specifically the gendered dynamics of domination and submission. This has allowed me to describe Bonhoeffer's psycho-social location in terms that shed light on his writings, namely in terms of the lonely, isolated "separative" self characteristic of those socialized into dominance, as well as to highlight the different experience of those groomed for submission. Such a model places both experiences within a framework whose primary purpose is explanation, not blame. Bonhoeffer is here referred to as "separative," or "dominant" or even "aggressive" not in order to denigrate him or to discredit his spiritual experience but as a way of locating him within important dynamics of utmost significance for his writings and his ongoing reception by others. Because his location depends on factors outside his control, and because his resulting isolated selfhood caused him real problems, it is possible within this framework to see Bonhoeffer as a sufferer within domination and not "only" a beneficiary of privilege.[12] Similarly, this psychological framework sees submission as also both a given of one's socialization and, on at least some subconscious level, an equally intentionally maintained human stance. Thus, while taking with utmost seriousness the ways abuse itself further degrades selfhood and reinforces submission, the perspective explored here refuses to cast those who suffer under abuse as mere "victims" devoid of human agency and initiative. Abuse can never be excused, and these words are in no way intended to blame abusees for others' attacks

12. For a perceptive account of the psychic distortions that often come with wealth and privilege, see van den Blink, "Rich Persons."

on them. But nevertheless I find these psychological resources helpful for locating both abuser and abusee within a broader psycho-social matrix entangling them both: convoluted nets from which God calls them forth, beloved and redeemed survivors of evil.

The experience of soluble selfhood is not limited to abuse victims. Depending on complex variables, it shapes the experience of many women to some extent and men (especially those in non-dominant social locations or who grew up with abuse) at some level as well. Ultimately, of course, all human psyches encompass both dominating and submissive elements. On the one hand, this allows even abuse victims to find relevance in Bonhoeffer's deconstruction of the dominating self in that they too suffer (though in very different configurations) from internalized aggression and, depending on their socio-economic status, may themselves also be in social positions of dominance all the more pronounced if they are Caucasian. But I suggest as well, on the other hand, that this study's feminist analysis is an important counter-perspective similarly proving helpful not only for abuse victims, nor only for women, but for the healing and liberation of long-suppressed and silenced aspects of every person, including those in positions of domination — even Dietrich himself. Paradoxically, it is only in reading Bonhoeffer consciously "against the grain," reversing his sense of the relative positions of self and other nearly every time they appear, that his writings prove life-giving for the submerged aspects of himself as well on this level.

Finally, I suggest the significance of this work in illumining the perspective from the "underside of selfhood" both in and of itself and as it encounters Bonhoeffer's theology and experience of selfhood and spiritual formation. This psychologically informed feminist reading of Bonhoeffer within the discipline of Christian spirituality allows Bonhoeffer interpreters to give up the illusion of his universal applicability and to recognize that it is precisely his limits that allow his insights to be appreciated in all their contextually-grounded power for himself and later readers. I hope this project provides an important contribution to Bonhoeffer studies in demonstrating his fuller humanity and the ways this shapes every dimension of his contemporary interpretation. I further hope that this contextualizing of Bonhoeffer may make possible new appropriation of his legacy that is unceasingly attentive to the dynamics of psycho-social formation (of Bonhoeffer himself, of the scholar, and of the intended or actual audience) and how those dynamics subtly or manifestly shape ongoing reception of him. Lastly, I hope that this study demonstrates the necessity of listening carefully to long-silenced voices and of the transformations that can result when they are well heard, transformations of dominant notions of self, other, sin, power, and the actual redeeming work of Jesus Christ in real human lives.

This book has begun to sketch the contours of a liberating "Bonhoeffer-ean" spirituality for soluble selves: one that by grace invites those whose gaze is locked down in abuse to behold the One who sees them, who comes to them, who breaks the power of evil and frees them. In Christ soluble selves hear that radical "for you" at the heart of any authentic Lutheran vision: the gift of unconditional, personal love that transforms lives in deepening conformation with Jesus himself, a costly discipleship. This is a life that takes seriously Bonhoeffer's insistence on ever-evolving discernment of reality and of the will of God (i.e., *was Christum treibt*, what conveys Christ) in situations of complexity and ambiguity. And it is a life that, in correspondence with this reality in the loving presence of God, itself becomes increasingly polyphonic in courage and worldly self-investment, even as it remains always inseparably connected to the *cantus firmus* whose hallmark is encompassing gratitude. I have found this journey with Bonhoeffer to be of transforming significance in my own life, a journey that has allowed me to find commonality with Dietrich *and* Shirley in constructing a profoundly Christian alternative for soluble selves to spiritualities of self-abandonment. I hope that the insights explored here will prove illuminating and liberating to others as well, so that long-entrenched cycles of violence may in time be broken and, with Mary, many may rejoice in God their Savior (Luke 1:47).

Bibliography

Primary Texts

Bonhoeffer, Dietrich. *Act and Being: Transcendental Philosophy and Ontology in Systematic Theology.* English editor Wayne Whitson Floyd Jr. Translated by H. Martin Rumscheidt. Vol. 2, Dietrich Bonhoeffer Works, English Edition (hereafter DBWE), general editor Wayne W. Floyd. Minneapolis: Fortress, 1996.

———. *Akt und Sein.* Edited by Hans-Richard Reuter. Vol. 2, Dietrich Bonhoeffer Werke (hereafter DBW), general editor Eberhard Bethge. Munich: Kaiser, 1988.

———. *Barcelona, Berlin, Amerika, 1928–1931.* Edited by Reinhart Staats and Hans-Christoph von Hase. Vol. 10, DBW. Munich: Kaiser, 1992.

———. *Berlin: 1932–33.* Edited by Carsten Nicolaisen and Ernst-Albert Scharffenorth. Vol. 12, DBW. Munich: Kaiser, 1997.

———. *Conspiracy and Imprisonment: 1940–1945.* German editors, Jørgen Glenthøj, Ulrich Kabitz, and Wolf Krötke. English editor, Mark S. Brocker. Translated by Lisa E. Dahill. Vol. 16, DBWE. Minneapolis: Fortress, 2006.

———. *Creation and Fall: A Theological Exposition of Genesis 1–3.* German editors, Martin Rüter and Ilse Tödt. English editor John W. deGruchy. Translated by Douglas Stephen Bax. Vol. 3, DBWE. Minneapolis: Fortress, 1997.

———. *Discipleship.* Edited by Geffrey B. Kelly and John D. Godsey. Translated by Barbara Green and Reinhard Krauss. Vol. 4, DBWE. Minneapolis: Fortress, 2001.

———. *Ethics.* Edited by Clifford J. Green. Translated by Reinhard Krauss, Charles West, and Douglas Stott. Vol. 6, DBWE. Minneapolis: Fortress, 2005.

———. *Ethik.* Edited by Ilse Tödt, Heinz Eduard Tödt, Ernst Feil, and Clifford J. Green. Vol. 6, DBW. Munich: Kaiser, 1992.

———. *Fiction from Tegel Prison.* German editors, Renate Bethge and Ilse Tödt. English editor, Clifford J. Green. Translated by Nancy Lukens. Vol. 7, DBWE. Minneapolis: Fortress, 1999.

———. *Illegale Theologen-Ausbildung: Finkenwalde 1935–1937.* Edited by Otto Dudzus and Jürgen Henkys, with Sabine Bobert-Stützel et al. Vol. 14, DBW. Munich: Kaiser, 1996.

———. *Illegale Theologen-Ausbildung: Sammelvikariate 1937–1940.* Edited by Dirk Schulz. Vol. 15, DBW. Munich: Kaiser, 1998.

———. *Letters and Papers from Prison.* Edited by Eberhard Bethge. Translated by Reginald Fuller et al. Enlarged ed. New York: Macmillian, 1971.

———. *Life Together/Prayerbook of the Bible.* German editors, Gerhard Ludwig Müller and Albrecht Schönherr. English editor, Geffrey B. Kelly. Translated by

Daniel W. Bloesch and James H. Burtness. Vol. 5, DBWE. Minneapolis: Fortress, 1996.

———. *London: 1933–35*. Edited by Hans Goedeking, Martin Heimbucher, and Hans-Walter Schleicher. Vol. 13, DBW. Munich: Kaiser, 1994.

———. *Nachfolge*. Edited by Martin Kuske and Ilse Tödt. Vol. 4, DBW. Munich: Kaiser, 1989.

———. *Sanctorum Communio: A Theological Study of the Sociology of the Church*. German editor, Joachim von Soosten. English editor, Clifford J. Green. Translated by Reinhard Krauss and Nancy Lukens. Vol. 1, DBWE. Minneapolis: Fortress, 1998.

———. *Testament to Freedom: The Essential Writings of Dietrich Bonhoeffer*. Edited by Geffrey B. Kelly and F. Burton Nelson. San Francisco: HarperSanFrancisco, 1990.

———. *Widerstand und Ergebung: Briefe und Aufzeichnungen aus der Haft*. Edited by Eberhard Bethge, Renate Bethge, Christian Gremmels. Vol. 8, DBW. Munich: Kaiser, 1997.

Bonhoeffer, Dietrich, and Maria von Wedemeyer. *Love Letters from Cell 92: The Correspondence between Dietrich Bonhoeffer and Maria von Wedemeyer, 1943–1945*. Edited by Ruth-Alice von Bismarck and Ulrich Kabitz. Translated by John Brownjohn. Nashville: Abingdon, 1992.

Secondary Texts

Abromeit, Hans-Jürgen. *Das Geheimnis Christi: Dietrich Bonhoeffers erfahrungs-bezogene Christologie*. Neukirchener Beiträge zur systematischen Theologie, 8. Neukirchen-Vluyn: Neukirchener, 1991.

Adams, Carol, and Marie M. Fortune, eds. *Violence Against Women and Children: A Christian Theological Sourcebook*. New York: Continuum, 1995.

American Psychological Association. *Ethical Principles of Psychologists*. American Psychologist Series 45.3. Washington, DC: American Psychological Association, 1990.

Apel, Willi, ed. *Harvard Dictionary of Music*. 2nd ed. Cambridge: Harvard University Press, 1972.

Ashley, M. Matthew. "The Turn to Spirituality? The Relationship Between Theology and Spirituality." In *Minding the Spirit: The Study of Christian Spirituality*, edited by Elizabeth A. Dreyer and Mark S. Burrows, 159–70. Baltimore: Johns Hopkins University Press, 2005.

Aveling, Harry. "Dietrich Bonhoeffer's Christology." *Colloquium* 16/1 (1983) 23–30.

Barnes, Kenneth C. "Dietrich Bonhoeffer and Hitler's Persecution of the Jews." In *Betrayal: German Churches and the Holocaust*, edited by Robert P. Erickson and Susannah Heschel, 110–28. Minneapolis: Fortress, 1999.

Barnett, Victoria. *Bystanders: Conscience and Complicity during the Holocaust*. Westport, CT: Greenwood, 1999.

———. *For the Soul of the People: Protestant Protest against Hitler*. Oxford: Oxford University Press, 1992.

Barrett, Mary Jo. "Healing from Trauma: The Quest for Spirituality." In *Spiritual Resources in Family Therapy*, edited by Froma Walsh, 193–208. New York: Guilford, 1999.

Barth, Karl. *Epistle to the Romans*. Translated from the 6th German ed. by Edwin C. Hoskins. London: Oxford University Press, 1933, 1960.

Bassin, Donna. "Woman's Images of Inner Space: Data Towards Expanded Interpretive Categories." *International Review of Psycho-analysis* 9/2 (1982) 191–204.

Bean, Constance A. *Women Murdered by the Men They Love*. New York: Haworth, 1992.

Beauvoir, Simone, de. *The Second Sex*. Translated by H. M. Parshley. New York: Knopf, 1952.

Beers, William. *Women and Sacrifice: Male Narcissism and the Psychology of Religion*. Detroit: Wayne State University, 1992.

Beller, Hava Kohav. *The Restless Conscience*, VHS. Santa Monica, CA: Direct Cinema, 1991.

Bem, Sandra. *The Lenses of Gender*. New Haven: Yale University Press, 1993.

Benhabib, Seyla. *Situating the Self: Gender, Community, and Postmodernism in Contemporary Ethics*. New York: Routledge, 1992.

Benjamin, Jessica. *The Bonds of Love: Psychoanalysis, Feminism, and the Problem of Domination*. New York: Pantheon, 1988.

———. *Like Subjects, Love Objects: Essays on Recognition and Sexual Difference*. New Haven: Yale University Press, 1995.

———. "Recognition and Destruction: An Outline of Intersubjectivity." In *Relational Perspectives in Psychoanalysis*, edited by Neil J. Skolnick and Susan C. Warshaw, 43–60. Hillsdale, NJ: The Analytic, 1992.

———. *Shadow of the Other: Intersubjectivity and Gender in Psychoanalysis*. London: Routledge, 1998.

Bergen, Doris L. *Twisted Cross: The German Christian Movement in the Third Reich*. Chapel Hill: University of North Carolina Press, 1996.

Bernstein, Doris. "The Female Superego: A Different Perspective." *International Journal of Psycho-analysis* 64 (1983) 187–202.

Bersani, Leo. *Baudelaire and Freud*. Berkeley: University of California Press, 1977.

Besier, Gerhard, et al., eds. '*Darum wagt es, Schwestern . . .*': *Zur Geschichte evangelischer Theologinnen in Deutschland*. Neukirchen-Vluyn: Neukirchener, 1994.

Bethge, Eberhard. "Bonhoeffer's Theology of Friendship." In *Friendship and Resistance: Essays on Dietrich Bonhoeffer*, 80–104. Grand Rapids: Eerdmans, 1995.

———. *Dietrich Bonhoeffer: A Biography*. Translated and revised by Victoria J. Barnett. Rev. ed. Minneapolis: Fortress, 2000.

———. "Turning Points in Bonhoeffer's Life and Thought." In *Bonhoeffer in a World Come of Age*, edited by Peter Vorkink II, with a foreword by John C. Bennett, 73–102. Philadelphia: Fortress, 1968.

Bethge, Renate. "Bonhoeffer and the Role of Women." *Church and Society* 85 (1995) 34–52.

———. "'Elite' and 'Silence' in Bonhoeffer's Person and Thought." In *Ethical Responsibility: Bonhoeffer's Legacy to the Churches*, edited by John D. Godsey and Geffrey B. Kelly, 293–306. New York: Mellen, 1981.

Bieler, Andrea. "Aspekte nationalsozialistischer Frauenpolitik in ihrer Bedeutung für die Theologinnen." In *'Darum wagt es, Schwestern . . . ': Zur Geschichte evangelischer Theologinnen in Deutschland*, edited by Gerhard Besier et al., 243–70. Neukirchen-Vluyn: Neukirchener, 1994.

Binder, Gerhart. *Irrtum und Widerstand: Die deutschen Katholiken in der Auseinandersetzung mit dem Nationalsozialismus.* Munich: Pfeiffer, 1968.

Blackburn, Vivienne. *Dietrich Bonhoeffer and Simone Weil: A Study in Christian Responsiveness.* New York: Lang, 2004.

Bloomquist, Karen. "'Let God Be God': The Theological Necessity of Depatriarchalizing God." In *Our Naming of God: Problems and Prospects of God-Talk Today*, edited by Carl E. Braaten, 45–60. Minneapolis: Fortress, 1989.

Bock, Gisela. "Ordinary Women in Nazi Germany: Perpetrators, Victims, Followers, and Bystanders." In *Women in the Holocaust*, edited by Dalia Ofer and Lenore J. Weitzman, 85–100. New Haven: Yale University Press, 1998.

Boesak, Allan. "What Dietrich Bonhoeffer Has Meant to Me." In *Bonhoeffer's Ethics: Old Europe and New Frontiers*, edited by Guy Carter et al., 21–29. Kampen: Kok Pharos, 1991.

Bongmba, Elias. "The Priority of the Other: Ethics in Africa. Perspectives from Bonhoeffer and Levinas." In *Bonhoeffer for a New Day*, edited by John W. de Gruchy, 175–89. Grand Rapids: Eerdmans, 1997.

"Bonhoeffer, Dietrich." In *Dictionary of the Holocaust: Biography, Geography, and Terminology*, edited by Erich Joseph Epstein and Philip Rosen. Westport, CN: Greenwood, 1997.

Bonhoeffer, Karl. "Lebenserinnerungen von Karl Bonhoeffer geschrieben für die Familie." In *Karl Bonhoeffer zum hundertsten Geburtstag am 31 März 1968*, edited by J. Zutt, H. Strauz, H. Scheller, 8–107. Berlin: Springer, 1969.

Bowman, Douglas C. *Bonhoeffer's Methodology for Describing the Nature of Man under Grace in the Modern Context.* PhD diss., San Francisco Theological Seminary, 1963.

Briggs, Sheila. "Images of Women and Jews in Nineteenth- and Twentieth-Century German Theology." In *Immaculate and Powerful*, edited by Clarissa Atkinson, Constance Buchanan, and Margaret Miles, 226–59. Boston: Beacon, 1985.

Brocker, Mark. *The Community of God, Jesus Christ, and Responsibility: The Responsible Person and the Responsible Community in Bonhoeffer's Ethics.* Ph.D. diss., University of Chicago, 1992.

———. "Sharing in the Sufferings of God." Lecture, Pacific Lutheran Theological Seminary, Berkeley, CA, January 12, 2001.

Brooks, Gary, and Louise Silverstein. "Understanding the Dark Side of Masculinity: An Interactive Systems Model." In *A New Psychology of Men*, edited by Ronald Levant and William Pollack, 280–333. New York: Basic, 1995.

Brown, Carole, and Carole R. Bohn, eds. *Christianity, Patriarchy and Abuse.* New York: Pilgrim, 1989.

Brown, Lyn Mikel. "Telling a Girl's Life: Self-Authorization as a Form of Resistance." *Women and Therapy* 11/3–4 (1991) 71–86.

———, and Carol Gilligan. *Meeting at the Crossroads: Women's Psychology and Girls' Development.* Cambridge, MA: Harvard University Press, 1992.

Browning, Don S. *Religious Thought and the Modern Psychologies*. Philadelphia: Fortress, 1987.

Brueggemann, Walter. "The Costly Loss of Lament." In *The Psalms and the Life of Faith*, edited by Patrick D. Miller, 98–111. Minneapolis: Fortress, 1995.

Burgin, Victor. "Object." In *Feminism and Psychoanalysis: A Critical Dictionary*, edited by Elizabeth Wright, 277–80. Oxford: Blackwell, 1992.

Bussert, Joy. *Battered Women: From a Theology of Suffering to an Ethic of Empowerment*. New York: DMNA, Lutheran Church in America, 1986.

Bynum, Caroline Walker. *Holy Feast and Holy Fast: The Religious Significance of Food to Medieval Women*. Berkeley: University of California Press, 1987.

———. *Jesus as Mother: Studies in the Spirituality of the High Middle Ages*. Berkeley: University of California Press, 1982.

Capps, Donald. *The Depleted Self: Sin in a Narcissistic Age*. Minneapolis: Fortress, 1993.

———. "Male Melancholia: Guilt, Separation, and Repressed Rage." In *Religion and Psychology: Mapping the Terrain*, edited by Diane Jonte-Pace and William Parsons, 147–59. New York: Routledge, 2001.

Carr, Anne. *A Search for Wisdom and Spirit: Thomas Merton's Theology of the Self*. Notre Dame: University of Notre Dame Press, 1988.

Carter, Guy, et al., eds. *Bonhoeffer's Ethics: Old Europe and New Frontiers*. Kampen: Kok Pharos, 1991.

Casalis, Georges. "Theology Under the Sign of Martyrdom: Dietrich Bonhoeffer." In *Martyrdom Today*, edited by Johannes-Baptist Metz and Edward Schillebeeckx, English language editor, Marcus Lefébure. Concilium: Religion in the Eighties. Vol. 163: 80–84. New York: Seabury, 1983.

Cascardi, Michele, and K. Daniel O'Leary. "Depressive Symptomatology, Self-Esteem, and Self-Blame in Battered Women." *Journal of Family Violence* 7/4 (1992) 249–59.

Chandler, Andrew, ed., with Anthony Harvey. *The Terrible Alternative: Christian Martyrdom in the Twentieth Century*. London: Cassell Academic, 1998.

Chapman, G. Clarke, Jr. "Bonhoeffer and Liberation Theology." In *Ethical Responsibility: Bonhoeffer's Legacy to the Churches*, edited by John D. Godsey and Geffrey B. Kelly, 147–95. New York: Mellen, 1981.

Charmaz, Kathy. "Book Reviews: Meeting at the Crossroads: Women's Psychology and Girls' Development." *Gender & Society* 7 (1993) 614–16.

Chase, Alta. "Women's Anxiety in Relation to Differentiation: Religious, Spiritual, and Other Resources." Ph.D. diss., Boston University School of Theology, 1993.

Chodorow, Nancy. *Feminism and Psychoanalytic Theory*. New Haven: Yale University Press, 1989.

———. *The Reproduction of Mothering: Psychoanalysis and the Sociology of Gender*. Berkeley: University of California Press, 1978.

Chopp, Rebecca S., and Sheila Greeve Davaney, eds. *Horizons in Feminist Theology: Identity, Tradition, and Norms*. Minneapolis: Fortress, 1997.

Coakley, Sarah. *Powers and Submissions: Spirituality, Philosophy and Gender*. Challenges in Contemporary Theology. Oxford: Blackwell, 2002.

Colapietro, Vincent M. "The Integral Self: Systematic Illusion or Inescapable Task?" *Listening* 25 (1990) 192–210.

Collins, Kenneth J., ed. *Exploring Christian Spirituality: An Ecumenical Reader.* Grand Rapids: Baker, 2000.

Conn, Joann Wolski. "Spiritual Formation." *Theology Today* 56/1 (1999) 86–97.

———. *Spirituality and Personal Maturity.* New York: Paulist, 1989.

———. *Women's Spirituality: Resources for Christian Development.* 2nd ed. New York: Paulist, 1996.

Conn, Walter E. *The Desiring Self: Rooting Pastoral Counseling and Spiritual Direction in Self-Transcendence.* New York: Paulist, 1998.

———. "Self-Love." *Pastoral Psychology* 46 (1998) 323–32.

Cooper-White, Pamela. *The Cry of Tamar: Violence against Women and the Church's Response.* Minneapolis: Fortress, 1995.

———. "Opening the Eyes: Understanding the Impact of Trauma on Development." In *In Her Own Time: Women and Developmental Issues in Pastoral Care,* edited by Jeanne Stevenson-Moessner, 87–102. Minneapolis: Fortress, 2000.

———. "Peer v. Clinical Counseling: Is There A Place for Both in the Battered Women's Movement?" *Response to the Victimization of Women and Children* 13/3 (1990) 2–6.

Cox, William F. "Spiritual Egocentrism: A Perspective on Spiritual Maturity." *Journal of Psychology and Theology* 12 (1984) 40–44.

Cuthbert, Carrie, and Kim Slote. *Intimate Partner Sexual Abuse: An International Survey and Literature Review.* Wellesley, MA: Wellesley Centers for Women, 1999.

Dahill, Lisa E. "Bonhoeffer and Resistance to Evil." *Journal of Lutheran Ethics* (August 2003) no pages. Online: http://www.elca.org/scriptlib/dcs/jle/article.asp?aid=59.

———. "Bonhoeffer's Late Spirituality: Challenge, Limit, and Treasure." *Journal of Lutheran Ethics* (December 2006) no pages. Online: http://www.elca.org/jle/article.asp?k=683. Accessed March 19, 2008.

———. "The Genre of Gender: Gender and the Academic Study of Christian Spirituality." In *Exploring Christian Spirituality: Essays in Honor of Sandra M. Schneiders, IHM,* edited by Bruce H. Lescher and Elizabeth Liebert, 98–118. Mahwah, NJ: Paulist, 2006.

———. "Jesus For *You:* A Feminist Reading of Bonhoeffer's Christology." *Currents in Theology and Mission* 34 (2007) 250–59.

———. "Particularity, Incarnation, and Discernment: Bonhoeffer's 'Christmas' Spirituality." *Studies in Christian-Jewish Relations* 2/1 (2007) 53–61.

———. "Probing the Will of God: Bonhoeffer and Discernment." *Dialog* 41/1 (2002) 42–49.

———. "Reading from the Underside of Selfhood: Bonhoeffer and Spiritual Formation." In *Minding the Spirit: The Study of Christian Spirituality,* edited by Elizabeth A. Dreyer and Mark S. Burrows, 249–66. Baltimore: Johns Hopkins University Press, 2004.

———. "Spirituality: Overview." *The Encyclopedia of Christianity.* 5 vols. Edited by Erwin Fahlbusch et al. Translated and edited in English by Geoffrey W. Bromiley. Grand Rapids: Eerdmans, 1999–2007, vol. 5 (Sh–Z).

———. "Spirituality in Lutheran Perspective." *Word & World* 18 (1998) 68–75.

———. *Truly Present: Practicing Prayer in the Liturgy*. Minneapolis: Augsburg Fortress, 2005.

Dahl, Darren. "Bonhoeffer and Human Being." *Consensus* 23/2 (1997) 73–89.

Davaney, Sheila Greeve. "The Limits of the Appeal to Women's Experience." In *Shaping New Vision: Gender and Values in American Culture*, edited by Clarissa W. Atkinson, et al. 31–50. Studies in Religion 5. Ann Arbor: UMI Research, 1987.

Davis, Kathy, Mary Evans, and Judith Lorber, eds. *Handbook of Gender and Women's Studies*. London: SAGE Publications, 2006.

de Gruchy, John W., "Bonhoeffer, Apartheid, and Beyond: The Reception of Bonhoeffer in South Africa." In *Bonhoeffer for a New Day*, edited by John W. de Gruchy, 353–65. Grand Rapids: Eerdmans , 1997.

———. ed. *Bonhoeffer for a New Day: Theology in a Time of Transition*. Papers Presented at the Seventh International Bonhoeffer Congress, Cape Town, 1996. Grand Rapids: Eerdmans , 1997.

de Santa Ana, Julio. "The Influence of Bonhoeffer on the Theology of Liberation." *The Ecumenical Review* 28 (1976) 188–97.

Doehring, Carrie. *Taking Care: Monitoring Power Dynamics and Relational Boundaries in Pastoral Care & Counseling*. Nashville: Abingdon, 1995.

Downey, Michael. *Understanding Christian Spirituality*. Mahwah, NJ: Paulist, 1997.

Dreyer, Elizabeth A., and Mark S. Burrows, eds. *Minding the Spirit: The Study of Christian Spirituality*. Baltimore: Johns Hopkins University Press, 2005.

Duff, Nancy J. "Recovering Lamentation as a Practice in the Church." In *Lament: Reclaiming Practices in Pulpit, Pew, and Public Square*, edited by Sally A. Brown and Patrick D. Miller, 3–14. Louisville: Westminster John Knox, 2005.

Duke Center for Spirituality, Theology, and Health. Online: http://www.dukespiritualityandhealth.org/publications/latest.html. Accessed March 29, 2008.

Dumas, André. *Dietrich Bonhoeffer: Theologian of Reality*. Translated by Robert McAfee Brown. New York: Macmillan, 1971.

———. "Religion and Reality in the Work of Bonhoeffer." In *A Bonhoeffer Legacy: Essays in Understanding*, edited by A. J. Klassen, 258–67. Grand Rapids: Eerdmans, 1981.

Erickson, Robert P., and Susannah Heschel, eds. *Betrayal: German Churches and the Holocaust*. Minneapolis: Fortress, 1999.

Erikson, Erik. "Womanhood and the Inner Space." In *Identity, Youth and Crisis*, 261–94. New York: Norton, 1968.

Esser, Annette, Anne Hunt Overzee, and Susan Roll, eds. *Re-Visioning our Sources: Women's Spirituality in European Perspective*. Kampen: Kok Pharos, 1997.

Evangelical Lutheran Church in America. *Evangelical Lutheran Worship*. Minneapolis: Augsburg Fortress, 2006.

Eugene, Toinette, and James Poling. *Balm for Gilead*. Nashville: Abingdon, 1998.

Fabella, Virginia, and Sun Ai Lee Park, eds. *We Dare to Dream: Doing Theology as Asian Women*. Hong Kong: Asian Women's Resource Centre for Culture and Theology; Asian Office of the Women's Commission of the Ecumenical Association of Third World Theologians, 1989.

Feige, Franz. *The Varieties of Protestantism in Nazi Germany: Five Theopolitical Positions*. New York: Mellen, 1990.

Ferguson, Margaret, and Jennifer Wicke, eds. *Feminism and Postmodernism*. Durham: Duke University Press, 1994.

Fischer, Kathleen. *Transforming Fire: Women Using Anger Creatively*. New York: Paulist, 1999.

———. *Women at the Well: Feminist Perspectives on Spiritual Direction*. New York: Paulist, 1988.

Fischer, Klaus P. *Nazi Germany: A New History*. New York: Continuum, 1995.

Fischer-Hüllstrung, H. "A Report from Flossenbürg." In *I Knew Dietrich Bonhoeffer*, edited by Wolf-Dieter Zimmermann and Ronald Gregor Smith. Translated by Käthe Gregor Smith, 230–32. London: Collins, 1966.

Floyd, Wayne Whitson. *Theology and the Dialectics of Otherness: On Reading Bonhoeffer and Adorno*. Lanham, MD: University Press of America, 1988.

For Shelter and Beyond: An Education Manual for Working with Women Who are Battered. Boston: Massachusettes Coalition of Battered Women Service Groups, 1981.

Ford, David F. *Self and Salvation: Being Transformed*. Cambridge Studies in Christian Doctrine. Cambridge: Cambridge University Press, 1999.

Fortune, Marie. *Is Nothing Sacred? When Sex Invades the Pastor-Parishioner Relationship*. San Francisco: Harper and Row, 1989.

———. *Love Does No Harm: Sexual Ethics for the Rest of Us*. New York: Continuum, 1995.

———. *Sexual Violence: The Unmentionable Sin*. New York: Pilgrim, 1983.

Fosshage, James L. "Self Psychology: The Self and Its Vicissitudes Within a Relational Matrix." In *Relational Perspectives in Psychoanalysis*, edited by Neil J. Skolnick and Susan C. Warshaw, 21–42. Hillsdale, NJ: Analytic, 1992.

Foster, Charles, et al. *Educating Clergy: Teaching Practice and Pastoral Imagination*. Carnegie Foundation for the Advancement of Teaching, Preparation for the Professions Series. San Francisco: Jossey-Bass, 2005.

Freud, Sigmund. "The Dissolution of the Oedipus Complex." *The Standard Edition of the Complete Psychological Works* (hereafter SE) 19: 173–82. London: Hogarth, 1924.

———. "Female Sexuality." SE 21 (1931) 77-174.

———. "Femininity." In *New Introductory Lectures on Psycho-Analysis*. SE 22 (1933) 3–182.

———. "Some Psychical Consequences of the Anatomical Distinction Between the Sexes." SE 19 (1924) 243–58.

Gebara, Ivone. *Out of the Depths: Women's Experience of Evil and Salvation*. Translated by Ann Patrick Ware. Minneapolis: Fortress, 2002.

Geertz, Clifford. "Thick Description." In *The Interpretation of Cultures*, 3–30. New York: BasicBooks, 1973.

Gilkes, Cheryl. *"If It Wasn't for the Women . . .": Black Women's Experience and Womanist Culture in Church and Community*. Maryknoll, NY: Orbis, 2001.

Gill, Anton. *An Honorable Defeat: A History of the German Resistance to Hitler, 1933–1945*. New York: Holt, 1994.

Gill-Austern, Brita. "Love Understood as Self-Sacrifice and Self-Denial: What Does It Do to Women?" In *Through the Eyes of Women: Insights for Pastoral Care*, edited by Jeanne Stevenson Moessner, 304–21. Minneapolis: Fortress, 1996.

————. "'She Who Desires': The Transformative Power of Subjectivity in Women's Psychological and Spiritual Experience." *American Baptist Quarterly* 16 (1997) 37–55.

Gilligan, Carol. *In a Different Voice: Psychological Theory and Women's Development.* Cambridge: Harvard University Press, 1982.

————. "Remapping the Moral Domain: New Images of the Self in Relationship." In *Reconstructing Individualism: Autonomy, Individuality, and the Self in Western Thought*, edited by Thomas Heller, et al., 237–52. Stanford: Stanford University Press, 1986.

Gilligan, Carol, Nona P. Lyons, and Trudy J. Hanmer, editors. *Making Connections: The Relational Worlds of Adolescent Girls at Emma Willard School.* Cambridge: Harvard University Press, 1990.

Gilligan, Carol, Annie G. Rogers, and Deborah L. Tolman, editors. *Women, Girls, and Psychotherapy: Reframing Resistance.* Binghampton, NY: Harrington Park, 1991.

Glazener, Mary. "On Being a Christian Today: Dietrich Bonhoeffer's Personal Faith." In *Reflections on Bonhoeffer: Essays in Honor of F. Burton Nelson*, edited by Geoffrey Kelly and C. John Weborg, 87–99. Chicago: Covenant, 1999.

Glenthøj, Jørgen. "Der unbegreiflich hohe Gedanke der Stellvertretung." In *Dietrich Bonhoeffer: Beten und Tun des Gerechten: Glaube und Verantwortung im Widerstand*, edited by Rainer Mayer and Peter Zimmerling, 48–61. Basel: Brunnen, 1997.

Godsey, John D. "Bonhoeffer and the Third World: West Africa, Cuba, Korea." In *Ethical Responsibility: Bonhoeffer's Legacy to the Churches*, edited by John D. Godsey and Geffrey B. Kelly, 257–65. Toronto Studies in Theology 6. New York: Mellen, 1981.

————. "Dietrich Bonhoeffer and Christian Spirituality." In *Reflections on Bonhoeffer: Essays in Honor of F. Burton Nelson*, edited by Geoffrey Kelly and C. John Weborg, 77–86. Chicago: Covenant, 1999.

Godsey, John D., and Geffrey B. Kelly, eds. *Ethical Responsibility: Bonhoeffer's Legacy to the Churches.* Toronto Studies in Theology 6. New York: Mellen, 1981.

Gold, Judith. "Book Forum: Review of Meeting at the Crossroads. Women's Psychology and Girls' Development." *American Journal of Psychiatry* 151 (1994) 281.

Goldberg, S. "Social Competence in Infancy: A Model of Parent-Infant Interaction." *Merrill-Palmer Quarterly* 23 (1977) 163–77.

Golden, Carla. "Relational Theories of White Women's Development." In *Lectures on the Psychology of Women,* edited by Joan C. Chrisler, et al., 229–42. New York: McGraw-Hill, 1996.

Goldenberg, Naomi. "A Theory of Gender as a Central Hermeneutic in the Psychoanalysis of Religion." In *Hermeneutical Approaches in the Psychology of Religion*, edited by J. A. Belzen, 65–84. Amsterdam: Rodopi, 1997.

Gosda, Petra. *'Du sollst keine anderen Götter haben neben mir': Gott und die Götzen in den Schriften Dietrich Bonhoeffers.* Neukirchen-Vluyn: Neukirchener, 1999.

Graff, Ann O'Hara, ed. *In the Embrace of God: Feminist Approaches to Theological Anthropology.* Maryknoll, NY: Orbis, 1995.

Grant, Jacquelyn. *White Women's Christ and Black Women's Jesus: Feminist Christology and Womanist Response.* American Academy of Religion Academy Series 64. Atlanta: Scholars, 1989.

Green, Clifford J. *Bonhoeffer: A Theology of Sociality.* Rev. ed. Grand Rapids: Eerdmans, 1999.

———. "Editor's Introduction." In Dietrich Bonhoeffer, *Sanctorum Communio.* *DBWE* 1: 1–20. Minneapolis: Fortress, 1998.

———. "Two Bonhoeffers on Psychoanalysis." In *A Bonhoeffer Legacy: Essays in Understanding*, edited by A. J. Klassen, 58–75. Grand Rapids: Eerdmans , 1981.

Griffin, Graeme M. "The Self and Jesus Christ: A Critical Consideration of the Nature of the Self and its Place in Christian Theology and Life: With Particular Reference to the Thought of Dietrich Bonhoeffer and Carl G. Jung." Th.D. diss., Princeton Theological Seminary, 1965.

Griffiths, Morwenna. *Feminisms and the Self: The Web of Identity.* London: Routledge, 1995.

Grodin, Debra, and Thomas R. Lindlof, eds. *Constructing the Self in a Mediated World.* Inquiries in Social Construction. Thousand Oaks, CA: Sage, 1996.

Grosz, Elizabeth. "Voyeurism/exhibitionism/the gaze." In *Feminism and Psychoanalysis: A Critical Dictionary*, edited by Elizabeth Wright, 447–50. Oxford: Blackwell, 1992.

Gunsberg, Linda. "Selected Critical Review of Psychological Investigations of the Early Father-Infant Relationship." In *Father and Child: Developmental and Clinical Perspectives*, edited by Stanley H. Cath et al. Boston: Little, Brown, 1982.

Gutierrez, Gustavo. "Theology from the Underside of History." In *The Power of the Poor in History*, translated by Robert R. Barr, 169–221. Maryknoll, NY: Orbis, 1983.

Hale, Lori Brandt. "Dietrich Bonhoeffer and the Question of the Other." Paper presented to the International Dietrich Bonhoeffer Society, Berlin, August 2000.

Hall, Therese E. "Gender Differences: Implications for Spiritual Formation and Community Life." *Journal of Psychology and Christianity* 16 (1997) 222–32.

Hanson, Bradley. "Spirituality as Spiritual Theology." In *Modern Christian Spirituality: Methodological and Historical Essays*, edited by Bradley C. Hanson, 45–52. American Academy of Religion Studies in Religion 62. Atlanta: Scholars, 1990.

———. "Theological Approaches to Spirituality: A Lutheran Perspective." *Christian Spirituality Bulletin* 2 (1994) 5–8.

Hardy, Douglas S. "A Winnicottian Redescription of Christian Spiritual Direction Relationships: Illustrating the Potential Contribution of Psychology of Religion to Christian Spiritual Practice." *Journal of Psychology and Theology* 28/4 (2000) 263–75.

Harstock, Nancy C. M. "Foucault on Power: A Theory for Women?" In *Feminism/ Postmodernism (Thinking Gender)*, edited and introduced by Linda J. Nicholson, 157–75. London: Routledge, 1990.

———. "Postmodernism and Political Change: Issues for Feminist Theory." In *Feminist Interpretations of Michel Foucault*, edited by Susan J. Hekman, 39–55. University Park: Pennsylvania State University Press, 1996.

Hay, David. "Experience." In *The Blackwell Companion to Christian Spirituality*, edited by Arthur Holder, 419–41. Malden, MA: Blackwell, 2005.

Hegy, Pierre, ed. *Feminist Voices in Spirituality.* Lewiston, NY: Mellen, 1996.

Heine, Susanne. "Female Masochism and the Theology of the Cross." Translated by Frederick J. Gaiser. *Word & World* 15 (1995) 299–305.

Herman, Judith. *Trauma and Recovery: The Aftermath of Violence—from Domestic Abuse to Political Terror*. New York: BasicBooks, 1992.

Heyward, Carter. *Speaking of Christ: A Lesbian Feminist Voice*. Edited by Ellen C. Davis. New York: Pilgrim, 1989.

Hilberman, Elaine. "The 'Wife-Beater's Wife' Reconsidered." *American Journal of Psychiatry* 137 (1980) 1336–47.

Hoff, Lee Ann. *Battered Women as Survivors*. London: Routledge, 1990.

Hoffmann, Peter. *The History of the German Resistance, 1933–1945*. Translated by Richard Barry. Cambridge, MA: MIT Press, 1977.

Holder, Arthur, ed. *The Blackwell Companion to Christian Spirituality*. Malden, MA: Blackwell, 2005.

Hood, Ralph W. Jr., et al. *The Psychology of Religion: An Empirical Approach*. New York: Guilford, 1996.

Horney, Karen. *Neurosis and Human Growth*. New York: Norton, 1950.

———. *The Neurotic Personality of Our Time*. New York: Norton, 1937.

———. "The Problem of Female Masochism." In *Feminine Psychology*, 214–33. New York: Norton, 1967.

Huff, Margaret Craddock. "The Interdependent Self: An Integrated Concept from Feminist Theology and Feminist Psychology." *Philosophy and Theology* 2 (1987) 160–72.

Huffaker, Lucinda Stark. *Creative Dwelling: Empathy and Clarity in God and Self*. AAR Academy Series. Atlanta: Scholars, 1998.

Hunsinger, George. "Koinonia Between Christ and His Community: Two Views of the Church." Paper presented at Barth/Bonhoeffer Conference, St. Paul, MN, July 26, 2000.

Hunt, Mary E. "Psychological Implications of Women's Spiritual Health." In *Women's Spirituality, Women's Lives*, edited by Judith Ochshorn and Ellen Cole, 21–32. New York: Haworth, 1995.

Isasi-Díaz, Ada María. *Mujerista Theology: A Theology for the Twenty-First Century*. Maryknoll, NY: Orbis, 1996.

Jack, Dana Crowley. *Silencing the Self: Women and Depression*. Cambridge, Harvard University Press, 1991.

Jacobs, Janet L. "The Effects of Ritual Healing on Female Victims of Abuse: A Study of Empowerment and Transformation." In *Gender and Religion*, edited by William H. Swatos, 127–41. New Brunswick, NJ: Transaction, 1994.

———. "The Endangered Female Self and the Search for Identity." In *The Endangered Self*, edited by Richard K. Fenn and Donald Capps, 37–46. Princeton: Princeton Theological Seminary, Center for Religion, Self, and Society, 1992.

———. *Victimized Daughters: Incest and the Development of the Female Self*. London: Routledge, 1994.

———. "The Violated Self and the Search for Religious Meaning." In *Sex, Lies and Sanctity: Religion and Deviance in Contemporary North America*, edited by Mary Jo Neitz and Marion S. Goldman, 237–50. Greenwich, CT: JAI, 1995.

Jacobs, Janet Liebman, and Donald Capps, eds. *Religion, Society, and Psychoanalysis: Readings in Contemporary Theory*. Boulder: Westview, 1997.

Janet, Pierre. *L'Automatisme Psychologique*. Paris: Félix Alcan, 1889.

Jasinski, Jana L., and Linda Williams, eds. *Partner Violence*. Wellesley, MA: Stone Center, 1998.

Johnson, Barbara. *A World of Difference*. Baltimore: Johns Hopkins University Press, 1987.

Johnson, Elizabeth A. "The Maleness of Christ." In *The Power of Naming: A Concilium Reader in Feminist Liberation Theology*, edited by Elisabeth Schüssler Fiorenza, 307–15. Maryknoll, NY: Orbis, 1996.

———. *She Who Is: The Mystery of God in Feminist Theological Discourse*. New York: Crossroad, 1992.

Jones, James W. *Religion and Psychology in Transition: Psychoanalysis, Feminism, and Psychology*. New Haven: Yale University Press, 1996.

Jones, L. Serene. "Trauma Theory and Christian Theology." Paper presented to the Feminist Theory and Religious Reflection Group of the American Academy of Religion, Nashville, November 18, 2000.

Jonte-Pace, Diane. "Analysts, Critics, and Inclusivists: Feminist Voices in the Psychology of Women." In *Religion and Psychology: Mapping the Terrain*, edited by Diane Jonte-Pace and William Parsons, 129–46. New York: Routledge, 2001.

———. "Maternal Absence, Castration, and the End of the World: A Freudian Reading of the Notion of the Endangered Self." In *The Endangered Self*, edited by Richard K. Fenn and Donald Capps, 116–28. Princeton: Princeton Theological Seminary, Center for Religion, Self, and Society, 1992.

———. "New Directions in the Feminist Psychology of Religion: An Introduction." *Journal of Feminist Studies in Religion* 31/1 (1997) 63–74.

———. "Object Relations, Mothering, and Religion: Toward a Feminist Psychology of Religion." *Horizons* 14/2 (1987) 310–27.

———. "Psychoanalysis after Feminism." *Religious Studies Review* 19/2 (1993) 110–15.

Jordan, Judith V. "Empathy and Self Boundaries." In *Women's Growth in Connection: Writings from the Stone Center*, 67–80. New York: Guilford, 1991.

———. "Some Misconceptions and Reconceptions of a Relational Approach." Unpublished paper, 1991. Stone Center.

———, Alexandra G. Kaplan, Jean Baker Miller, Irene P. Stiver, and Janet L. Surrey. *Women's Growth in Connection: Writings from the Stone Center*. New York: Guilford, 1991.

Jordan, Judith V., ed. *Women's Growth in Diversity: More Writings from the Stone Center*. New York: Guilford, 1997.

Josselson, Ruthellen. "The Embedded Self: I and Thou Revisited." In *Self, Ego, and Identity: Integrative Approaches*, edited by Daniel K. Lapsley and F. Clark Power, 91–106. New York: Springer, 1988.

———. *Finding Herself: Pathways to Identity Development in Women*. San Francisco: Jossey-Bass, 1987.

Joy, Morny. "Feminism and the Self." *Theory and Psychology* 3 (1993) 275–302.

Kaplan, Alexandra G. "The 'Self-in-Relation': Implications for Depression in Women." In *Women's Growth in Connection: Writings from the Stone Center*, 206–22. New York: Guilford, 1991.

Keller, Catherine. *From a Broken Web: Separation, Sexism and Self*. Boston: Beacon, 1986.

———. "'To Illuminate Your Trace': Self in Late Modern Feminist Theology." *Listening* 25 (1990) 211–24.

———. "Toward a Postpatriarchal Postmodernity." In *Spirituality and Society: Postmodern Visions*, edited by David Ray Griffin, 63–80. Albany, NY: SUNY Press, 1988.

Kelly, Geffrey B. "Freedom and Discipline: Rhythms of a Christocentric Spirituality." In *Ethical Responsibility: Bonhoeffer's Legacy to the Churches*, edited by John D. Godsey and Geffrey B. Kelly, 307–36. Toronto: Mellen, 1981.

———. "Prayer and Action for Justice: Bonhoeffer's Spirituality." In *The Cambridge Companion to Dietrich Bonhoeffer*, edited by John W. de Gruchy, 246–68. Cambridge: Cambridge University Press, 1999.

Kelly, Geffrey B., and F. Burton Nelson. *The Cost of Moral Leadership: The Spirituality of Dietrich Bonhoeffer*. With a foreword by Renate Bethge. Grand Rapids: Eerdmans, 2003.

Kennedy, Roger. "Becoming a Subject: Some Theoretical and Clinical Issues." *International Journal of Psychoanalysis* 81 (2000) 875–92.

———. *The Elusive Human Subject: A Psychoanalytic Theory of Subject Relations*. London: Free Association, 1998.

Keshgegian, Flora A. *Redeeming Memories: A Theology of Healing and Transformation*. Nashville: Abingdon, 2000.

Kierkegaard, Søren. *The Sickness Unto Death*. In *Fear and Trembling/The Sickness Unto Death*, translated by Walter Lowrie. Princeton: Princeton University Press, 1968.

Kirstein, Ronald D. "Heinz Kohut's Nuclear Self: A Self Psychology/Spiritual Model of Maturity." Ph.D. diss., Graduate Theological Union, 1993.

Klein, Julie Thompson. *Interdisciplinarity: History, Theory and Practice*. Detroit: Wayne State University Press, 1990.

Kohut, Heinz. *The Analysis of the Self*. New York: International Universities Press, 1971.

———. *The Restoration of the Self*. New York: International Universities Press, 1977.

Kuhlmann, Helga. "Die Ethik Dietrich Bonhoeffers—Quelle oder Hemmschuh für feministisch-theologische Ethik?" *Zeitschrift für evangelische Ethik* 37 (1993) 106–20.

Kyung, Chung Hyun. *Struggle to Be the Sun Again: Introducing Asian Women's Theology*. Maryknoll, NY: Orbis, 1990.

Lamb, Michael. "The Development of Parental Preferences in the First Two Years of Life." *Sex Roles* 3 (1977) 495–97.

Lane, Belden C. "Galesville and Sinai: The Researcher as Participant in the Study of Spirituality." *Christian Spirituality Bulletin* 2 (1994) 18–20.

Lapsley, Daniel K., and F. Clark Power, eds. *Self, Ego, and Identity: Integrative Approaches*. New York: Springer, 1988.

Leistner, Herta, et al., eds. *Laß spüren deine Kraft: feministische Liturgie: Grundlagen, Argumente, Anregungen*. Frauenstudien und Bildungszentrum der EKD, Arbeitskreis Feministische Liturgie. Gütersloh: Gütersloher, 1997.

Lescher, Bruce H., and Elizabeth Liebert, eds. *Exploring Christian Spirituality: Essays in Honor of Sandra M. Schneiders, IHM.* Mahwah, NJ: Paulist, 2006.

Lewis, Michael, and Leonard A. Rosenblum, eds. *The Effect of the Infant on Its Caregiver.* New York: Wiley, 1974.

Liaboe, Gary P., and James D. Guy. "Masochism and the Distortion of Servanthood." *Journal of Psychology and Theology* 13/4 (1985) 255–62.

Liebert, Elizabeth. "Coming Home to Themselves: Women's Spiritual Care." In *Through the Eyes of Women: Insights for Pastoral Care,* edited by Jeanne Stevenson Moessner, 257–84. Minneapolis: Fortress, 1996.

Linklater, Kristin. *Freeing the Natural Voice.* New York: Drama, 1976.

Lobel, Kerry, ed. *Naming the Violence: Speaking Out about Lesbian Battering.* Seattle: Seal, 1986.

Lowe, Mary Elise. "Woman Oriented Hamartiologies: A Survey of the Shift from Powerlessness to Right Relationship." *Dialog: A Journal of Theology* 39/2 (2000) 119–39.

Lundborg, Paul S. "Spiritual Formation: An Ancient Practice for Lutheran Parish Life Today." D.Min. thesis, San Francisco Theological Seminary, 1992.

MacCannell, Dean, and Juliet Flower MacCannell. "Violence, Power and Pleasure: A Revisionist Reading of Foucault from the Victim Perspective." In *Up against Foucault: Explorations of Some Tensions between Foucault and Feminism,* edited by Caroline Ramazanoğlu, 203–38. London: Routledge, 1993.

Mananzan, Mary John, et al., eds. *Women Resisting Violence: Spirituality for Life.* Maryknoll, NY: Orbis, 1996.

Manvell, Roger, and Heinrich Fraenkel. *The Canaris Conspiracy: The Secret Resistance to Hitler in the German Army.* New York: McKay, 1969.

Markus, Hazel, and Daphna Oyserman. "Gender and Thought: The Role of the Self-Concept." In *Gender and Thought: Psychological Perspectives,* edited by Mary Crawford and Margaret Gentry, 100–27. New York: Springer, 1989.

Marsh, Charles. "The Overabundant Self and the Transcendental Tradition: Dietrich Bonhoeffer on the Self-Reflective Subject." *Journal of the American Academy of Religion* 60 (1992) 659–72.

———. *Reclaiming Dietrich Bonhoeffer: The Promise of His Theology.* Oxford: Oxford University Press, 1994.

Martin, Bernice. "Whose Soul Is It Anyway? Domestic Tyranny and the Suffocated Soul." In *On Losing the Soul: Essays in the Social Psychology of Religion,* edited by Richard K. Fenn and Donald Capps, 69–96. Albany: SUNY Press, 1995.

Mayer, Rainer. "Beten und Tun des Gerechten: Glaube und Verantwortung bei Dietrich Bonhoeffer." In *Dietrich Bonhoeffer: Beten und Tun des Gerechten: Glaube und Verantwortung im Widerstand,* edited by Rainer Mayer and Peter Zimmerling, 11–34. Basel: Brunnen, 1997.

Mayer, Rainer, and Peter Zimmerling, eds. *Dietrich Bonhoeffer: Beten und Tun des Gerechten: Glaube und Verantwortung im Widerstand.* Basel: Brunnen, 1997.

———. *Dietrich Bonhoeffer, Mensch hinter Mauern: Theologie und Spiritualität in den Gefängnisjahren.* Basel: Brunnen, 1993.

McFague, Sallie. *Models of God: Theology for an Ecological, Nuclear Age.* Philadelphia: Fortress, 1987.

———. *Super, Natural Christians: How We Should Love Nature*. Minneapolis: Fortress, 1997.

McFayden, Alistair. *Bound to Sin: Abuse, Holocaust, and the Christian Doctrine of Sin*. Cambridge Studies in Christian Doctrine 6. Cambridge: Cambridge University Press, 2000.

McGinn, Bernard. "The Letter and the Spirit: Spirituality as an Academic Discipline." In *Minding the Spirit: The Study of Christian Spirituality*, edited by Elizabeth A. Dreyer and Mark S. Burrows, 25–41. Baltimore: Johns Hopkins University Press, 2005.

McGrath, Alister E. *Christian Spirituality: An Introduction*. Oxford: Blackwell, 1999.

McNeill, John J. "Psychotherapy and the Spiritual Journey." *Journal of Religion and Health* 37 (1998) 333–44.

Medley, Mark. "Becoming Human Together: Imaging the Triune God." In *Perspectives in Religious Studies* 23/3 (1996) 289–316.

Meyer-Wilmes, Hedwig. "Excessive Violence Against Women in the Name of Religion." In *Religion as a Source of Violence?* edited by Wim Beuken and Karl Josef Kuschel, 55–63. Maryknoll, NY: Orbis, 1997.

Meyers, Diana Tietjens, ed. *Feminists Rethink the Self*. Feminist Theory and Politics. Boulder: Westview, 1997.

Miller, Jean Baker. *Connections, Disconnections, and Violations: Work in Progress, no. 33*. Wellesley, MA: Stone Center, 1988.

———. "The Construction of Anger in Women and Men." In *Women's Growth in Connection: Writings from the Stone Center*, 181–96. New York: Guilford, 1991.

———. "The Development of Women's Sense of Self." In *Women's Growth in Connection: Writings from the Stone Center*, 11–26. New York: Guilford, 1991.

———. *Toward a New Psychology of Women*. 2nd edition. Boston: Beacon, 1986.

———. "Women and Power." In *Women's Growth in Connection: Writings from the Stone Center*, 197–205. New York: Guilford, 1991.

——— et al. "Some Misconceptions and Reconceptions of a Relational Approach." Unpublished paper. Stone Center, 1991.

Miller-McLemore, Bonnie J. "Shaping the Future of Religion and Psychology: Feminist Transformations in Pastoral Psychology." In *Religion and Psychology: Mapping the Terrain*, edited by Diane Jonte-Pace and William Parsons, 181–201. New York: Routledge, 2001.

Mitchell, Juliet. *Psychoanalysis and Feminism*. New York: Pantheon, 1974.

Mitchell, Stephen A. "True Selves, False Selves, and the Ambiguity of Authenticity." In *Relational Perspectives in Psychoanalysis*, edited by Neil J. Skolnick and Susan C. Warshaw, 1–20. Hillsdale, NJ: Analytic, 1992.

Mollenkott, Virginia Ramey. *The Divine Feminine: The Biblical Imagery of God as Female*. New York: Crossroad, 1983.

Moseley, Romney M. *Becoming a Self Before God: Critical Transformations*. Nashville: Abingdon, 1991.

Mount Carmel Ministries. *Daily Texts: Bible Verses & Prayers for Each Day of the Year*. Alexandria, MN: Mount Carmel Ministries, 2008.

Mücke, Anke. "Lebenssituationen von Frauen in der Weimarer Republik." In *'Darum wagt es, Schwestern . . .': Zur Geschichte evangelischer Theologinnen in Deutschland*, edited by Gerhard Besier et al., 71–108. Neukirchen-Vluyn: Neukirchener, 1994.

Müller, Christine-Ruth. *Dietrich Bonhoeffers Kampf gegen die nationalsozialistische Verfolgung und Vernichtung der Juden: Bonhoeffers Haltung zur Judenfrage im Vergleich mit Stellungnahmen aus der evangelischen Kirche und Kreisen des deutschen Widerstands.* Munich: Kaiser, 1990.

Mulvey, Laura. "Visual Pleasure and Narrative Cinema." In *Visual and Other Pleasures,* 14–26. London: Macmillan, 1989.

National Coalition Against Domestic Violence. *National Coalition Against Domestic Violence Fact Sheet.* Washington, DC: National Coalition Against Domestic Violence, 1991.

Nelson, F. Burton. "Bonhoeffer and the Spiritual Life: Some Reflections." *Journal of Theology for Southern Africa* 30 (1980) 34–38.

Neuger, Christie Cozad. "Narratives of Harm: Setting the Developmental Context for Intimate Violence." In *In Her Own Time: Women and Developmental Issues in Pastoral Care,* edited by Jeanne Stevenson-Moessner, 65–86. Minneapolis: Fortress, 2000.

Noddings, Nel. *Women and Evil.* Berkeley: University of California Press, 1989.

Ochs, Carol. *Song of the Self: Biblical Spirituality and Human Holiness.* Valley Forge: Trinity , 1994.

———. *Women and Spirituality.* 2nd ed. Lanham, MD: Rowman & Littlefield, 1997.

Ochshorn, Judith, and Ellen Cole, eds. *Women's Spirituality, Women's Lives.* New York: Haworth, 1995.

Page, Rose. "Direction in the Various Stages of Spiritual Development." *Contemplative Review* 12 (1979) 11–18.

Pangritz, Andreas. "'Who Is Jesus Christ for Us Today?'" In *The Cambridge Companion to Dietrich Bonhoeffer,* edited by John W. de Gruchy, 134–53. Cambridge: Cambridge University Press, 1999.

———. "Aspekte der 'Arkandisziplin' bei Dietrich Bonhoeffer." *Theologische Literaturzeitung* 119 (1994) 755–68.

Park, Andrew Sung. *From Hurt to Healing: A Theology of the Wounded.* Nashville: Abingdon, 2004.

———, and Susan L. Nelson, eds. *The Other Side of Sin: Woundedness from the Perspective of the Sinned-Against.* Albany: SUNY Press, 2001.

Peck, William Jay. "The Role of the 'Enemy' in Bonhoeffer's Life and Thought." In *A Bonhoeffer Legacy: Essays in Understanding,* edited by A. J. Klassen, 345–62. Grand Rapids: Eerdmans, 1981.

Pelikan, Herbert Rainer. *Die Frömmigkeit Dietrich Bonhoeffers: Äußerungen, Grundlinien, Entwicklung.* Vienna: Herder, 1982.

Pellauer, Mary. *Lutheran Theology Facing Sexual and Domestic Violence.* Chicago: Commission for Women, Evangelical Lutheran Church in America, 1998.

———, Barbara Chester, and Jane Boyajian. *Sexual Assault and Abuse: A Handbook for Clergy and Religious Professionals.* San Francisco: HarperSanFrancisco, 1987.

Pence, Gary. "Is Sin an Abusive Doctrine?" *Dialog* 38 (1999) 294–97.

Peterman, Janet S. *Speaking to Silence: New Rites for Christian Worship and Healing.* Louisville: Westminster John Knox, 2007.

Peters, Tiemo Rainer. "Der andere ist unendlich wichtig. Impulse aus Bonhoeffers Ekklesiologie für die Gegenwart." In *Die Präsenz des verdrängten Gottes: Glaube, Religionslosigkeit und Weltverantwortung nach Dietrich Bonhoeffer*, edited by Christian Gremmels and Ilse Tödt, 166–84. Munich: Kaiser, 1987.

Phillips, John A. *Christ for Us in the Theology of Dietrich Bonhoeffer*. New York: Harper & Row, 1967.

Pieper, Josef. *Zucht und Maß: Über die vierte Kardinalstugend*. Leipzig: Hegner, 1939.

Plaskow, Judith. *Sex, Sin, and Grace: Women's Experience and the Theologies of Reinhold Niebuhr and Paul Tillich*. Lanham, MD: University Press of America, 1980.

———, and Carol P. Christ, eds. *Weaving the Visions: New Patterns in Feminist Spirituality*. San Francisco: HarperCollins, 1989.

Poole, Roger. "Bonhoeffer and the Arcane Discipline." In *Ethical Responsibility: Bonhoeffer's Legacy to the Churches*, edited by John D. Godsey and Geffrey B. Kelly, 271–92. Toronto: Mellen, 1981.

Post, Stephen G. "The Inadequacy of Selflessness: God's Suffering and the Theory of Love." *Journal of the American Academy of Religion* 56/2 (1994) 213–28.

Principe, Walter H. "Broadening the Focus: Context as a Corrective Lens in Reading Historical Works in Spirituality." In *Minding the Spirit: The Study of Christian Spirituality*, edited by Elizabeth A. Dreyer and Mark S. Burrows, 42–48. Baltimore: Johns Hopkins University Press, 2005.

Pryor, Robin. "The Process of Formation." *Ministerial Formation* 80 (1998) 35–39.

Raab, Kelley A. *When Women Become Priests: The Catholic Women's Ordination Debate*. New York: Columbia University Press, 2000.

Ragsdale, Katherine Hancock, ed. *Boundary Wars: Intimacy and Distance in Healing Relationships*. Cleveland: Pilgrim, 1996.

Ramshaw, Gail. *God Beyond Gender: Feminist Christian God-Language*. Minneapolis: Fortress, 1995.

Rasmussen, Larry. *Dietrich Bonhoeffer—His Significance for North Americans*. With Renate Bethge. Minneapolis: Fortress, 1990.

Reynolds, Terrence. *The Coherence of Life Without God Before God: The Problem of Earthly Desires in the Later Theology of Dietrich Bonhoeffer*. Lanham, MD: University Press of America, 1989.

Ricoeur, Paul. "Lamentation as Prayer." In *Thinking Biblically: Exegetical and Hermeneutical Studies*, André LaCocque and Paul Ricouer, 211–32. Translated by David Pellauer. Chicago: University of Chicago Press, 1998.

Rieker, Patricia P., and Elaine (Hilberman) Carmen. "The Victim-to-Patient Process: The Disconfirmation and Transformation of Abuse." *American Journal of Orthopsychiatry* 56 (1986) 360–70.

Riley, Bruce T. *The Psychology of Religious Experience in its Personal and Institutional Dimensions*. American University Studies 49. Bern: Lang, 1988.

Rizzuto, Ana-Maria. "Exploring Sacred Landscapes." In *Exploring Sacred Landscapes: Religious and Spiritual Experiences in Psychotherapy*, edited by Mary Lou Randour, 16–33. New York: Columbia University Press, 1993.

Roberts, Robert C., and Mark R. Talbot, eds. *Limning the Psyche: Explorations in Christian Psychology*. Grand Rapids: Eerdmans, 1997.

Rose, Jacqueline. *Sexuality and the Field of Vision*. London: Verso, 1987.

Ruether, Rosemary Radford. *Sexism and God-Talk: Toward a Feminist Theology.* Boston: Beacon, 1983.

Rutter, Peter. *Sex in the Forbidden Zone: When Men in Power Abuse Women's Trust.* Los Angeles: Jeremy Tarcher, 1989.

St. Clair, Michael. *Human Relationships and the Experience of God: Object Relations and Religion.* Mahwah, NJ: Paulist, 1994.

Saiving, Valerie. "The Human Situation: A Feminine View." In *Womanspirit Rising: A Feminist Reader in Religion,* edited by Carol Christ and Judith Plaskow, 25–42. San Francisco: Harper and Row, 1979.

Sander, Louis W. "Polarity, Paradox, and the Organizing Process in Development." In *Frontiers of Infant Psychiatry,* edited by Justin D. Call et al., 333–46. New York: Basic, 1983.

Schindler, Regine. "Verhaftet und verlobt: Zum Briefwechsel zwischen Dietrich Bonhoeffer und Maria von Wedemeyer, 1943–1945." In *Theologie und Freundschaft. Wechselwirkungen: Eberhard Bethge und Dietrich Bonhoeffer,* edited by Christian Gremmels and Wolfgang Huber, 154–69. Munich: Kaiser, 1994.

Schmidt, William S. *The Development of the Notion of Self: Understanding the Complexity of Human Interiority.* New York: Mellen, 1994.

Schneiders, Sandra M., I.H.M. "Approaches to the Study of Christian Spirituality." In *The Blackwell Companion to Christian Spirituality,* edited by Arthur Holder, 15–33. Malden, MA: Blackwell, 2005.

————. "A Hermeneutical Approach to the Study of Christian Spirituality." In *Minding the Spirit: The Study of Christian Spirituality,* edited by Elizabeth A. Dreyer and Mark S. Burrows, 49–60. Baltimore: Johns Hopkins University Press, 2005.

————. *The Revelatory Text: Interpreting the New Testament as Sacred Scripture.* 2nd ed. Collegeville, MN: Liturgical, 1999.

————. "Spirituality as an Academic Discipline: Reflections from Experience." *Christian Spirituality Bulletin* 1 (1993) 10–15.

————. "Spirituality in the Academy." *Theological Studies* 50 (1989) 676–97.

————. "The Study of Christian Spirituality: Contours and Dynamics of a Discipline." In *Minding the Spirit: The Study of Christian Spirituality,* edited by Elizabeth A. Dreyer and Mark S. Burrows, 5–24. Baltimore: Johns Hopkins University Press, 2005.

Scholder, Klaus. *A Requiem for Hitler: And Other New Perspectives on the German Church Struggle.* Translated by John Bowden. Philadelphia: Trinity, 1989.

Schrag, Calvin O. *The Self After Postmodernity.* New Haven: Yale University Press, 1997.

Schramm, Brooks. "Lament's Hope." In *Spirituality: Toward a 21ˢᵗ Century Lutheran Understanding,* edited by Kirsi Stjerna and Brooks Schramm, 60–70. Minneapolis: Lutheran University Press, 2004.

Schüssler Fiorenza, Elisabeth. "Ties That Bind: Domestic Violence against Women." In *Women Resisting Violence: Spirituality for Life,* edited by Mary John Mananzan, et al., 39–55. Maryknoll, NY: Orbis, 1996.

Schwartz, Richard C. "Releasing the Soul: Psychotherapy as a Spiritual Practice." In *Spiritual Resources in Family Therapy,* edited by Froma Walsh, 223–39. New York: Guilford, 1999.

Schwöbel, Christoph, and Colin E. Gunton, eds. *Persons, Divine and Human: King's College Essays in Theological Anthropology*. Edinburgh: T. & T. Clark, 1991.

Scott, Jamie S. "Dietrich Bonhoeffer, *Letters and Papers from Prison*, and Paul Ricoeur's 'Hermeneutics of Testimony.'" In *Paul Ricoeur and Narrative*, edited by Morny Joy, 13–25. Calgary: University of Calgary Press, 1997.

Serra, Piera. "Physical Violence in the Couple Relationship: A Contribution Toward the Analysis of the Context." *Family Process* 32/1 (1993) 21–34.

Sheldrake, Philip. *Spirituality and History: Questions of Interpretation and Method*. Rev. ed. London: SPCK, 1996.

———. *Spirituality and Theology: Christian Living and the Doctrine of God*. Maryknoll, New York: Orbis, 1998.

Sheldrake, Philip, ed. *The New Westminster Dictionary of Christian Spirituality*. Louisville: Westminster John Knox, 2005.

Siegele-Wenschkewitz, Leonore. "'Die Ehre der Frau, dem Manne zu dienen': Zum Frauenbild Dietrich Bonhoeffers." In *Wie Theologen Frauen sehen*, edited by Renate Jost and Ursula Kubera, 98–126. Freiburg: Herder, 1993.

———, and Gerda Stuchlik, eds. *Frauen und Faschismus in Europa*. Pfaffenweiler: Centaurus, 1990.

Silverman, Kaja. *The Acoustic Mirror: The Female Voice in Psychoanalysis and Cinema*. Bloomington: Indiana University Press, 1988.

Skolnick, Neil J., and Susan C. Warshaw, eds. *Relational Perspectives in Psychoanalysis*. Hillsdale, NJ: Analytic, 1992.

Slane, Craig J. *Bonhoeffer as Martyr: Social Responsibility and Modern Christian Commitment*. Grand Rapids: Brazos, 2004.

Smith, Laurene E. "'We Are Where God Is': Sacred Dimensions of Battered Women's Lives." In *Sacred Dimensions of Women's Experience*, edited by Elizabeth Dodson Gray, 210–19. Wellesley, MA: Roundtable, 1988.

Snorton, Teresa E. "Self-Care for the African-American Woman." In *In Her Own Time: Women and Developmental Issues in Pastoral Care*, edited by Jeanne Stevenson-Moessner, 285–94. Minneapolis: Fortress, 2000.

Solari-Twadell, Phyllis Ann, ed. *Parish Nursing: Promoting Whole Person Health Within Faith Communities*. Thousand Oaks, CA: Sage, 1999.

Spahr, Jane Adams. "Approaches to the Spirituality of Lesbian Women: Implications for Ministry." D.Min. thesis, San Francisco Theological Seminary, 1987.

Spiritual Directors International. *Guidelines for Ethical Conduct*. Bellevue, WA: Spiritual Directors International, 2007.

Stern, Daniel N. "The Early Development of Schemas of Self, Other, and 'Self with Other.'" In *Reflections on Self Psychology*, edited by Joseph D. Lichtenberg and Samuel Kaplan, 49–84. Hillsdale, NJ: Analytic, 1983.

———. *The First Relationship: Infant and Mother*. Cambridge: Harvard University Press, 1977.

———. *The Interpersonal World of the Infant: A View from Psychoanalysis and Developmental Psychology*. New York: Basic, 1985.

Stern, Lori. "Disavowing the Self in Female Adolescence." *Women and Therapy* 11/3–4 (1990) 105–17.

Stiver, Irene P. "Work Inhibitions in Women." In *Women's Growth in Connection: Writings from the Stone Center*, 223–36. New York: Guilford, 1991.

Stortz, Martha Ellen. "Practicing Christians: Prayer as Formation." In *The Promise of Lutheran Ethics*, edited by Karen Bloomquist and John R. Stumme, 55–71, 192–94. Minneapolis: Fortress, 1998.

Stout, Karen. "Intimate Femicide: A National Demographic Overview." *Violence Update* 1/6 (1991).

Straus, Murray, Richard J. Gelles, and Suzanne K. Steinmetz. *Behind Closed Doors: Violence in the Family*. New York: Doubleday, 1980.

Strauss, Jaine, and George R. Goethals, eds. *The Self: Interdisciplinary Approaches*. New York: Springer, 1991.

Surrey, Janet L. "The Relational Self in Women: Clinical Implications." In *Women's Growth in Connection: Writings from the Stone Center*, 35–43. New York: Guilford, 1991.

———. "Relationship and Empowerment." In *Women's Growth in Connection: Writings from the Stone Center*, 162–80. New York: Guilford, 1991.

———. "The 'Self-in-Relation': A Theory of Women's Development." In *Women's Growth in Connection: Writings from the Stone Center*, 51–66. New York: Guilford, 1991.

Szepansky, Gerda. *Frauen leisten Widerstand, 1933–1945: Lebensgeschichten nach Interviews und Dokumenten*. Frankfurt: Fischer Taschenbuch, 1983.

Taves, Ann. "Varieties of Protestant Religious Experience." In *Fits, Trances, & Visions: Experiencing Religion and Explaining Experience from Wesley to James*, 308–47. Princeton: Princeton University Press, 1999.

Taylor, Charles. *Sources of the Self: The Making of Modern Identity*. Cambridge: Harvard University Press, 1989.

Taylor, Jill McLean, Carol Gilligan, and Amy M. Sullivan. *Between Voice and Silence: Women and Girls, Race and Relationship*. Cambridge: Harvard University Press, 1995.

Thalmann, Rita. *Etre Femme sous le IIIe Reich*. Paris: Laffont, 1982.

Thistlethwaite, Susan Brooks. "Every Two Minutes: Battered Women and Feminist Interpretation." In *Feminist Interpretation of the Bible*, edited by Letty M. Russell, 96–107. Philadelphia: Westminster, 1986.

Thisleton, Anthony C. *Interpreting God and the Postmodern Self: On Meaning, Manipulation and Promise*. Grand Rapids: Eerdmans, 1995.

Tolman, Deborah, and Elizabeth Debold. "Made in Whose Image?" Paper presented to the American Psychological Association. August, 1991.

Tönnies, Ferdinand. *Community and Society*. Edited and translated by Charles P. Loomis. New Brunswick, NJ: Transaction, 1988.

Townes, Emilie M., ed. *Embracing the Spirit: Womanist Perspectives on Hope, Salvation, and Transformation*. Maryknoll, NY: Orbis, 1997.

United Nations Population Fund. *Lives Together, Worlds Apart: Men and Women in a Time of Change. The State of World Population 2000*. New York: United Nations, 2000.

van den Blink, A. J. "Rich Persons." In *Dictionary of Pastoral Care and Counseling*, edited by Rodney J. Hunter et al., 1085–87. Nashville: Abingdon, 1990.

———. "Trauma Reactivation in Pastoral Counseling: Implications for Theory and Practice." *American Journal of Pastoral Counseling* 1/2 (1998) 23–39.

van der Kolk, Bessel A., and Onno van der Hart. "Pierre Janet and the Breakdown of Adaptation in Psychological Trauma." *American Journal of Psychiatry* 146 (1989) 1530–40.

van Eyden, René. "Dietrich Bonhoeffer's Understanding of Male and Female." In *Bonhoeffer's Ethics: Old Europe and New Frontiers*, edited by Guy Carter et al., 200–207. Kampen: Kok Pharos, 1991.

von Goethe, Johann W. *Wilhelm Meisters Lehrjahre*. Edited by Ehrhard Bahr. Stuttgart: Reclam, 1982, 1990.

von Schlabrendorff, Fabian. *Offiziere gegen Hitler, nach einem Erlebnisbericht*, with Gero von Schulze-Gaevernitz. Zurich: Europa, 1946.

Walker, Lenore. *Battered Woman Syndrome*. New York: Springer, 1984.

Walsh, Mary-Paula. *Feminism and Christian Tradition: An Annotated Bibliography and Critical Introduction to the Literature*. Westport, CN: Greenwood, 1999.

Watson, Robert A. "Toward Union in Love: The Contemplative Spiritual Tradition and Contemporary Psychoanalytic Theory in the Formation of Persons." *Journal of Psychology and Theology* 28/4 (2000) 282–92.

Weaver, Darlene Fozard. *Self Love & Christian Ethics*. New Studies in Christian Ethics 23. Cambridge: Cambridge University Press, 2002.

Westberg, Granger E., and Jill Westberg McNamara. *The Parish Nurse: Providing a Minister of Health for Your Congregation*. Minneapolis: Augsburg, 1990.

Westcott, Marcia C. "On the New Psychology of Women: A Cautionary View." *Feminist Issues* 10 (1990) 3–18.

Westermann, Claus. *Lamentations: Issues and Interpretation*. Translated by Charles Muenchow. Minneapolis: Fortress, 1994.

Wind, Renate. "'Es war eigentlich nur Hoffnung': Maria von Wedemeyer, 23 April 1924–16 November 1977." In *Ich bin was ich bin: Frauen neben großen Theologen und Religionsphilosophen des 20. Jahrhunderts*, edited by Esther Röhr, 305–44. Gütersloh: Gütersloher, 1997.

Winnicott, Donald W. "The Capacity to Be Alone." In *The Maturational Process and the Facilitating Environment: Studies in the Theory of Emotional Development*. New York: International Universities Press, 1965.

———. "Ego Distortion in Terms of True and False Self." In *The Maturational Process and the Facilitating Environment: Studies in the Theory of Emotional Development*, 140–52. New York: International Universities Press, 1965.

———. *Playing and Reality*. Harmondsworth, UK: Penguin, 1974.

Woggon, Frank Milstead. "The Will to be Known: Toward a Pastoral Anthropology of the Self." *Pastoral Psychology* 44 (1995) 45–61.

Women's Action Coalition, ed. *WAC Stats: The Facts About Women*. New York: New Press, 1993.

Wood, Alberta D., and Maureen C. McHugh. "Woman Battering: The Response of the Clergy." *Pastoral Psychology* 42/3 (1994) 185–96.

Wulff, David M. *Psychology of Religion: Classic and Contemporary*. New York: Wiley, 1997.

Wüstenberg, Ralf K. "'Religionless Christianity': Dietrich Bonhoeffer's Tegel Theology." In *Bonhoeffer for a New Day*, edited by John W. de Gruchy, 57–71. Grand Rapids: Eerdmans, 1997.

————. *A Theology of Life: Dietrich Bonhoeffer's Religionless Christianity*. Translated by Doug Stott. Grand Rapids: Eerdmans, 1998.

Young, Josiah. *No Difference in the Fare: Dietrich Bonhoeffer and the Problem of Racism*. Grand Rapids: Eerdmans, 1998.

Young-Bruehl, Elisabeth. Review of Jessica Benjamin, *Like Subjects, Love Objects*. *Journal of the American Psychoanalytic Society* 46 (1998) 634–38.

Zerner, Ruth. "Regression und Kreativität." In *Dietrich Bonhoeffer. Fragmente aus Tegel*, edited by Renate Bethge and Eberhard Bethge, 181–216. Munich: Kaiser, 1978.

Zimmerling, Peter. "Gottesliebe und irdische Liebe: Religiosität und Erotik bei Dietrich Bonhoeffer." In *Dietrich Bonhoeffer: Beten und Tun des Gerechten: Glaube und Verantwortung im Widerstand*, edited by Rainer Mayer and Peter Zimmerling, 35–47. Basel: Brunnen, 1997.

————. "Die Spiritualität Bonhoeffers in den Gefängnisjahren: Beten, das Gerechte tun und auf Gottes Zeit warten: Ein Werkstattsbericht." In *Dietrich Bonhoeffer, Mensch hinter Mauern: Theologie und Spiritualität in den Gefängnisjahren*, edited by Rainer Mayer and Peter Zimmerling, 35–68. Basel: Brunnen, 1993.

Zimmermann, Wolf-Dieter, and Ronald Gregor Smith, eds. *I Knew Dietrich Bonhoeffer*. Translated by Käthe Gregor Smith. London: Collins, 1966.

Index